SAVAGISM AND CIVILIZATION

A Study of the Indian and the American Mind

CIVILIZATION, *n.* The act of civilizing, or the state of being civilized; the state of being refined in manners, from the grossness of savage life, and improved in arts and learning.

SAVAGE, *n.* A human being in his native state of rudeness, one who is untaught, uncivilized or without cultivation of mind or manners. The *savages* of America, when uncorrupted by the vices of civilized men, are remarkable for their hospitality to strangers, and for their truth, fidelity and gratitude to their friends, but implacably cruel and revengeful toward their enemies. . . .

SAVAGISM, *n.* The state of rude uncivilized men; the state of men in their native wildness and rudeness.

—Noah Webster, *An American Dictionary of the English Language*, 1828

SAVAGISM AND CIVILIZATION

A Study of the Indian
and the American Mind

ROY HARVEY PEARCE

THE JOHNS HOPKINS PRESS
BALTIMORE AND LONDON

For ARTHUR O. LOVEJOY

Can Speculation satisfy,
Notion without Reality?

Manufactured in the United States of America

The Johns Hopkins Press, Baltimore, Maryland 21218
The Johns Hopkins Press Ltd., London

ISBN 0-8018-0524-4 (cloth)
ISBN 0-8018-0525-2 (paper)

Originally published, 1953, as *The Savages of America: A Study of the Indian and the Idea of Civilization*

Revised Edition, 1965
Second printing, 1967

Johns Hopkins Paperbacks edition, 1967
Second printing, 1971

Foreword

THIS IS a book about a belief. I have tried to recount how it was and what it meant for civilized men to believe that in the savage and his destiny there was manifest all that they had long grown away from and yet still had to overcome. Civilized men, of course, believed in themselves; they could survive, so they knew, only if they believed in themselves. In America before the 1850's that belief was most often defined negatively—in terms of the savage Indians who, as stubborn obstacles to progress, forced Americans to consider and reconsider what it was to be civilized and what it took to build a civilization. Studying the savage, trying to civilize him, destroying him, in the end they had only studied themselves, strengthened their own civilization, and given those who were coming after them an enlarged certitude of another, even happier destiny—that manifest in the progress of American civilization over all obstacles.

Now, coming after those who came after, knowing what we know, being what we are, we are bound to question that certitude. We readily comprehend, after the fact, something of the forces of violence and denial which supported it—even as we live among the achievements which in good part it made possible. Yet because our own failures and discontents drive us to search out its strengths and weaknesses, its potential for creation and destruction, we must first take care to understand it well enough to ask the right questions. Only then may we hope to find the right answers. We are not in a position either to justify the past or to instruct it. We can only assent to its certitudes and ask ourselves how they comport with our own. One of the ways of coming to understand a certitude is to study the belief which nourished it. This is such a study.

1

To write the history of a belief one must develop a clearly outlined chronology and scheme of analysis, yet not force the materials of the history into that sort of precisely articulated rise-and-fall, cause-and-effect pattern which their very existence denies. The chronological limits and the kind of analysis which I have set for this study are intended to make for such a plan.

The chronological limits 1609 and 1851 mark the dates of publication of Richard Johnson's *Nova Brittania* and of Lewis Henry Morgan's *League of the Iroquois.* These books—both dedicated in significant part to explaining the savage to civilized men—are, to be sure, neither the first of their kind nor the last; for there is never a first or a last in the history of such explanations. Nor are they unique. They are symptomatic, cumulative, typical of their kinds and the concerns of their times. As the work of men who were trying to comprehend events significant for life in America, these two books are effects and expressions of current history—that which was being made even as it was being recorded. Their dates of publication mark off one phase in the history of American interest in the Indian—and thus, in effect, one phase of the American's interest in himself. That phase in its largest implications, the American obsession with the problem of the civilized vs. the savage, is my subject here.

It is as a means to the clear analysis of those implications that I have given the terms Idea, Symbol, and Image somewhat specialized, narrow meanings—though not so specialized and narrow, I trust, that the intellectual and cultural historian will find them unfamiliar and the general reader will think them difficult. The terms are meant to categorize, however roughly, stages in the history of an idea as it becomes part of a system of thought and action. By Idea I mean a predication, explicit or implicit, which offers a solution of a major human problem. By Symbol I mean a vehicle for an Idea: a concrete, emotionally powerful sign for an abstract proposition. By Image I mean a vehicle for a Symbol: a particular mode of expounding and comprehending a Symbol and the Idea it bodies forth. In this study, as the epigraph facing the title page indicates, the Idea is that which Noah Webster and all those for whom he spoke called the savage and his savagism; the Symbol is the Indian; and the Images are those found in social, historical, and imaginative writing of the period. The system of thought and action is, of course, that which we associate with the ideology of progress and civilization in American culture through the 1850's. This study, then, is an effort to realize one phase of a project which was initiated in Charles and Mary Beard's *The American Spirit* (1948). In their Preface the Beards called their book " an effort to grasp . . . the intellectual and moral qualities that Americans have deemed necessary to civilization in the United States."

The study is thus planned according to the structure of thought and action, the functioning of intellectual and moral qualities, which it essays to analyse, describe, and understand. The first chapter stands apart as a sketch of colonial antecedents and origins. The next six chapters are chronologically central; the first three of these treat of the circumstances and nature of the idea of savagism as it came to be symbolized by the Indian; the next three treat of developing images of the symbol. Here, in effect, I have intended to set down a theme and its variations—and to suggest how that theme, savagism, is in effect a countertheme to a larger one, civilization. The last chapter, which explicitly considers the mutual implications of the ideas of savagism and of civilization, therefore stands apart as summary and coda.

If the method is analytic, it is because the structure of thought and action treated is itself analytic. Indeed, that structure constitutes, in Marianne Moore's words, a " scholastic philosophy of the wilderness "—or, in the title of one of Melville's major texts, a " Metaphysics of Indian-Hating." And it is one of my hopes for this study that, as it proceeds, calm and collecting, it might serve as an acknowledgment of the burden which the story it tells puts upon us. For it is a fact of our lives that, in Penn Warren's words, we were all of us born in " the shadow of the great forest," and have yet to come out.

2

In writing the history of a belief, the historian perforce reveals a complex of tensions, contradictions, inconsistencies, confusions, and errors. Yet such revelation cannot make him feel superior to the men whose belief he is studying. If he has done his job tolerably well, he will see in some small measure how it was and why it mattered to believe thus. Knowing the past, he will be able to sympathize with it; sympathizing with it, he will accept it; accepting it, he will perhaps be able to begin to free himself of the limitations which it sets about him and to use more intelligently the opportunities it offers him. Here I can do no better than to repeat the words of the historian to whom this study is dedicated:

> . . . though the history of ideas is a history of trial-and-error, even the errors illuminate the peculiar nature, the cravings, the endowments, and the limitations of the creature that falls unto them, as well as the logic of the problems in reflection upon which they have arisen; and they may further serve to remind us that the ruling modes of thought of our own age, which some among us are prone to regard as clear and coherent and firmly grounded and final, are unlikely to appear in the eyes of posterity to have any of these attributes. The adequate record of even the confusions of our forebears may help, not only to clarify those confusions, but to engender a salutary doubt whether we are wholly immune from different but equally great confusions. For though we have more empirical information at our disposal, we have not different or better minds; and it is, after all, the action of the mind upon facts that makes both philosophy and science—and, indeed, largely makes the " facts."

This study, then, attempts to record adequately what Professor Lovejoy might term the " facts " of Savagism and Civilization in American culture through the 1850's—and thus to illuminate the peculiar nature, the cravings, the endowments, and the limitations of our forebears and of ourselves.

3

In preparing this book for reissue, I have modified the order of the front matter, revised this Foreword, modified phrasing here and there, expanded the final chapter, and corrected a few (happily, there were few) typographical errors and errors of fact. I am grateful to the reviewers who pointed out the latter. In particular, I am grateful to Arthur Moore and Bruce Denbo—whose most thoughtful invitation I had to decline but nonetheless took advantage of.

This has been a co-operative enterprise, if only in the sense that many have co-operated with me so that I could get it done I am deeply grateful to:

The American Council of Learned Societies and the Committee on Midwestern Studies of Michigan State College for grants which made possible travel and research off home-grounds;

The Regents of the University of California for a grant which secured bibliographical assistance;

The Graduate School of The Ohio State University for a grant which aided the first publication of this study;

The editors of *ELH, Journal of English and Germanic Philology, South Atlantic Quarterly, Journal of the History of Ideas, PMLA,* for permission to use passages from articles which appeared in their journals; and the Columbia University Press for permission to use a portion of an essay of mine which appeared in the *English Institute Annual for 1949;*

The staffs of the Library of The Johns Hopkins University, the Library of the Peabody Institute, the Library of the Maryland Historical Society, the Library of Congress, the Ayer Collection of the Newberry Library, the Huntington Library, the Library of The Ohio State University, and the libraries of the University of California at Berkeley and Los Angeles for help in finding my way through their collections;

Ruth Lapham Butler for being an ideal curator;

James McBlair, Robin Blaser, Jack Spicer, Helen Weinberg, John Edwards, Martha Heyneman, and Conrad Tanzy for bibliographical assistance;

Charles Anderson, Don Cameron Allen, Raymond Dexter Havens, George Carter, Robert Elliott, Glenn Leggett, William Hildreth, William Charvat, Jay Vogelbaum, Kurt Wolff, Josephine Miles, Charles Muscatine, Harold Kelling, James Hart, John Raleigh, Kathryn Turner, Edwin Harrison Cady, and Stephen Gilman for reading, dissecting, and helping to reconstitute portions of the manuscript and for generous and disturbing advice;

Marie Vandenberg Pearce for making it probable that I would finish this book; and

Arthur O. Lovejoy for making it possible that I could begin it.

ROY HARVEY PEARCE

February, 1953
November, 1964

Postscript for the Paperback Edition

I have, in this paperback edition, made no changes in the 1965 text of this book except to restore the title I had in mind when, long ago, I was writing it. For the book is a study of one of those unattractive "isms" which taught our forebears how to make up their minds, and also how to act, most often without awareness of the confused meanings of their thinking or of the ambiguous consequences of their deeds. The lesson we may learn, I suggest, is that we have learned the lesson too well. The apologetics entailed is still too much with us. We still are confronted by "savages"; we still are the bearers of "civilization"; we still seek ever to develop a theory of the relation of the one to the other, a theory whereby the violence that has inevitably ensued will be at once rationalized, understood, and excused—above all, made bearable. I have said that we are not in a position to instruct the past. But I continue to think that, in a history such as this one, we may well be instructed by it.

September, 1966

Table of Contents

PART 1

Antecedents and Origins, 1609–1777

"Tho' they be Brutish Persons; yet, they are of Mankind, and so objects of Compassion. It is an act of Love to our own nature to seek their Salvation. . . ."

The Reverend Solomon Stoddard, 1723

Rescue Group (*Erected 1853*) Horatio Greenough

I

Spirituals and Temporals: *The Indian in Colonial Civilization*

THE RENAISSANCE Englishmen who became Americans were sustained by an idea of order. They were sure, above all, of the existence of an eternal and immutable principle which guaranteed the intelligibility of their relations to each other and to their world and thus made possible their life in society. It was a principle to be expressed in the progress and elevation of civilized men who, striving to imitate their God, would bring order to chaos. America was such a chaos, a new-found chaos. Her natural wealth was there for the taking because it was there for the ordering. So were her natural men.

Thus colonial Americans were from the very beginning beset by an Indian problem at once practical and theoretical. Practically, they had to overcome this natural man and to live with him; theoretically, they had to understand him. And they brought with them a pattern of culture, an idea of order, in which theory and practice were taken to be identical. They were certain that man could realize his highest potentialities in only that sort of society which they had left behind them in England. Here in America, it would be possible to realize such a society at its purest and most abundant. Aware to the point of self-consciousness of their specifically civilized heritage, they found in America not only an uncivilized environment, but uncivilized men—natural men, as it was said, living in a natural world. And they knew that the way to civilize a world was to civilize the men in it. Theoretically, savages, as men, were capable of being civilized; practically, they were bound to be. But practice did not support theory. Indians were not civilized, but destroyed.

Such, in general, was the colonial experience with the Indian; such had been the experience of revolutionary Americans when, in the 1770's, they set out to establish their glorious new-world civilization. The colonial concern with the savage Indian was a product of the tradition of Anglo-French primitivistic thinking—an attempt to see the savage, the ignoble savage, as a European *manqué*. When, by the 1770's, the attempt had obviously failed, Americans were coming to understand the Indian as one radically different from their proper selves; they knew he was bound inextricably in a primitive past, a primitive society, and a primitive environment, to be destroyed by God, Nature, and Progress to make way for Civilized Man. Americans after the 1770's worked out a theory of the savage which depended on an idea of a new order in which the Indian could have no part.

Since it is an aspect of a specifically nationalistic self-consciousness, the American understanding of the Indian after the 1770's is the major concern of this study. First, however, we must look at the antecedents and origins of that understanding in the Renaissance theory of the ignoble savage and its colonial variations. Everywhere in the colonies we can see efforts to understand the Indian as one to be lived with, one whose way of life is simply a corrupt variant of the particular way of life of his civilized neighbors, one who can surely be brought to civilization. Equally, we can see the sad failure of such efforts. The record is one of a failure in theory which made for a failure in practice.

1

The Indian whom the sixteenth-century voyagers came to know was, more than anything else, a creature whose way of life showed Englishmen what they might be were they not civilized and Christian, did they not fully partake of the divine idea of order. Viewed in the light of that ordered, civil nature toward which all men, as men, must aspire, he seemed to have fallen as far away from his proper state as he could and yet remain human. The lesson to be learned everywhere in the Americas was a deep and powerful one for civilized Christians whose intellect was essentially medieval but whose world was fast becoming the one we call modern. For in the New World the Englishman might search in vain for microcosms within the macrocosm, for men whose lives reproduced in little the order of the universe. In America, he might see clearly what he himself would become did he not live according to his highest nature. The Indian became important for the English mind, not for what he was in and of himself, but rather for what he showed civilized men they were not and must not be.[1]

Aboriginal Americans, so English voyagers were again and again to find, denied their holy, human selves and lived like beasts; they were, in the traditional terminology, more animal than rational. The northeastern Indians encountered on Frobisher's second voyage to America are described thus:

> If they for necessities sake stand in need of the premisses, such grasse as the Countrey yeeldeth they plucke up and eate, not deintily, or salletwise to allure their stomacks to appetite: but for necessities sake without either salt, oyles or washing, like brute beasts devouring the same. They neither use table, stoole, or table cloth for comlines: but when they are imbrued with blood knuckle deepe, and their knives in like sort, they use their tongues as apt instruments to lick them cleane: in doing whereof they are assured to loose none of their victuals.[2]

Moreover, these Indians "live in Caves of earth, and hunt for their dinners or praye, even as the beare or other wild beastes do," and "dare do any thing that their conseites will allowe, or courage of man maie execute."[3] The southeastern Indians described by

[1] I have discussed the sixteenth-century conception of the primitive in "Primitivistic Ideas in the *Faerie Queene*," *JEGP*, XLIV (1945), 139-51. I follow that essay here.

[2] Richard Hakluyt, *The Principal Navigations* (Glasgow, 1904), VII, 224.

[3] *Ibid.*, VII, 370; and Thomas Churchyard, *A Prayse, and Reporte of Maister Martyne Forboishers* [sic] *Voyage to Meta Incognita* (London, 1578), sig. B iv.

Henry Hawks " are soone drunke, and given to much beastlinesse, and void of all goodnesse." [4] And the savages whom Cabot brought to England are said merely to have been of " demeanour like to bruite beastes." [5] This, with hardly a variation, is a regular theme of the voyage narratives. Even the Virginia Indians described so cheerfully in Thomas Hariot's famous *Brief and True Report* (1588)[6] are, for Hariot, interesting as they avoid beastliness, not as they approach humanity. American Indians were everywhere found to be, simply enough, men who were not men, who were religiously and politically incomplete. If it was a brave new world, Caliban was its natural creature, Ferdinand one of its discoverers and planters.

America had to be planted so that sub-humans could be made human. This was one of the civilized Englishman's greatest burdens. In Letters Patent issued in 1606 for the colonizing of Virginia, the King urged the furtherance of a work " which may, by the Providence of Almighty God, hereafter tend to the Glory of His Divine Majesty, in propagating of Christian Religion to such people, as yet live in darkness, and miserable ignorance of the true knowledge and worship of God, and may in time bring the Infidels and Savages living in those parts, to human civility and to a settled and quiet Government . . . ." [7] The practical problem of bringing savages to civilization was to be solved by bringing them to the Christianity which was at its heart. Success in empire-building and trade was to be measured by success in civilizing and Christianizing; success in civilizing and Christianizing would assure success in empire-building and trade. Meantime, the Indian, in his savage nature, stood everywhere as a challenge to order and reason and civilization.

The idea of savage nature and savage destiny which seventeenth-century planters took with them to America is most clearly

[4] Hakluyt, IX, 386.

[5] *Ibid.*, VII, 155.

[6] *Ibid.*, VIII, 374-83.

[7] *Calendar of State Papers, Col. Series, America and West Indies, 1675-1676, also Addenda 1574-1675*, No. 48.

and fully set down by the Reverend Samuel Purchas—he who carried on the editing of voyage narratives begun by the Reverend Richard Hakluyt. Towards the end of the long series of narratives which make up *Hakluytus Posthumus, or Purchas His Pilgrimes* (1625), Purchas inserts an apologia for English colonization of Virginia.[8] Christian Englishmen, he declares, originally had not the right to despoil heathen Indians of their lands; for ownership of the land is a right in nature, not in God. Hence the Indians cannot be held responsible for not working their land according to God's revealed will; they live only according to the law of nature. Still, the English, as Christians knowing God's will, have an obligation to work that land; for it is almost bare of inhabitants and it is rich in all those things which make for "merchandise." And further, as Christians, they have the obligation to bring the Indians from a state of nature to a state of Christian civility. At first Indians in Virginia had recognized this English obligation, and the English had recognized the Indians' natural right to their lands; the English had obtained lands by legal purchase—all according to the law of nature. But then, in the Virginia massacre of 1622, the Indians had risen against the English, forgetting even that law of nature by which they had lived and in terms of which the English had treated peacefully with them. Now, Purchas is sure, the English have the right to do virtually as they please—or rather, virtually as God would be pleased to have them do.

God is to be glorified as His rich and abundant Virginia is properly used, as Englishmen live richly on that land. He is to be glorified, moreover, as Englishmen try to force to civility and Christianity these savages who refuse even to be proper natural men. Here Purchas writes like a voyager of the 1570's and 80's. The Indians are "so bad people, having little of Humanitie but shape, ignorant of Civilitie, of Arts, of Religion; more brutish then the beasts they hunt, more wild and unmanly then that unmanned wild Countrey, which they range rather than inhabite; captivated

[8] *Hakluytus Posthumus, or Purchas His Pilgrimes* (Glasgow, 1906), XIX, 218-65.

also to Satans tyranny in foolish pieties, mad impieties, wicked idlenesse, busie and bloudy wickednesse; hence have wee fit objects of zeale and pitie . . . ."[9] Zeal and pity are to be rewarded with the riches of Virginia—this God has arranged:

> All the rich endowments of Virginia, her Virgin-portion from the creation nothing lessened, are wages for all this worke: God in wisedome having enriched the Savage Countries, that those riches might be attractives for Christian suters, which there may sowe spirituals and reape temporals.[10]

For giving God and civilization to the Indian, the colonial Englishman was to receive the riches of a new world. Already he had God and civilization and rejoiced in the power they gave him. Looking at the Indian in his lack of such power, the Englishman could be sure of what he himself was; looking at himself, he could be sure of what the Indian should be. In America, from the very beginning the history of the savage is the history of the civilized.

2

The handful of adventurers who came to plant Virginia in 1607 were sure that they could live peacefully with the Indians; for they were sure that the Indians needed them and their civilization. Mercantile profits, political aggrandizement, and civilizing and Christianizing the savage heathen—these were all integrally part of that glorious plan whereby the new world might be given the intelligible order of the old.[11] In 1609, Sir Thomas Gates, as Governor of the colony, was told by the Virginia Company that

[9] *Ibid.*, XIX, 231.

[10] *Ibid.*, XIX, 232.

[11] For a contemporary statement of this design, see *A True and Sincere Declaration of the Purpose and Ends of the Plantation Begun in Virginia* [1610] in Alexander Brown, *The Genesis of the United States* (Boston, 1840), 339-40. For a general account, see Perry Miller, "The Religious Impulse in the Founding of Virginia: Religion and Society in the Early Literature," *William and Mary Quarterly*, Ser. 3, V (1948), 492-522; and "Religion and Society in the Early Literature: The Religious Impulse in the Founding of Virginia," *ibid.*, Ser. 3, VI (1949), 24-41.

his missionaries should work with Indian children, that he must even have children taken from their parents if necessary, since they were " so wrapped up in the fogge and miserie of their iniquity, and so tirrified with their continuall tirrany[,] chayned under the bond of Deathe unto the Divell " that they very likely would have to be forced, when young, into the good Christian life.[12] By 1619 at least fifty missionaries had been sent to Virginia to take charge of thirty Indian children who were being educated into Christianity and civilization.[13] Money was being collected in England for a school for the children; and in June 1622 a missionary-rector was appointed.[14] But it was too late. For in April, 1622 the Virginia Indians had attempted to wipe out the English colonists, and failing, had assured their own destruction.

The period from 1607 to 1622, as a matter of fact, had been one of uneasy peace.[15] The Virginia Indians were antagonistic but learned soon that they could not dislodge the English, whose armor protected them from arrows and whose will and determination protected them from the confusions and mistakes attendant upon exploration and pioneering. On their part, although they did not recognize Indian title to land, the English still tried always to purchase such land before taking it over, thus to respect Indian dignity and natural law. They were aware of the power of Powhatan and, after him, of Opechancanough, whose intent it was to league all Indians against them; still they felt that John Rolfe's marriage to Powhatan's daughter, Pocahontas, in 1613 secured once and for all such treaties as they had arranged with Powhatan. But peace was secured only because Powhatan hoped that the colonial experiment would fail through English ineptitude. When

[12] *Records of the Virginia Company*, III (Washington, 1933), 14-15.

[13] *Ibid.*, III, 116, 128, 165-66.

[14] See Wesley Frank Craven, *The Southern Colonies in the Seventeenth Century, 1607-1689* (Baton Rouge, La., 1949), pp. 142-44; and Samuel Eliot Morison, *The Founding of Harvard College* (Cambridge, 1935), pp. 411-15.

[15] Accounts of the details vary. I follow those in Matthew P. Andrews, *Virginia, the Old Dominion* (New York, 1937), pp. 23-24, 30, 56-57, 66-70, 99-107, 104-107; and Craven, *The Southern Colonies*, p. 146.

Powhatan died in 1616, his successor, Opechancanough, continued the policy of watching and waiting. Meantime, the English became surer and surer that their peaceful, civilizing, Christianizing ways were winning over the Indians; and they encouraged the Indians to come to them as good friends. Then, on April 1, 1622 (March 22, O. S.) suddenly and without warning the Indians rose over a hundred-mile area and killed all Englishmen they could—at least 347. That the massacre failed to wipe out all the English was owing, God willing, to the last-minute warning of an Indian convert. God willed, moreover, English vengeance in punitive expeditions in 1622 and 1623. The problem now became one of simple survival. The savages had committed themselves. As the Reverend Samuel Purchas triumphantly pointed out, they no longer had any rights, since they had broken even the law of nature by which, as natural men, they should have lived.

The assurance with which Englishmen had first gone to the Virginia Indians was that of the Protestant humanist with his supreme confidence in the order of nature:

> And surely [it had been written in a promotional tract of 1609] so desirous is man of civill society by nature, that he easily yields to discipline and government, if he see any reasonable motive to induce him to the same . . . for it is not the nature of men, but the education of men, which make them barbarous and uncivill, and therefore chaunge the education of men, and you shall see that their nature will be greatly rectified and corrected; seeing therefore men by nature so easily yielde to discipline and government upon any reasonable shewe of bettering their fortunes, it is everie mans dutie to travell both by sea and land, and to venture either with his person or with his purse, to bring the barbarous and savage people to a civill and Christian kinde of government, under which they may learne how to live holily, justly, and soberly in this world, and to apprehend the meanes to save their soules in the world to come, rather than to destroy them, or utterly to roote them out . . . .[16]

After 1622, however, it seemed to most Englishmen in Virginia

[16] Robert Gray, *A Good Speed to Virginia* [1609], ed. W. F. Craven (New York, 1937), Sig. [C 1v]–C 2r.

that destruction of the Indians was warranted. This free and open pioneering declaration is characteristic of a new sentiment:

Because our hands which before were tied with gentlenesse and faire usage, are now set at liberty by the treacherous violence of the Savages, not untying the Knot, but cutting it: So that we, who hitherto have had possession of no more ground then their waste, and our purchase at a valuable consideration to their owne contentment, gained; may now by a right of Warre, and law of Nations, invade the Country, and destroy them who sought to destroy us.[17]

The Indian became for seventeenth-century Virginians a symbol not of a man in the grip of devilish ignorance, but of a man standing fiercely and grimly in the path of civilization.[18] In 1644 when Opechancanough tried again to wipe out the English, the Virginians were ready, and rather easily put him down, captured him, and allowed him to be killed by his guard. His successor sued for peace and was granted it for an annual tribute and, inevitably, for all the land that the English might want. From this time on, with nearby Indians secured as allies against possible incursions by Indians from the north and west, Virginia Indian troubles were strictly frontier troubles, somehow distant from the civilized affairs of Jamestown and the tidewater plantations. In 1675 an Indian uprising forced frontier planters to unite in their own defense and to defy the royal governor who would not give them adequate support; the result, of course, was Bacon's rebellion, in which the Indian problem came to be only incidental. Steadily the Indian problem became the western problem which it was for American society in the later eighteenth and early nineteenth centuries. Steadily such missionary work as was to be done was becoming a matter of distant, enlightened philanthropy and

[17] Edward Waterhouse, " A Declaration of the State of the Colonie and Affaires in Virginia " [1622], *Records of the Virginia Company,* III, 556-57.

[18] See John Martin, " The Manner Howe to Bringe the Indians into Subjection," a report prepared for the Virginia Company, December 15, 1622, *ibid.*, III, 704-706.

charity.[19] Meantime, Virginians, in mastering their new land, had mastered its aboriginal inhabitants.

When, in 1622, Virginians discovered they had to destroy or be destroyed, they ceased trying to understand the Indian; for such understanding presumably would avail them little. Hence such accounts of Indians as they wrote come before 1622 and reflect the early, optimistic views of men who are certain that savages can be readily civilized. The accounts from 1607 through 1622 are few and simply to the point.

In his *Nova Brittania* (1609) Richard Johnson reports briefly and straightforwardly. Virginia, he writes, " is inhabited with wild and savage people, that live and lie up and downe in troupes like heards of Deere in a Forrest: they have no law but nature, their apparell skinnes of beasts, but most goe naked: the better sort have houses, but poore ones, they have no Arts nor Science, yet they live under superior command such as it is, they are generally very loving and gentle, and do entertaine and relieve our people with great kindnesse: they are easy to be brought to good, and would fayne embrace a better condition." [20] In his *The New Life of Virginea* (1612) Johnson makes practical suggestions for bringing such natural men to a better condition. Seeing no need for violence, he advises the Virginia planters, " In steed of Iron and steele you must have patience and humanitie to manage their crooked nature to your form of civilitie . . . ." [21]

Henry Spelman's manuscript *Relation of Virginea* (1613) fills in random but particular observations on Indian Life—on religion, habitations, marriage customs, naming of children, care of the sick, burial, government, executions, agriculture, quarrels, war, pastimes—yet his prime interest is still in the fact that there *is* a minimal sense of order and discipline, something analogous to civilized order, in Indian society. Of religion, he observes that

[19] See, for example, Lieutenant-Governor Alexander Spotswood's discussion of his interest in work with Indian children in a letter to the Bishop of London, November 11, 1711, *Virginia Historical Society Collections*, n. s., I (1882), 126.

[20] Peter Force, *Tracts*, I, no. 6, p. 11.

[21] *Ibid.*, I, no. 7, pp. 18-19.

although " for yᵉ most part they worship yᵉ divell," such worship is, however bad, still worship. And concerning Indian " Justis and goverment," he is pleased to discover that although he had thought the Indians were by nature lawless, yet he has found laws justly administered among them.[22]

The most hopeful view is that of Alexander Whitaker, minister at Henrico, in his *Good Newes from Virginia* (1613). Whitaker observes that the Indians acknowledge a " great good God " but that they fear the Devil more; they worship him and are virtually slaves of their " Priests," who " are no other but such as our English Witches are." Then:

Wherefore my brethren, put on the bowells of compassion, and let the lamentable estate of these miserable people enter in your consideration: One God created us, they have reasonable soules and intellectuall faculties as well as wee; we all have *Adam* for our common parent: yea, by nature the condition of us both is all one, the servants of sinne and slaves of the divell . . . .

But if any of us should misdoubt that this barbarous people is uncapable of such heavenly mysteries, let such men know that they are farre mistaken in the nature of these men, for besides the promise of God, which is without respect of persons, made as well to unwise men after the flesh, as to the wise, &c. let us not thinke that these men are so simple as some have supposed them: for they are of body lustie, strong, and very nimble: they are a very understanding generation, quicke of apprehension, suddaine in their dispatches, subtile in their dealings, exquisite in their inventions, and industrious in their labour.

What kind of a society do these savage servants of Satan have?

Finally, there is a civill governement amongst them which they strictly observe, and shew thereby that the law of Nature dwelleth in them: for they have a rude kinde of Common-wealth, and rough governement, wherein they both honour and obey their Kings, Parents, and Governours, both greater and lesse, they observe the limits

[22] I have used the text of Spelman's relation printed in *Travels and Works of Captain John Smith*, ed. Arber and Bradley (Edinburgh, 1910), " Introduction," I, ci-cxiv.

of their owne possessions, and incroach not upon their neighbours dwellings . . . .

Thus there are in the Virginia Indians glimmerings of the light of civilized nature—glimmerings of an idea of rational, holy order with its government, laws, and sense of private property. Clearly "these unnurtured grounds of reason" in the Indians urge upon all Christians the hope and necessity of bringing them to Christian civility and its glories. Whitaker promises more details; but he is sure now of the essentials.[23]

The details are systematically given by Captain John Smith; the system assumed is that of the naturally minimal order of savage life, with its natural aspiration towards the higher life of Christian civility. Smith's central account is in his *Map of Virginia, with a Description of the Countrey, the Commodities, People, Government and Religion* (1612).[24] (This is virtually the same account he gives in the *General History of Virginia* [1616].) He begins with names of tribes and statistics, and then proceeds to descriptions: his Indians are comely, brown (but all born white), close shaven, very strong and agile, inconstant, timorous, quick of apprehension, "all *Savage*," covetous, malicious, as honest as could be expected. He is fascinated and revolted by their gaudy dress, their barbaric ornaments, and their monstrous body painting. He observes that they live in groups of six to twenty in houses "built like our Arbors" and that they have gardens which they work together. The men fish, hunt, war, and occupy themselves generally with "such manlike exercises"; and "the women and children do the rest of the worke." In this careful manner Smith goes methodically through the whole range of Indian culture as he has observed it: diet, weapons, tools, utensils, boat-building, cloth-making, fishing, hunting, war, music, entertainment, and medicine.

But what interests him most is Indian religion and government, to which he devotes two separate sections of his account. "There

[23] *Good Newes from Virginia* [1613] (New York, 1936), pp. 24-27.

[24] *Travels and Works of Captain John Smith*, ed. Arber and Bradley, I, 65-84.

is," he says, " yet in *Virginia* no place discovered to bee so *Savage* in which the *Savages* have not a religion . . . ." " But," he points out immediately, " their chiefe God they worship is the Divell." Devil-worship, in fact, deforms the whole of a religion dominated by evil priests who are agents of Satan and who must be paid Satanic homage. So the religious ceremonies of these people are diabolical, with outrageous costumes, conjuring, singing and dancing—even human sacrifice. They believe that only the chiefs and priests live after death, and these with the Devil whom they worship; the common people, they suppose, do not have life after death. There is hope for Christian conversion; some have sought it already. But for the present " . . . in this lamentable ignorance doe these poore soules sacrifice themselves to the Divell, not knowing their Creator."

Indian government, although savage, is more enlightened than Indian religion:

Although the countrie people be very barbarous; yet have they amongst them such government, as that their Magistrates for good commanding, and their people for due subjection and obeying, excell many places that would be counted very civill.

It is a monarchical government, with an emperor ruling over kings. The emperor is Powhatan; and he is supreme, ruling not by written laws, but by custom. " Yet when he listeth, his will is a law and must bee obeyed: not only as a king, but as halfe a God they esteeme him." Each king and his people hold their land directly from the emperor; and they live within its limits, fearing always to violate any of his commands; for he is hard and cruel. He has tried, Smith notes, to frighten the English, but he has failed, and peace has been secured. Throughout his account Smith has been sure that it will always remain so.

But it did not remain so. The massacre of 1622 made the hope of Christianization and civilization seem unreal beyond practical reason. Essentially, the problem presented by the Indian came to be taken as one not of securing peace but of surviving. So Virginians concerned themselves little with knowing the Indian; for he was literally not worth knowing. Not until the early eighteenth century, when eminent Virginian gentlemen-scholars, surveying their land and its past, looked curiously at the Indian's role in that past and at the difference between the civilized and the savage, was there exhibited a serious or sustained interest in the Indian, his nature, and his fate.

3

Settlers in Maryland were more fortunate in their relations with the Indians than the Virginians; and Maryland accounts and reactions reflect this good fortune. The Anglicans and Catholics who came to found Maryland in 1634 encountered peaceably disposed Indians, eager to welcome them. As a matter of fact, the local Indians, the Patuxents, hoped for English aid against the raids of their fierce neighbors, the Susquehannocks. Anxious to secure their colonial establishments, the English were pleased to protect the Indians; knowing about Indian troubles to the south, they were determined to make good their decision to use the Indians kindly. They took proper precautions, erected fortifications to protect themselves just in case trouble should develop; ". . . yet," in the words of a contemporary promotional tract, "they ceased not to procure to put these jealousies out of the Natives minds, by treating and using them in the most courteous manner they could, and at last prevailed therein and setled a very firme peace and friendship with them." [25] Indian lands were always treated for and purchased. In the 1650's the proprietor, Lord Baltimore, acting ever in the grand feudal style, ordered about 10,000 acres set aside as a kind of Indian reservation; but this scheme was lost in the midst of political battles for the control of the colony.[26] Troubles with Indians on the northern and southern and western frontiers developed in the 1640's and in the 1670's; on both occasions successful punitive expeditions were sent out. The expedition of the 1670's, conducted jointly with Virginia, was part of the chain of events that led to Bacon's Rebel-

[25] *A Relation of Maryland* [1635], in *Narratives of Early Maryland, 1633-1684*, ed. C. C. Hall (New York, 1910), p. 76.

[26] Matthew P. Andrews, *History of Maryland: Province and State* (New York, 1929), p. 63.

lion. But in Maryland itself, by and large, the peace was kept, and the Marylander's view of the Indian reflected that peace.

Although there was in Maryland, too, the high intention of converting the savages, that intention never was realized as part of Lord Baltimore's official policy. Christianization became a matter of private enterprise—largely Catholic enterprise.[27] Anglicans and Puritans, the latter having moved into Maryland during the middle of the century, sent out few missionaries. But Catholics, tolerated in Maryland as nowhere else, thought that this colony was to be that one where Jesuit missionaries might work their will. The narrative (1634) by a Jesuit priest who was part of the first colonizing expedition is full of the high hopes of one who sees the Indians simply as infidels waiting to be converted.[28] The Jesuits were for a time free to work among the Indians, and they worked hard and successfully enough for one of them to report in 1639:

Whoever shall contemplate in thought the whole earth, will perhaps nowhere find men more abject in appearance than these Indians; who nevertheless have souls (if you consider the ransom paid by Christ) no less precious than the most cultivated Europeans. They are inclined indeed to vices, though not very many, in such darkness of ignorance, such barbarism and in so unrestrained and wandering a mode of life; nevertheless in their disposition they are docile, nor will you perceive in them, except rarely, the passions of the mind transported in an extraordinary manner . . . . They are readily swayed by reason, nor do they withhold their assent obstinately from the truth set forth in a credible manner. This natural disposition of the tribe, aided by the seasonable assistance of divine grace, gives us hope of a most desirable harvest hereafter, and animates us in the highest degree to continue our labors in this vineyard.[29]

But for all this confidence, with its touch of Jesuitical enthusiasm for primitives who are easily open to conversion because they

[27] *Ibid.*, p. 42.

[28] Father Andrew White, *A Briefe Relation of the Voyage unto Maryland* [1634], in *Narratives of Early Maryland*, pp. 40-45.

[29] *Annual Letter of the English Province of the Society of Jesus, 1639*, *ibid.*, pp. 129-30.

have not yet acquired civilized vices, the Jesuits were not allowed to proceed freely.[30] In their attempts to get directly to the Indians, they had secured land grants directly from them. Lord Baltimore, though a Catholic himself, was forced to object; for he was to be absolute ruler in Maryland. Jesuit authorities in England acceded to his objection; Jesuits in Maryland surrendered their Indian lands; and although they continued to work among the Indians, they could not realize their hopes for large-scale conversions such as were being managed in Canada and South America.[31]

If Jesuits could not take advantage of peaceful relations with the Indians, secular Marylanders could. The anonymous author of *A Relation of Maryland* (1635), writing some thirteen years after the Virginia massacre, can still believe in the inevitable union of religion and empire.[32] He objects, he says, to such accounts as that of Captain Smith, because Smith always writes from an assumption that war with the Indians is an essential fact of colonial life. (Here the author of the *Relation* misreads Smith; but he has an axe to grind.) Smith's account is simply in error, he feels; if the Indians are treated well, introduced to civility, husbandry, and the " mechanick trades," they may become very useful to the English. As it is now, they live only under the law of Nature and that " discretion " which derives therefrom. Add the virtues of Christianity to their natural virtues, and you have a " brave people." He concludes:

that since God Almighty hath made this Countrey so large and fruitfull, and that the people be such as you have heard them described; It is much more Prudence, and Charity, to Civilize, and make them Christians, then to kill, robbe, and hunt them from place to place, as you would doe a wolfe. By reducing of them, God shall be served, his Majesties Empire enlarged by the addition of many thousand

[30] See Gilbert Chinard, *L'Amérique et le Rêve Exotique dans la Littérature Française au XVIIe et au XVIIIe Şiècle* (Paris, 1934), pp. 122-87.

[31] The exact proceedings here are puzzling. See for a cogent analysis, Charles M. Andrews, *The Colonial Period of American History,* II (New Haven, 1936), 313.

[32] " Of the Naturall disposition of the Indians," in *Narratives of Early Maryland*, pp. 83-90.

Subjects, as well as of large Territories, our Nation honoured, and the Planters themselves enriched by the trafficke and commerce which may be had with them.[33]

The optimism here perhaps derives from the promotional intentions of the *Relation* itself. But, in a larger sense, it reflects the assurance of Christianization and civilized progress which invariably shaped the earliest American understanding of the Indian. That Maryland optimism is not so grim as that of Virginia, so peaceful as that of Pennsylvania, or so fierce as that of New England, is owing primarily to the fact that there was virtually no Indian " problem " in colonial Maryland. Significantly, all that could be said of the Indian in Maryland was said as early as 1635.[34]

4

The New England Puritan of the 1630's knew, in the very intensity of his Puritanism, that he too must be a civilizer and Christianizer, and thus a savior of the Indians, and that God would show him the truest way with the savage. He knew that Pilgrim experience with the Indians, some ten years before, had been fortunate: God had sent a " wonderful plague " among the savages to destroy them and to leave most of their lands free for civilized occupation.[35] The Puritan received, as he must have expected to receive, the same kind of help. Yet he helped himself too.

Although in 1634 John Winthrop could write to an English friend, " [the natives] are neere all dead of the small Poxe, so as the Lord hathe cleared our title to what we possess," [36] still Indians

[33] *Ibid.*, p. 90.

[34] In the only other detailed account I have seen, that in George Alsop's *Character of the Province of Maryland*, the Indian is not taken seriously. See *ibid.*, pp. 365-71.

[35] Edward Winslow to George Morton (?), December 11, 1621, in Alexander Young, *Chronicles of the Pilgrim Fathers* (Boston, 1841), pp. 232-33; The Great Patent of New England, November 3, 1620, as quoted *ibid.*, p. 184, f. n. 3; and a Plymouth sermon of Robert Cushman (1621), *ibid.*, pp. 258-59.

[36] Winthrop to Sir Nathaniel Rich, May 22, 1634, *Winthrop Papers*, III (Massachusetts Historical Society, 1943), 167.

to the south and north, who were plagued mainly by the English themselves, remained relatively strong and independent and had to be faced down. Twice in the century formal frontier war was waged: in 1637, against the Pequots, who were easily slaughtered at Mystic by Mason's expedition; and in 1675-1676, against the Wampanoags and their leader King Philip, who were destroyed in their turn, though not quite so easily as the Pequots had been. And continually there was trouble on a small scale; the problem was to keep various tribes split up and thus weak in striking power, to protect frontier settlements from marauding bands, to combat papist French influence to the north, and gradually to take over lands as the proper time came. Steadily, as the colonies developed in holdings and in power, the English moved further inland from their coastal settlements and took over more Indian land. Warfare resulted. But this too was part of God's Way with New England.

For here the Puritans carried to its extreme the logic of seventeenth-century Christian imperialism. God had meant the savage Indians' land for the civilized English and, moreover, had meant the savage state itself as a sign of Satan's power and savage warfare as a sign of earthly struggle and sin. The colonial enterprise was in all ways a religious enterprise. For Puritans, as for Pilgrims before them, land tenure was finally to be demonstrated from theology.[37] Indian lands were to be bought if local savages should pretend to ownership, but to be bought only as a means of keeping peace with those savages.[38] The fact was that the Indians possessed their lands only as a natural right, since that possession existed anterior to and outside of a properly civilized state and since that possession was not in accordance with God's commandment to men to occupy the earth, increase, and multiply; what

[37] "Reasons and Considerations Touching the Lawfulness of Removing Out of England into the Parts of America," *Mourt's Relation* [1622], in Young, *Chronicles of the Pilgrim Fathers*, pp. 243-46.

[38] See, for example, the letters of instruction sent to John Endicott from the Massachusetts Bay Company, April 17 and May 28, 1629, in Alexander Young, *Chronicles of the First Planters of the Colony of Massachusetts Bay* (Boston, 1846), pp. 159 and 176.

followed, then, was that the land was technically *vacuum domicilium*, and that the English, who would farm the land and make it fructify, who would give it order, were obliged to take over.[39] Thus, characteristically, the Puritan in his eager orthodoxy was little interested in natural law and went directly to divine law, to divine logic. For John Winthrop, in 1629, it was a matter of such logic:

. . . the whole earth is the Lord's garden, and he hath given it to the sons of Adam to be tilled and improved by them. Why then should we stand starving here for the places of habitation, (many men spending as much labor and cost to recover or keep sometimes an acre or two of lands as would procure him many many hundreds of acres, as good or better, in another place,) and in the mean time suffer whole countries, as profitable for the use of man, to lie waste without any improvement.[40]

Convinced thus of his divine right to Indian lands, the Puritan discovered in the Indians themselves evidence of a Satanic opposition to the very principle of divinity. In a world in which the divine plan was so clear, in a world through which the Bible would guide all men in all things, in a world in which civilization and the divinely illuminated human reason had to count for everything, the Indian might well be a terrifying anomaly, at best a symbol of what men might become if they lived far from God's Word. Yet he also was a man who had to be brought to the civilized responsibilities of Christian manhood, a wild man to be improved along

[39] The problem is surveyed by Chester E. Eisinger, "The Puritans' Justification for Taking the Land," *Essex Institute Historical Collections,* LXXXIV (1948), 131-43. The best single statement of the Puritan position is in John Winthrop's "General Considerations for the Plantation in New-England," [1629], in Young, *Chronicles of the First Planters,* pp. 271-78. Winthrop's authorship of the "General Considerations" is demonstrated and variant texts are given in *Winthrop Papers,* II (Massachusetts Historical Society, 1931), 106-21. Young's text seems to be that which G. W. Robinson, editor of the *Winthrop Papers,* calls draft D, from the Higginson Papers. Young's text varies slightly, but never significantly, from draft D as printed in the *Winthrop Papers.*

[40] "General Considerations," in Young, *Chronicles of the First Planters,* p. 272.

with wild lands, a creature who had to be made into a Puritan if he was to be saved. Save him, and you saved one of Satan's victims. Destroy him, and you destroyed one of Satan's partisans.

The logic was inexorable and unrelieved. Wherever the Indian opposed the Puritan, there Satan opposed God; Satan had possessed the Indian until he had become virtually a beast; Indian worship was devil worship. The faintly optimistic (and propagandistic?) reports about Indian religion which were published in London early in the seventeenth century soon were drowned out in the general recounting of its evils.[41] Satanism, it was abundantly evident, was at the core of savage life.[42] And it was not hard to associate the physical state of the Indian, his living a cold, hard life, with his spiritual state; hence, everywhere one might see in the flesh what it meant to be a devil-worshipper. Racial and cultural tension mounted throughout the century, until, in the 1690's, the very presence of Indian devil-worshippers was taken as part of the evidence of that great visitation of witches to New England, which we call the Witchcraft Craze. Indian witch doctors clearly were sharing diabolically in the wonders of the invisible world.[43]

When frontier New Englanders suffered at the hands of Indians, they inevitably interpreted their suffering as God's warning

[41] For an optimistic report, see Edward Winslow, *Good Newes from New England* [1624], in Young, *Chronicles of the Pilgrim Fathers*, pp. 354-67. For the contradiction of this view, see Francis Higginson, *New-England's Plantation* [1630], in Young, *Chronicles of the First Planters*, pp. 241-64; Philip Vincent, *A True Relation of the late Battell Fought in New England* [1638], in Charles Orr, *History of the Pequot War* (Cleveland, 1897), pp. 98-99; John Underhill, *Newes from America* [1638], *ibid.*, pp. 47-86; Thomas Lechford, *Plain Dealing: or, Newes from New-England* [1642], *Massachusetts Historical Society Collections*, Ser. 3, III (1833), 102-106; and John Josselyn, *An Account of Two Voyages to New-England* [1674], *ibid.*, Ser. 3, III (1833), 293-311.

[42] Morison, *The Founding of Harvard College*, p. 415.

[43] George Lyman Kittredge, *Witchcraft in Old and New England* (Cambridge, 1929), pp. 362-63, 371; Cotton Mather, *Decennium Luctuosum* [1699], in *Narratives of the Indian Wars, 1675-1699*, ed. Charles H. Lincoln (New York, 1913), p. 242.

to New England through Satan. Of the hard captivity of Mary Rowlandson in 1676, the contemporary editor of her narrative concluded:

I may say, that as none knows what it is to fight and pursue such an enemy as this, but they that have fought and pursued them: so none can imagine what it is to be captivated, and enslaved to such atheisticall, proud, wild, cruel, barbarous, bruitish (in one word) diabolicall creatures as these, the worst of the heathen . . . .[44]

Thus for those who lived in the frontier settlements to the west and south and to the north in Maine, it came to be, simply enough, destroy or be destroyed; this was yet another skirmish in man's Holy War against Satan, now on a new-world battlefield. When, as late as 1703, it was recommended that troublesome Indians be hunted down with dogs, the argument from Christian violence was an old one. Some sixty-five years before a military man had argued with saintly authority in defense of the massacre of the Pequots:

It may be demanded, Why should you be so furious? . . . Should not Christians have more mercy and compassion? But I would refer you to David's war. When a people is grown to such a height of blood, and sin against God and man, and all confederates in the action, then he hath no respect to persons, but harrows them, and saws them, and puts them to the sword, and the most terriblest death that may be. Sometimes the Scripture declareth women and children must perish with their parents. Sometimes the case alters; but we will not dispute it now. We had sufficient light from the word of God for our proceedings.[45]

[44] *Soveraignty and Goodness of God* [1682], reprinted from ed. 1795 as *A Narrative of the Captivity and Restoration of Mrs. Mary Rowlandson, ibid.*, p. 116. Cf. the Stockwell narrative in Increase Mather's *Essay for the Recording of Illustrious Providences* (London, 1684), pp. 39-58; and the preface to John Williams' *Redeemed Captive Returning to Zion* (Boston, 1707).

[45] The recommendation is that of the Reverend Solomon Stoddard in a letter to Governor Dudley, *Massachusetts Historical Society Collections*, Ser. 4, II (1854), 235-37. The argument is that of John Underhill, second

So Puritans made history. So they wrote it too. Puritan historians and reporters, determined to understand their nature and destiny, uniformly saw Indian troubles in light from the word of God. Edward Johnson, for example, equated the Pequot War with the Antinomian disturbance as Puritan trials with Satan. John Mason appended to his history of the Pequot War a list of " special providences " by means of which the English had won their victory. Nathaniel Saltonstall insisted that however heavily the hand of the Lord lay upon his Puritan sinners, still He had commissioned them to destroy the crafty, bestial, diabolical creatures who opposed them. William Hubbard was sure that King Philip's War was nothing less than a Satanic plot against God's Chosen People, and both Mathers took the Indian wars as evidence that Satan was putting up a last fight against his Puritan adversary.[46] For the Puritan, history was everywhere cosmically and eternally meaningful. A Satanic principle was part of that meaningfulness; and the New England Indians somehow embodied that principle.

Out of such an understanding of civilized man in New England arose the Puritan understanding of savage man. There was, at the outset, no difficulty in accounting for the genesis of the savage. Almost universally it was agreed that the Indians were of the

in command to Mason at the proceedings at Mystic, in his *Newes from America* [1638], in Orr, *History of the Pequot War*, p. 81.

[46] Johnson, *Wonder-Working Providence* [1654], ed. J. F. Jameson (New York, 1910), p. 80; Mason, *Brief History of the Pequot War* [1736], in Orr, *History of the Pequot War*, pp. 1-46; Saltonstall, *A Continuation of the State of New-England* [1676], in *Narratives of the Indian Wars, 1675-1699*, p. 54; Hubbard, *Narrative of the Indian Wars in New England* [1677] (n. p., 1814), p. 61; Increase Mather, *Brief History of the War with the Indians* (London, 1676), *passim* and *Relation of the Troubles Which Have Hapned in New England* (London, 1677), *passim*; Cotton Mather, *Decennium Luctuosum* (London, 1699), *passim.* This is a mere sampling, of course. Johnson's equation of the Pequot War with the Antinomian troubles is not unique with him: Cf. letter from John Higginson to John Winthrop (*c.* May 1637), *Winthrop Papers,* III (Massachusetts Historical Society, 1943), 404-407; and Thomas Shepard's " Memoir of Himself " (*c.* 1645-1650), in Young, *Chronicles of the First Planters*, p. 550.

race of men, descendants, in order, of Adam, Noah, and those Asiatic Tartars who had come to America by a land-bridge from northern Asia.[47] This opinion, orthodox in the seventeenth century,[48] allowed Puritans to account simply for the savage, heathenish state of the Indian. Was he not perhaps the farthest of all God's human creatures from God Himself? Descended from wanderers, had he not lost his sense of civilization and law and order? Had he not lost, except for a dim recollection, God Himself? And wasn't he, as a direct result of this loss, in the power of Satan? Seen only thus, as one item in a God-centered course of experience, the Indian took on an awful meaning for the Puritan mind.

The Puritan writer on the Indian was therefore less interested in the Indian's culture than in the fallen spiritual condition which that culture manifested. Such early accounts of the Indian as those contained in Edward Winslow's *Good Newes from New England* (1624), Francis Higginson's *New-England's Plantation* (1630), and William Wood's *New England's Prospect* (1634) describe the appearance, social organization, and customs of the local Indians sketchily and, considering the tone of later accounts, somewhat optimistically. They depict heathen Indians, almost wiped out by the plague, living without the benefits of civilization, fearing their enemies, who will certainly welcome the English and the way of life they bring. But as the century wore on, Puritans were troubled by disputes, warfare, and what we can see now as the stubborn integrity of some Indian cultures. It was clear to many Puritans that all Indians were victims beyond rescue of their low condition and that not much was to be gained by studying them. By the 1680's even Daniel Gookin, in charge of Christian Indian settlements for the United Colonies and known to be soft toward

[47] A general survey of contemporary received opinion on Indian origins is Daniel Gookin's, in the first chapter of his *Historical Collections of the Indians of New England* [MS., *c.* 1680?], *Massachusetts Historical Society Collections,* Ser. 1, I (1792), 141-226.

[48] See John H. Powell's sketch *On the Origin of the American Indians* (Philadelphia, 1946); and Don Cameron Allen's definitive study in his *The Legend of Noah* (Urbana, Ill., 1949), pp. 113-37.

the savages, could give only a despairing account of Indian culture. His " Of the Language, Customs, Manners, and Religion of the Indians " [49] is straightforward and gloomy. The Indians, he concludes, have been and continue to be, with a few Christianized exceptions, brutish and barbarous; they indulge in polygamy; they are revengeful; the men only hunt and fish and fight while the women cook and do a little planting; they are all thieves and liars and by now they have virtually all become drunkards. True enough, they are hospitable and have some faintly systematic way of government. Yet their heathen worship and their submitting to powwows, who are nothing but witches and wizards holding familiarity with Satan, damn them forever. Gookin is interested in the Indians insofar as they fail to be potential Puritans.

What mattered was not the intrinsic character of the New England Indians, but rather the meaning that character might have for the whole of New England life. Thus the account of tarnished noble savages in Thomas Morton's *New English Canaan* (1632), of hypercholeric warriors in Philip Vincent's *True Relation* (1638), of natural men in Thomas Lechford's *Plain Dealing* (1643) and in John Josselyn's *Account of Two Voyages* (1674) —each of these attempts by non-Puritans to describe New England Indians disinterestedly would have seemed to Puritans mistaken. Precisely because the Puritan was so deeply concerned with the meaning of the Indian for the whole of his culture, he hardly could conceive of describing that Indian disinterestedly. The Puritan understanding of savage man is most fully recorded in the history of the bitter failure of Puritans to bring the Indians to God.

The record of individual New England missionary efforts is abundant but scattered, involving almost as many organizations as men.[50] Apparently money was first sent to New England for mis-

[49] This is the third chapter of Gookin's *Historical Collections of the Indians in New England, Massachusetts Historical Society Collections*, Ser. 1, I (1792), 149-56.

[50] I follow here the summaries in W. DeLoss Love, *Samson Occom and the Christian Indians of New England* (Boston, 1899), pp. 12-13; and George Parker Winship, " Introduction," *The New England Company of*

sionary work in the 1630's, when Roger Williams and perhaps John Eliot were going to the Indians. In 1636 Plymouth Colony enacted laws to provide for the preaching of the Gospel among the Indians, and in 1643 Thomas Mayhew began his mission on Martha's Vineyard and Nantucket. Little or nothing was achieved, however, until November 1644 when the Massachusetts General Court asked the ministers to recommend measures for converting the Indians. Two years later the General Court directed the ministers to elect two of their number every year to engage in gospel work among the heathen. In 1646 John Eliot, having learned a local Indian dialect, began systematically to preach to them. Then, in 1649, Edward Winslow, acting as London agent for the United Colonies, managed to get Parliament to authorize the incorporation of " The President and Society for the Propagation of the Gospel in New England," and this organization, poorly administered, financed missionary work in New England until the Restoration. With the Restoration, the charter of " The President and Society " was declared invalid and a royal Charter was granted, in February 1662, to the " Company for Propagacion of the Gospell in New England, and parts adjacent, in America." Until 1779, when the Revolutionary War caused remittances to America to be cut off, this Company carried on most of the financing of New England missions. A " Society for Promotion of Christian Knowledge," formed in England in 1698, the " Society in Scotland for Propagating Christian Knowledge," formed in 1709, and an abortive " Society for Propagating Christian Knowledge," incorporated in Massachusetts in 1762, likewise contributed to the holy cause. (The " Society for the Propagation of the Gospel in Foreign Parts " was an Anglican corporation founded in 1701, which sent its missionaries mainly to the Indians in the middle colonies and which gave up work with the Indians late in the eighteenth century.) All these organizations issued, finally, in " The Society for Propagating the Gospel among the Indians, and Others, in North America," founded in 1787. A great number of

1649 and John Eliot, Publications of the Prince Society, XXXVI (1920), vi-xliv.

intentions and organizations certainly, but few practical results. Only with self-consciously dedicated souls like Eliot and the Mayhews in the seventeenth century and with evangelical missionaries like Sargeant and Brainerd in the eighteenth, did the Gospel reach the heathen. There were, it seemed, only a few workers for this vast, wild vineyard.

For all his assurances that it was his holy mission to convert the heathen, the Puritan felt that the business seemed to be proceeding with agonizing delay. Why? he wondered. And, as always, he had answers from Scripture. Indian troubles, Indian opposition, and Indian recalcitrance were taken as God-ordained reminders to the Puritan that his way on this earth was a hard way; hence the Indian was to be literally and continually the devil's advocate for a people who needed to be reminded of their own sinfulness and of the agonizing hope of regeneration and election. Moreover, in the 1640's it seemed that there was specific scriptural authority for the delay in Indian conversion. The wild prophecy of Revelation 15 was interpreted as meaning that there could be no large-scale conversion of the heathen until the Jews themselves had been converted and until the Anti-Christ had been destroyed.[51] The notion still persisted in the 1670's during King Philip's War, when Increase Mather tried to dismiss it by pointing out that, in spite of the troubles which had resulted in the war, there nevertheless was a " glorious Sprinkling " of Indian converts in New England.[52]

It was indeed a " Sprinkling "—the result of work carried on by a few men who felt a deep personal need to go to the Indians directly. Yet even these few men were so sure of their Puritan

[51] See Thomas Lechford, *Plain Dealing* [1642], *Massachusetts Historical Society Collections,* Ser. 3, III [1833], 79-80; Roger Williams, *Christenings Make Not Christians* [1645], ed. H. M. Dexter, *Rhode Island Historical Tracts,* Ser. 1, no. 14 (1881), pp. 19-20; and John Cotton, *The Way of the Congregational Churches Cleared* (London, 1648), Part I, p. 78.

[52] *A Brief History of the War with the Indians in New England* [1676], in *The History of King Philip's War,* ed. S. G. Drake (Boston, 1862), p. 39.

way that they could not see the Indian as anything but imperfect copies of themselves. John Eliot, for example, worked for the Indians from 1634 on, was able in the 1640's to preach to them in their own language, translated the Old and the New Testaments into the local Massachusetts dialect, founded a Christian-Indian town in 1651 and saw thirteen others founded by 1674, and even ventured in 1659 to suggest that it would be possible to form the purest of Christian Commonwealths on the basis of his experiments in organizing Indian towns. Yet it is clear that he viewed savage life as one of satanic degradation and that he knew the Indians to be, as Cotton Mather pointed out in his biography of Eliot, "doleful creatures [who were] the veriest *ruines of mankind*, which [were] to be found any where upon the face of the earth."[53] Even a man like Roger Williams, who strove for savage as well as for civilized rights, was appalled by Indians in their "hideous *worships* of *creatures* and *devils*."[54] The missionaries' triumph was that they did not let such feelings keep them from their sacred duty.

Their faith was simple. If English missionaries could go to the Indians, first organize their living into some civil pattern, and then teach them the Word, they might pull them from the embrace of Satan. An ordered civil life was the basic condition of a holy life; civilization was properly a means to holiness. The Civil and the Holy Covenants of man with God were parts of a cosmic principle of order. If such a faith could sustain a Puritan society, certainly it could create an Indian society.

Yet for all the missionaries' faith in themselves, their society, and the savage's potentialities for civilization and God, the few who worked with the Indians seemed bound to fail. By the end of the seventeenth century everyone knew it. The trials of King Philip's War had hardened Puritan hearts; even the Christian Indians, well on the way to salvation, were mistreated.[55] A list

[53] *Magnalia* (Hartford, 1820), I, p. 504.

[54] *The Bloody Tenant Yet More Bloody* [1652], *Publications of the Narragansett Club*, Ser. 1, IV (1870), p. 85.

[55] See Daniel Gookin, *An Historical Account of the Doings and Sufferings of the Christian Indians* [MS., *c.* 1680], *American Antiquarian*

drawn up in 1698 gives only 2500 as the number of converts in the Indian towns, and points out that most of these are dying off rapidly.[56] Indian drunkenness, which had been sadly remarked before, came regularly to be denounced in a kind of ritualistic Puritan breast-beating.[57] For all this, Puritans could blame not themselves but the non-Puritan English traders among them;[58] or, going farther, could insist that both the failure of the missions and the successes of the corrupt traders were proofs of Puritan decadence, God's warning to New Englanders to mend their ways.[59] The frightening paradox was that the savage heathen was lowered, not raised, by his contact with the civilized Christian.

Yet we may observe that the cause of Puritan failure went deeper than the introduction of disease, drunkenness, and vice. It stemmed from the very quality of Puritan understanding of the Indian, necessarily from high Puritanism itself, from the desperate need of those who had settled New England to hold on to their special beliefs about the nature and destiny of man if they were to hold on to their God-ordained way of life. They had to assume

Society Collections, II (1836), 423-534; and *A True Account of the Most Considerable Occurrences* [1676], in S. G. Drake, *The Old Indian Chronicle* (Boston, 1867), pp. 247-85.

[56] Nicholas Noyes, *New Englands Duty and Interest* (Boston, 1698), appendix.

[57] Compare, for example, such early accounts as Thomas Lechford, *Plain Dealing* [1642], *Massachusetts Historical Society Collections*, Ser. 3, III (1833), 105, and John Josselyn, *An Account of Two Voyages* [1674], *ibid.*, Ser. 3, III (1833), 304, with such late accounts as Daniel Gookin, *Historical Collections of the Indians in New England* [c. 1680], *ibid.*, Ser. 1, I (1792), 151; Samuel Danforth, *The Woful Effects of Drunkenness, a Sermon* (Boston, 1710); *The Diary of Samuel Sewall, Massachusetts Historical Society Collections*, Ser. 5, V (1878), 108 and 115, VI (1879), 438; Samuel Penhallow, *The History of the Wars of New England* [1726] (Cincinnati, 1859), p. 125; and Experience Mayhew, *Indian Converts* (London, 1727), pp. xvii-xviii.

[58] *A Monitory, and Hortatory Letter to Those English, Who Debauch the Indians by Selling Strong Drink Unto Them* (Boston, 1700), pp. 10-12.

[59] Increase Mather, *Ichabod, or, a Discourse Shewing What Cause There Is To Fear That the Glory of the Lord Is Departing from New-England* (Boston, 1702), pp. 71-73.

that the Indian's nature was absolutely one and the same with their nature; the integrative orthodoxy of their society demanded such an absolute. Herein they might very well be desperate enough to fool themselves. Or so a Royal Commission noted in 1665, reporting first that in heterodox Rhode Island " is the greatest number of Indians[,] yet they never had any thing allowed towards the civilizing and converting of the Indians," and then that in orthodox Massachusetts:

They convert Indians by hiring them to come & heare Sermons; by teaching them not to obey their Heathen Sachims, & by appointing Rulers amongst them over tenns, twenties, fifties, &c. The lives, Manners, & habits of those, who they say are converted, cannot be distinguished from those who are not, except it be by being hyred to heare Sermons, which the more generous natives scorne.[60]

This is perhaps unfair, certainly antagonistic. Yet it indicates, if from an anti-Puritan viewpoint, how the Puritan might confuse appearance with reality. And it points, however obliquely, to an essential fact: that the seventeenth-century Puritan, in trying to recover for the Indian a civil and religious purity which he was sure he had already recovered for himself, was simply defining one reality in terms of another, the primitive in terms of the civilized, the Indian in terms of the Puritan. And, in the nature of things, he was bound to be wrong, and so to fail in his holy enterprise.

However, there was yet to be a renewed hope. Essentiallv an evangelical hope of saving a dying Indian for God, it rose as part of the last-ditch efforts of some Puritans to remain Puritans in spite of the reasonable theology and material progress that made them out to be gloomily and inhumanly old-fashioned. They would help manage a miracle, save the worst of Satan's creatures, and thus gloriously justify their Puritanism.

During the first quarter of the eighteenth century, reports to the English missionary societies which were financing evangelical work recounted, proposed, and promised great things—increased use of native missionaries, a kind of reservation system, some

[60] *Maine Historical Society Collections*, Ser. 2, IV (1889), 294.

thirty congregations newly established in southern New England, more attempts to get to the eastern Indians whom the French papists had debauched, cooperation with Dutch missionaries working among the Five Nations, and attempts to combat the effects of liquor, dishonest traders, and disease.[61] Even so, it was clear that God was angry with New England for her failure to Christianize the heathen when He had clearly indicated in Scripture that it was to be done.

And as we dread to go to Hell our selves [wrote the Reverend Solomon Stoddard in 1723], it should be awful to us to consider their Damnation. Love and Pity calls for it, that we should help them out of their Danger. We should pity *Beasts* in Misery, much more *Men*: Tho' they be Brutish Persons; yet, they are of Mankind, and so objects of Compassion. It is an act of Love to our own nature to seek their Salvation . . . .[62]

Who were the Indians who were thus to be saved? There was, for example, Joseph Quasson who had been bound to a white man when his father died in debt, who in his servitude had learned how to read and had come to know God. Freed, however, he had become a roisterer and a drunkard and by 1726 a condemned murderer. The account of Quasson which we have was written from his death cell by a friendly minister. And the point that the minister makes is this: the fact that Quasson had been bound to a white man; that his trial was delayed three years after the

[61] Samuel Sewall to Sir William Ashurst, head of the Company for the Propagation of the Gospel, May 3, 1700, *Massachusetts Historical Society Collections*, Ser. 6, I (1886), 231-33; [Increase Mather, Cotton Mather, and Nehemiah Walker], *A Letter About the Present State of Christianity, among the Christianized Indians of New England* (Boston, 1705); and Experience Mayhew, *Indian Converts* (London, 1727), pp. xvii-xviii.

[62] *Question, Whether God is not Angry with the Country for doing so little towards the Conversion of the Indians* (Boston, 1723), p. 8. Cf. letter from Cotton Mather to Robert Wodrow, Professor of Divinity at Glasgow, September 17, 1715, *Massachusetts Historical Society Collections*, ser. 7, VIII (1912), 328-29; and Thomas Paine, *The Temporal Safety of the Lord's People* (Boston, 1732) for variations on the same theme.

murder; that he was given seven weeks to live after being condemned; that liquor was taken away from him—all this shows how hard the Lord was working for his salvation.[63] And there was Sarah Coomes, the dying six-year-old of whom Experience Mayhew wrote in 1727:

She lay sick a considerable while before she died; and in that time continued to crave Instructions in things of God and the eternal World, and to express her Assent to, and acquiesce in them. She in particular expressed her steadfast Belief of the Doctrines of Christ's Person, Suffering, and Intercession for Sinners; and when she prayed, she called upon God to have Mercy upon her for his sake.[64]

This is Puritanism *in extremis*.

Along with the enthusiasm of the Great Awakening, this revivalistic interest in Indian conversion marks a final stage in the history of Puritanism. The work of New England born and trained Congregationalist missionaries had shifted by 1725 to the western parts of the middle colonies, where, joining with Scotch-Irish Presbyterian missionaries from the middle colonies, they worked toward that union of Congregationalist and Presbyterian missionary efforts which was to become official at the end of the century. The infusion of Presbyterian Calvinism must have done much to hearten the Congregationalist missionaries. For the ministers involved, John Sargeant, David Brainerd, Charles Beatty, and Jonathan Edwards chief among them, conversion was everything and civilizing nothing; the high Puritan faith in the uses of civilization as a means to conversion had disappeared almost entirely. Savages were to be converted on the frontier, apart from the immediately baneful influence of civilization. In a report which he prepared for the Society in Scotland for Propagating Christian Knowledge, Brainerd is primarily concerned with "experimental religion," which is to say, demonstrable religious conversion. He tells, for example, of his violent preaching to Indians, August 8, 1745, in Crosweeksung, New Jersey; he was pleased

[63] Samuel Moody, *A Summary Account of the Life and Death of Joseph Quasson, Indian* (Boston, 1726).

[64] *Indian Converts* (London, 1727), p. 264.

that the Indians were not able to " withstand the shock of this surprising operation . . . . They were almost universally praying and crying for mercy in every part of the house, and many out of doors, and numbers could neither go nor stand." [65] He was thus living up to the precepts of Ebenezer Pemberton who had preached at his ordination, insisting that conversion was to be achieved only by powerful preaching: " They [the preachers] are to 'compel sinners to come in' by a lively representation of the power and grace of an almighty Redeemer." [66] In his own short life, so his editor, biographer, and intended father-in-law, Jonathan Edwards, was pleased to note, the desperately consumptive Brainerd showed evidence, above all, of those authentic religious affections which were the only means to salvation. In an edition of the *Life of Brainerd*, published after Edwards' death, there was included further contemporary evidence of this need for violent conversion of the heathen—this in Charles Beatty's " Further remarks respecting Indian affairs." Beatty argues in so many words that Indians must be converted before being civilized; for they hate civilization and Christianity equally and must be convinced of the misery of their spiritual state before they can realize the misery of their civil state. Only " gospellizing " will succeed where civilizing has failed.[67] Having virtually destroyed the Indian by trying to bring a new civil life to him, the New England missionaries, encouraged by their Scotch-Irish Presbyterian brethren, were now to call the Holy Spirit directly to the Indian in order that they might give him that new life immediately. Certainly a miracle was needed.

Thus the Puritan's understanding of the Indian issued into the revivalism and anti-rationalism which in the end marked his

[65] *Mirabilia Dei Inter Indicos* [1746], in Jonathan Edwards, ed., *An Account of the Life of Mr. David Brainerd* [1749], (Edinburgh, 1798), pp. 376-77. Cf. an analogous account by John Brainerd, the brother of David, *John Brainerd's Journal* (*1761-1762*), *a Reprint* (Newark, N. J., 1941).

[66] *A Sermon Preached in Newark, June 12, 1774,* in *An Account of the Life of Mr. Brainerd*, pp. 525-45.

[67] *Ibid.*, appendix, pp. 52-[60]. Beatty's " Remarks " are part of his *Journal of a Two Months' Tour* (London, 1768), here reprinted.

understanding of himself. Always his mind had worked from the inside out, from God, Scripture, and reason to man and nature. Whatever he saw outside, he had somehow already seen inside. Understanding the Indian as he was related to man and nature, the Puritan thus succeeded, if he did succeed, only in knowing a little more about God, Scripture, and reason, and in understanding himself.

5

It is the Pennsylvania Quakers who should have best succeeded in bringing the Indian to God and to civilization. Yet they too failed. The reason for this failure follows, simply enough, from the nature of Quaker culture and the Quaker idea of the good life. In coming to America, the Quakers too hoped to bring the Indians out of heathenism and into a saving awareness of the divine principle within them. The Quaker problem was not to discover and describe the differences between savage and civilized men, but rather to discover and make known likenesses in terms of which all men could live the good, peaceful life together and in terms of which savages might be "convinced" into civilization. Quakers travelled widely among Indians, worked hard, but bothered themselves not at all with theorizing, with constructing complex systems for converting the savage heathen into the civilized Christian. They could believe in cultural complexity no more than they could believe in political complexity. They could offer the Indians not ritual and dogma, but love. Hence, so far as our record here is concerned, they finished where they had begun, with a simple faith in the saving awareness of the divine principle within all men. Meantime, the Indians on the frontiers of Pennsylvania were destroyed by that very cultural and political complexity in which the Quakers could not believe.

Travelling Quakers from the first worked earnestly to establish friendly relations with the Indians. Settling in 1677 in West Jersey, they were careful to treat honestly and fairly for such Indian lands as they had been granted by the Crown. And, more often than not, Indians in turn helped the Quakers, showing them how to live on the frontier; and there was peace. As a Quaker wrote back to England in 1678: "Without any carnal weapon we entered the land and inhabited therein, as safe as if there had been thousands of garrison; for the Most High preserved us from harm both of man and beast." [68] In such a spirit Pennsylvania itself was established. Quaker missionary work among the Indians, however, antedates Quaker colonization in America—having begun sporadically in 1659. George Fox himself encouraged his brethren to "go and discourse with some of the heathen kings, desiring them to gather their council and people together, that you may declare God's everlasting truth, and his everlasting way of life and salvation to them." [69] In 1672 and 1673 Fox himself visited North America and preached to the Indians. With the settling of Pennsylvania in 1681, Quaker missionary work and Quaker political relations with the Indians became officially one and were so for seventy-five years. In the words of a treaty of 1728, it was agreed "That all paths should be open and free to both Christians and Indians." [70]

Christians and Indians were alike men, alike in the principle of divinity within them. It was to be prayed and worked for that the Indians would become civilized Christians. But no good Friend could be so proud, so sure of himself in this world, as to violate the rights of another man because he was no Christian, or because he lacked the qualities of a civilized man. The love of a Friend would find a way. So William Penn addressed the Indians whom he knew:

> There is a great God, and Power, which hath made the world and all things therein, to whom you, and I, and all people owe their being and well-being, and to whom you and I must one day give an account, for all that we have done in the world.
>
> This great God hath written his law in our hearts, by which we are taught and commanded to love, and to help, and to do good to one another. Now this great God hath been pleased to make me con-

[68] *Some Account of the Conduct of the Religious Society of Friends towards the Indian Tribes in the Settlement of the Colonies of East and West Jersey and Pennsylvania* (London, 1844), p. 16.

[69] *Ibid.*, p. 20.

[70] *Ibid.*, p. 32.

cerned in your part of the world; and the King of the country where I live hath given me a great province therein: but I desire to enjoy it with your love and consent, that we may always live together as neighbours and friends; else, what would the great God do to us, who hath made us (not to devour and destroy one another, but) to live soberly and kindly together in the world? [71]

For all this, Quaker missionary efforts were in the long run as ineffective as Quaker politics. Indian converts were virtually nonexistent, since the savage knew that a religion meant ceremony and ritual, and since the Quakers offered only the law which God had placed in the heart. If Indians were to worship Christ, it would have to be Christ symbolized, made dramatic, and brought to life, not that private Christ who shone only as an Inner Light. Likewise, a civilization bound by the sense of innumerable meetings could mean little to Indians among whom social relationships were defined by strict traditions and forms. Quaker freedom and Quaker love were at once too much and too little for the savages whom they were to reach and to save.

We have, so far as I am aware, no attempt by a Quaker to analyze the nature of the savage and its meaning for the civilized man. It would seem that it never occurred to the good Quaker to think in general terms of differences between the savage and the civilized. We do have, however, abundant accounts of Quaker meetings with Indians and abundant incidental observations and conclusions. For example, the travelling Friend John Richardson in a long account of his "trials and exercises," recalls the end of a conference between William Penn and a few Indians. Penn had given the Indians match coats and "some Brandy or Rum, or both," which they had taken "quietly and in a solid manner." Richardson observes:

that they did not, nor I suppose never do speak, two at a time, nor interfere in the least one with another that way in all their Councils, as has been observed. Their Eating and Drinking was in much Stillness and Quietness.

[71] William Wistar Comfort, *William Penn, 1644-1718: A Tercentenary Estimate* (Philadelphia, 1944), p. 44.

I much desire that all *Christians* (whether they may be such in Reality or Profession only) may endeavour to imitate these People in those Things which are so commendable, which may be a Means to prevent Loss of Time and expedite Business; as much as may be endeavouring to prevent one speaking at a time in Meetings of Conference and Business.[72]

Too, we have Penn's 1683 report on the simple, happy Pennsylvania Indians who " are under a dark Night in Things relating to *Religion*, to be sure, the *Tradition* of it; [who yet] believe [in] a *God* and *Immortality*, without the Help of Metaphysics." [73] Characteristically, the Quaker saw the possible good in savage customs and in savage religion. For he wanted to live with the savages and to find in them the essential humanity he knew was there.

Quaker efforts and Quaker hopes were crushed by the power politics of Anglo-French dealings with the Pennsylvania Indians during the first half of the eighteenth century. Under William Penn's son, mercantile interests were coming more and more to dominate the politics of the colony. " Practical " men in Pennsylvania, administrators whose interests were with the Proprietors of the colony, not with its Quaker inhabitants, made peace with the Iroquois in 1732 because the Iroquois and their allies controlled the balance of savage power on the frontier; hence the Quakers could only stand by and see all their good work with the Delawares undone—by, among other things, the infamous Walking Purchase of 1737. The Delawares, bitter that Pennsylvanians, forgetting their pledges of friendship, had betrayed them to the outlander Iroquois, rapidly came under the influence of the French; life on the frontier, now inhabited by Scotch-Irish pioneers, came to be bloody and hard. The Quakers, holding to their pacifist principles, could not give full and prompt support to plans

[72] *An Account of the Life of That Ancient Servant of Jesus Christ, John Richardson* (London, 1758), pp. 137-38. Cf. for analogous observations and conclusions, Emily Moore, ed., *Travelling with Thomas Story* (Letchworth, 1947), pp. 54-56.

[73] *A Collection of the Works of William Penn* (London, 1726), II, 699-706. I quote from p. 703.

for frontier defence, to Braddock's expedition in 1755, for example; they still hoped (they still had to hope, being Quakers) to kill the Indian danger with loving kindness. In the midst of Anglo-French imperialistic rivalry which centered in the middle colonies, the Quakers were unaware of the insignificance of their pacifist aims and hopes. Of necessity, they became politically less and less effective; their failure with the Indians was, as a matter of fact, only one of many failures, all relating to their insisting on being Friends to all rival parties, when none would be friends to them. In 1756 there was war, and Pennsylvania, having firmly secured Iroquois friendship, was offering large bounties for Delaware scalps.[74] A principle of survival had overridden a principle of divinity.

With the coming of the French and Indian War, the Quakers soon achieved that status of neutral observer which was implicit in their position from the very beginning. Wealthy Quaker merchants in Philadelphia founded in 1756 "The Friendly Association for gaining and preserving Peace with the Indians by Pacific Measures." (The following year a similar, but less active, New Jersey Association was founded by John Woolman and others.) Supported with large funds for gifts and councils, the Association got permission to treat with the marauding Delawares and Shawnees on the frontier and succeeded in making a peace. Such peace as there was on the Pennsylvania frontier during the French and Indian War was due largely to the efforts of the Association; yet after the initial success, the administrators of the colony allowed the Quakers to take part in negotiations with the Indians only informally, as advisors and observers. Finally even the Friendly Association, with infinite good intentions and high hopes, could not keep peace between Indians and ruthless men on the frontier. With such affairs as the massacre of harmless Connestoga Indians by the so-called Paxton Boys in 1763 and Pontiac's Rebel-

[74] I follow here the analysis of Julian Boyd, "Indian Affairs in Pennsylvania, 1736-1762," in *Indian Treaties Printed by Benjamin Franklin, 1736-1762* (Philadelphia, 1938), pp. iii-lxxviii; and Frederick B. Tolles, *Meeting House and Counting House, The Quaker Merchants of Colonial Philadelphia, 1682-1763* (Chapel Hill, 1948), pp. 21-28.

lion in the northwest, the Friendly Association passed out of existence. However, a tradition had been established; the Quakers were often to figure officially in future Indian-white relations as interested neutrals. This was logical enough; for from the beginning what had interested the Quakers was not the rights of Indians nor the rights of white men, but rather the divine rights of all men.[75]

The Quaker experience furnishes still another lesson in practical failure. Ironically enough, that failure was rooted in what Quakers assumed (and assume) to be the very principle of success—the awareness of the divine principle in all men. Believing thus, they were constrained to be pacifists, not to make over the Indians in their own images but rather simply to try to bring them to an awareness of that divine principle. The simplicity of such a principle was beyond most savages, certainly, as it was (and always has been) beyond most civilized men, even, if we may look closely at the record of Quaker mercantilism in the first half of the eighteenth century, beyond many Quakers. We have early and direct contemporary testimony concerning this failure. In the 1680's, the Dutch travellers, Dankers and Sluyter, noted that the Quakers were bound to fail with the Indians either because the Quakers themselves could not live up to their ideals, or, if they could, the Indians could neither respect nor understand actions rising from those ideals:

> The Indians hate the Quakers very much on account of their deceit and covetousness, and say they are not Englishmen, always distinguishing them from all other Englishmen, as is also done by almost all other persons. The Indians say " they are not Christians, they are like ourselves." [76]

To point out that the Indians say of the Quakers, " they are like ourselves " is certainly to mark a failure. But it is also to mark a success. In a world dominated by imperialistic and mercantilistic

[75] See Theodore Thayer, " The Friendly Association," *Pennsylvania Magazine of History and Biography*, LXVII (1943), 356-76.

[76] *Journal of a Voyage to New York in 1679-80, Memoirs of the Long Island Historical Society*, I (1867), 244.

drives and consequent hatred of savages who stand in the path of empire, the precise mark of success is failure.

6

The imperialist, mercantilist forces which had destroyed Quaker efforts to save the Indian for civilization had, in fact, been moving everywhere in the American colonies. As it developed, official British policy came to treat the Indian not so much in terms of civilization as of trade. In the western parts of the middle colonies and in the colonies to the south of Virginia, traders were officially encouraged to keep up good relations with the Indians, and settlers were by and large told to keep off Indian lands. Inevitably settlers followed traders onto Indian lands or traders were dishonest; inevitably there resulted such an Indian-colonial conflict as the bloody Yamasee War of 1715-1716. But Indian resistance in the long run figured for little. By the time of the French and Indian War, which was itself being fought over control of trade in America, Indians were involved only as trading victims of both sides. British imperialism won out against French imperialism. British Superintendents of Indian Affairs in the North and in the South were appointed in the middle 1750's; control of Indian affairs was thus centralized and the future of the Indian trade secured. But still traders were dishonest and Indian lands were encroached upon by settlers. Affairs got out of hand once more in Pontiac's Conspiracy of 1763-1765. The record is one of quarrels, treaties, stop-gap measures to keep the peace, inter-colonial squabbles over Indian trade and Indian lands, and the beginnings of what was to be an inexorable progress westward.

The problem, then, became one of understanding the Indian, not as one to be civilized and to be lived with, but rather as one whose nature and whose way of life was an obstacle to civilized progress westward. What was observed was that the virtues of high civilization, as well as its vices, destroyed savage life, destroyed what could be frankly admitted to be savage virtues. How explain this paradox of the admitted incompatibility of admitted virtues? This is the problem of the savage as it comes to exist for colonial Americans towards the middle of the eighteenth century. Their achievement is that they begin to state the problem clearly and objectively, to think not only of possible likenesses between the savage and the civilized, but of necessary differences. So stated, the problem was to be handed on to Americans after 1775 and then to be solved in such a way as to form a grand rationale for the progress of American civilization over what was called American savagism.

7

In Robert Beverly's *History of the Present State of Virginia* (1705), there is the first attempt by a colonial American to write a " complete " account of the nature of the Indian.[77] After tracing the history of seventeenth-century Indian-white relations in Book I of his *History,* and emphasizing throughout that the English were equally responsible with the Indians for the bloodiness of those relations, Beverly moves, in Book III, to a synoptic account " Of the Indians, their Religion, Laws, and Customs, in War and Peace." He details, to use his headings, Persons and Dress, Marriages and Children, Town Buildings and Fortifications, Cooking and Food, Travelling, Reception, and Entertainment, Learning and Language, War and Peace, Religion and Worship, Diseases and Cures, Sports and Pastimes, Laws and Authority, Treasure and Riches, and Crafts. The rich details are presented as objectively as Beverly can manage, drawn from observation and the best authorities, and are treated systematically, so we would say, as they range from appearance through material culture to institutions and customs.

Beverly's main concern is to understand the Indians as natural men. Yet he is not willing wholly to condemn them for being natural men. He is especially pleased to record certain parallels

[77] Beverly's account of the Virginia Indians was in part written to correct materials in John Oldmixon's *British Empire in America* (1708), which Beverly had seen in manuscript in 1703. Beverly's brother-in-law, William Byrd II, had supplied Oldmixon with materials for his account. Beverly was asked to revise the Oldmixon account, but found it not worth revising. In his *British Empire* Oldmixon speaks disparagingly of Beverly, but nonetheless borrows verbatim from him. See Louis B. Wright, ed. *The Present State of Virginia* (Chapel Hill, N. C., 1947), pp. xvii, 349.

between savage life and classical, heroic life. He notes, for example, that Indian cooking and Indian food resemble those of the Spartans, and observes of the wondrous custom of offering maidens of the village to distinguished visitors; " After this manner perhaps many of the Heroes were begotten in old times, who boasted themselves to be the Sons of some Way-faring God." [78] He has his *History* illustrated with Gribelin's copies of De Bry's copies of John White's drawings of sixteenth-century Virginia Indians; in Gribelin's copies the original Indians have virtually been classicized out of existence; they *are* Spartans. Arguing against both orthodox and rationalistic religionists, Beverly decides that Indian religion is neither brutal devil-worshipping nor deistical freethinking; rather it simply is the religion of savage ignorance.

In the end, he faces the present state of the Virginia Indians as he sees it:

> Thus I think I have given a succinct account of the *Indians*; happy, I think, in their simple State of Nature, and in their enjoyment of Plenty, without the Curse of Labour. They have on several accounts reasons to lament the arrival of the Europeans, by whose means they seem to have lost their Felicity, as well as their Innocence. The *English* have taken away great part of their Country, and consequently made everything less plenty amongst them. They have introduc'd Drunkenness and Luxury amongst them, which have multiply'd their Wants, and put them upon desiring a thousand things, they never dreamt of before . . . . [79]

Civilization, Christianization, even marriage of Indians and whites, remain as great hopes of saving savages for God and civilization.[80] But Beverly knows that if the Indians give up their savage life, they will be giving up not only the evil, but also the good in that life.

Like Beverly, John Lawson in his *New Voyage to Carolina* (1708) is interested, first, in the nature of savage life and, second,

[78] *Ibid.*, p. 189.

[79] *Ibid.*, p. 233.

[80] Beverly deleted mention of miscegenation in the 1722 edition of the *History*.

in the effect of civilization on that life. As Surveyor-General of North Carolina, Lawson travelled extensively throughout the colony, keeping a detailed journal of his travels. In the journal there is an abundance of observations on the Indian; appended to the journal, there is a lengthy, systematic account which brings together those observations.

Lawson too begins with descriptions of appearance, moves to details of material culture, and ends with a discussion of institutions—family, marriage, government, religion, and morals. His primary concern is with concrete particulars, since, he thinks, there have been published by irresponsible reporters too many second- and third-hand accounts. He does not wish to praise the Indians nor to condemn them; he is interested in seeing them for what they are. Thus he finds the Carolina Indians to be a simple people, with simple virtues and simple vices. They do not envy other men their riches or achievements; they are concerned only to develop their own abilities as warriors or hunters, to live out their lives, not fearing the death which they know must come to them. If they are cruel to their prisoners, torturing them mercilessly, it is because they know that death is the easy, natural way out, and they wish to make the way out as difficult as possible. If they are "revengeful," it is because they never forget injuries, not because they are full of such "Heats and Passions" as possess Europeans. If their religion is savage, it is because they are unenlightened aborigines, living in a cruel, hard world. And thus far Englishmen in America have brought them only death. So Lawson can sum up:

In short, they are an odd sort of People under the Circumstances they are at present, and have such uncouth Ways in their Management and Course of Living, that it seems a Miracle to us, how they bring about their Designs, as they do, when their Ways are commonly quite contrary to ours. I believe, they are, (as to this Life,) a very happy People; and were it not for the Feuds amongst themselves they would enjoy the happiest state, (in this World) of all Mankind. They met with Enemies when we came amongst them; for they are no nearer Christianity now, than they were at the first Discovery, to all Appearance. They have learned several Vices of the Europeans, but not one Vertue, as I know of.[81]

What is to be done? Lawson is explicit:

. . . if we will admit Reason to be our Guide, she will inform us that these Indians are the freest People in the World, and so far from being Intruders upon us that we have abandoned our own Native Soil, to drive them out, and possess theirs, neither have we any true Balance in Judging of these poor Heathens, because we neither give Allowance for their Natural Disposition, nor the Sylvan Education, and strange Customs (uncouth to us) they lie under and have ever been trained up to; these are false Measures for Christians to take, and indeed no man can be reckoned a Moralist only, who will not make choice and use of better Rules to walk and act by.[82]

Traders must conduct their business so as to show Indians "the Steps of Vertue, and the Golden Rule, to do as we would be done by." Like Beverly before him, Lawson recommends civilization and Christianization, even intermarriage of whites and Indians. Like Beverly, he is sure that the savage can be civilized. But he sees that savage life has an integrity of its own, an integrity which is essentially different from that of the civilized life which will necessarily destroy it.

This matter of the essential integrity of savage life, for good and for bad, became increasingly the main concern of eighteenth-century Americans writing on the Indian. William Byrd II, working up his *History of the Dividing Line* for publication, sees the Indians as warring, cruel, sneaking, basely malicious, cunning, yet somehow valorous—in their religion as in everything, "contented with Nature as they find her." [83] Cadwallader Colden, as a kind of Indian agent in New York, writes, in the second edition of his *History of the Five Indian Nations* (1747), of the aristocratic, cruelly domineering Iroquois, natural men who are impassioned

[81] *Lawson's History of North Carolina* (Richmond, Va., 1937), pp. 251-52.

[82] *Ibid.*, p. 256.

[83] William Byrd's *Histories of the Dividing Line*, ed. William K. Boyd (Raleigh, N. C., 1929), pp. 112-23, 218-22, 306-308.

lovers of freedom and warfare, polished orators, virtually heroes out of Homer.[84] The jurist-historian William Smith follows Colden in his *History of the Province of New York* (1757), but finds nothing ennobled in savage heroes, out of Homer or not.[85] Louis Evans, writing a *Brief Account of Pennsylvania* (1753), takes a dim view of Indians as true republicans who will not submit to any authority except that rising out of their natural selves.[86] Likewise, Benjamin Franklin, in his "Observations Concerning the Increase of Mankind, Peopling of Countries, etc." (1755), observes of the Indians that "their wants . . . [are] supplied by the Spontaneous Productions of Nature" and that naturally they don't want to be civilized.[87] Writers in 1764 and 1765, concerned with the effects of Pontiac's Rebellion, point out that the Indian must be fought not with honorably civilized but with dishonorably savage techniques of war. Even so, they admit that savages will fight heroically to defend the simple liberty which they love.[88] Indian-white difficulties were seen more and more to arise from the difference between two conceptions of the good life, a difference so great as always to force war to the death. In 1765, Lieutenant Henry Timberlake had travelled enough among the Cherokees to see the matter from the savage's point of view:

[84] Colden's account is contained in a "Short View of the Form of Government of the Five Nations, and of their Laws, Customs, etc." which forms the introduction to the second edition of his *History of the Five Indian Nations* (London, 1747).

[85] *History of the Province of New-York* (London, 1757), pp. 35-38.

[86] *Brief Account* [1753], in L. H. Gipson, *Louis Evans* (Philadelphia, 1939), pp. 90-94.

[87] I follow the text (from the Shaftesbury Papers) given in A. O. Aldridge, "Franklin's Letter on Indians and Germans," *American Philosophical Society Proceedings*, XIV (1950), 391-95.

[88] Gavin Cochrane, "Treatise on the Indians of North America," Ayer Collection MS. 176 (Newberry Library, Chicago); Robert Rogers, *Concise Account of North America* (London 1765), pp. 205-64; William Smith, "Of the Temper and Genius of the Indians," in *An Historical Account of the Expedition against the Ohio Indians* [1765] (Cincinnati, 1868 [from ed. London, 1766]), pp. 95-110;; Henry Timberlake, *The Memoirs of Lieutenant Henry Timberlake* [1765] (Johnson City, Tenn., 1927), pp. 75-102.

. . . who would seek to live by labour, who can live by amusement? The sole occupations of an Indian life, are hunting, and warring abroad, and lazying at home. Want is said to be the mother of industry, but their wants are supplied at an easier rate.[89]

Some ten years later, James Adair, a trader among the Cherokees, could go even farther than Timberlake and see savage society as the modern counterpart of Old Testament society. Trying, in his *History of the American Indians,* to demonstrate a grand parallel between Indian and ancient Hebrew life and thus to prove the Hebraic origin of the Indian (against the commonly accepted theory of Tartar origin), Adair prefers simple Hebraic-savage honesty to complex British-civilized corruption. Indeed, he finds in Indian life much that would be desirable in civilized British life. For Indians are governed by the "plain and honest law of nature."

. . . their whole constitution breathes nothing but liberty; and when there is that equality of condition, manners, and privileges, and a constant familiarity in society, as prevails in every Indian nation, and through all our British colonies, there glows such a chearfulness and warmth of courage in each of their breasts, as cannot be described.[90]

But such a version of primitive nobility among the Cherokees is easily contradicted by at least one other traveller among them (and other southeastern Indians), Bernard Romans, in his *Concise Natural History of East and West Florida* (1775). Romans thinks that these savages are so much unnatural men that they must have been separately created. And as for their day-to-day lives:

But alas! What a people do we find them, a people not only rude and uncultivated, but incapable of civilization: a people that would think themselves degraded to the lowest degree, were they to imitate us in any respect whatsoever, and that look down on us and all our manners with the highest contempt: and of whom experience has taught us, that on the least opportunity they will return like the dog to

[89] Henry Timberlake, *Memoirs,* p. 99.

[90] James Adair, *History of the American Indians* (London, 1775), p. 379.

his vomit. See there the boasted, admired state of nature, in which these brutes enjoy and pass their time here.[91]

Romans' view is extreme, of course. But for him, as for all eighteenth-century colonial writers, the Indian was, as he always had been, a natural man. Now, more and more, he was seen to be deeply and perhaps permanently attached to his savage nature. All writers, Romans excepted, might still hope and trust that somehow he could be detached from that nature and brought to civilization. Yet they were beginning to see that the gap between the savage and civilized might not be so easily bridged, that, in fact, it might not be a gap but an ocean, a continent, which could never be crossed.

8

Through the first three-quarters of the eighteenth century, the problem of the relation of the Indian to American life came more and more often to be stated thus. It was, in its simplest, most general terms, the problem of the relation of savage to civilized life. Savages were inextricably bound in what was to be called savagism. They might have a kind of good life in that state; for there were specifically savage virtues, natural virtues, even if there were not specifically noble savages. Yet one could not doubt that morality and virtue were everywhere essentially one and the same, if men, sprung from Adam, were everywhere essentially one and the same. How hold to a God-ordained moral absolute and to an assurance of common humanity, and still understand whatever good there might be in savage societies? How relate that good to the obviously greater good of civilized societies? How believe in two ideas of order? This was the special problem facing Americans who, from 1775 through the 1850's, tried to understand the Indians' place in American life, who at once saw and were part of the westward progress of civilization over savagism.

The American solution was worked out as an element in an idea of progress, American progress. Cultures are good, it was

[91] Bernard Romans, *Concise Natural History of East and West Florida* (New York, 1775), p. 39.

held, as they allow for full realization of man's essential and absolute moral nature; and man realizes this nature as he progresses historically from a lesser to a greater good, from the simple to the complex, from savagism to civilization. Westward American progress would, in fact, be understood to be reproducing this historical progression; and the savage would be understood as one who had not and somehow could not progress into the civilized, who would inevitably be destroyed by the civilized, the lesser good necessarily giving way to the greater. Civilized men who gave in to the temptations of savagism and its simplicities would likewise be destroyed. For the Indian was the remnant of a savage past away from which civilized men had struggled to grow. To study him was to study the past. To civilize him was to triumph over the past. To kill him was to kill the past. History would thus be the key to the moral worth of cultures; the history of American civilization would thus be conceived of as three-dimensional, progressing from past to present, from east to west, from lower to higher.

As this idea of civilized progress came to be an article of American belief, so did the idea of savagism from which it took substance and to which it gave strength. It was an idea of progress which came into being as Americans were moved to consider their own life as it might relate to Indian life; to understand that relationship practically, theoretically, and symbolically; and to act in accordance with that understanding. Americans would, in short, be obliged at one and the same time to make their destiny, to know it, and to live it out. The effort of colonial Americans had mainly been directed toward proving that savage and civilized destiny were one. That effort failed as a matter of course. And Americans after 1775, trying to know their unique destiny, would come to know it in terms of savages who could have no share in it.

PART 2

The Life and Death of the American Savage, 1777-1851

"Civilization or death to all American Savages."

Soldiers' Toast, July 4, 1779.

"We have taught them neither how to live, nor how to die."

Lewis Cass, Governor of Michigan Territory, 1826.

II

A Melancholy Fact:

The Indian in American Life

AMERICANS who were setting out to make a new society could find a place in it for the Indian only if he would become what they were—settled, steady, civilized. Yet somehow he would not be anything but what he was—roaming, unreliable, savage. So they concluded that they were destined to try to civilize him and, in trying, to destroy him, because he could not and would not be civilized. He was to be pitied for this, and also to be censured. Pity and censure were the price Americans would have to pay for destroying the Indian. Pity and censure would be, in the long run, the price of the progress of civilization over savagism.

1

Fighting a Revolution, barely able to handle the British, Americans hoped to neutralize the Indian's power and to settle with him later. The British, on their side, tried to convince him that a victory for land-hungry colonials would mean the end of his way of life. British agents and administrators were skilled in handling Indians; they guaranteed continued preservation of Indian territory, rights, and trade; their appeals were powerful, direct, and realistic. The result was that on most fronts colonial Americans found themselves troubled by Indians allied with the British. They managed to put down the British-manipulated Cherokee uprising in 1776, to withstand repeated British-encouraged frontier raids, even to attack the Indians on their own, as in Sullivan's 1779 expedition to destroy the corn and villages of Iroquois loyal to the British. They also came to recognize that the Indian's power could never be simply neutralized, and that they would soon have to settle with him once and for all.

The Indian's fortune after the Revolution was to learn that he had no right to exist independently and to live as and where he pleased. The official American view was still the British colonial view: that Indian land was to be considered as conquered territory. Yet Indians, in the 1780's encouraged by British agents operating from British-held territory in the north and south, firmly held that their land belonged to them and must be purchased outright. Treaties were made, and boundaries were set by the new American government; and treaties were promptly broken and boundaries disregarded by frontier citizens who had little respect for their government and less for what Hugh Henry Brackenridge termed in 1782 "the animals, vulgarly called Indians."[1]

This was to be the abiding relationship between red Indians and white Americans. In the settled east, where Indians had been done away with, it was hoped that their western lands could gradually be taken over and that they might as gradually be civilized and absorbed into the oncoming white population. Congress acted toward this end in 1786 when it placed control of Indian affairs solely in the hands of the national government. Yet individual states, needing to grab land, continued to treat with Indians and to get what they could; and individual frontiersmen took what they found worth taking. The Northwest Ordinance of 1787 and the Constitution of 1789 set forth an Indian policy whose central tenet was that Indian title to western land, even though it be conquered land, had to be extinguished formally before Americans might move onto it and that, further, Indians were to be settled on farms and to be civilized as their lands were taken over. Impatient frontiersmen broke the law while they forced Indians to obey it.

There was no time to civilize. Americans moving westward in effect forced the Indians to try, however vainly, to hold on to those ways of savage life which civilizing theoretically would end. En-

[1] Hugh Henry Brackenridge, *Indian Atrocities* [1782] (Cincinnati, 1867), p. 62.

couraged by the British, tribes in the Ohio country went so far as to repudiate early treaties with the United States and to insist that all land west of the Ohio was to be theirs forever. Desperately strong in their determination to survive, they were able to defeat the punitive expeditions of Harmar in 1790 and of St. Clair in 1791, but were completely routed by Wayne's army in 1794. At the resulting Treaty of Greenville in 1795, deserted by the British, they surrendered almost all of the Ohio country. In the southeast, tribes led by the Creeks were encouraged by Spain to resist the onrush of the pioneers of the new republic. Yet by 1790 they too were willing to accept by treaty the rule of the United States.

Treaties meant little to pioneering Americans, who moved without hesitation onto Indian lands and took what they pleased. When, for example, representatives of Kickapoos, Weas, and Delawares refused in 1802 to cede further land to the Territory of Indiana, its Governor, William Henry Harrison, informed them that the lands already belonged to the United States and would be taken over by force if necessary. Actions like Harrison's, implementing the frontier drive to land, power, and elbow room, again pushed Indians in the northwest into united resistance, this time under Tecumseh and his half brother, the Prophet. Even with British help, this attempt to resist American encroachment failed too; the final defeat of the northwest Indians became only one incident in the War of 1812. Likewise in the War of 1812, Creeks in the southeast, allied with the British once more, were put down by Andrew Jackson and his Indian haters. One of the sovereignties finally achieved in the War of 1812 was that of American over Indian. A Fourth of July toast (the tenth of the evening) drunk by officers in Sullivan's expedition in 1779 had expressed essentially what was to be proved a great and eternal frontier truth: "Civilization or death to all American Savages." [2]

Theoretically, death was to be by the attrition rising out of gradual, ordered, intelligently-controlled expansion westward. The process, it was fully granted, would be painful but nonetheless

[2] The banquet is reported in the journal of Major James Norris, in Frederick Cook, ed., *Journals of the Military Expedition of Major General John Sullivan* (Auburn, N. Y., 1887), pp. 225-26.

necessary. Early it achieved official, formal recognition, so that in 1789 Henry Knox, Secretary of War and thus in charge of Indian affairs, could serenely declare:

Although the disposition of the people of the States, to emigrate into the Indian country, cannot be effectually prevented, it may be restrained and regulated.

It may be restrained, by postponing new purchases of Indian territory, and by prohibiting the citizens from intruding on the Indian lands.

It may be regulated, by forming colonies, under the direction of Government, and by posting a body of troops to execute their orders.

As population shall increase, and approach the Indian boundaries, game will be diminished, and new purchases may be made for small considerations. This has been, and probably will be, the inevitable consequence of cultivation.

It is, however, painful to consider, that all the Indian tribes, once existing in those States now the best cultivated and most populous, have become extinct. If the same causes continue, the same effects will happen; and, in a short period, the idea of an Indian on this side the Mississippi will only be found in the page of the historian.[3]

Actually, death was more violent than Knox had planned. The Louisiana Purchase of 1803 made it possible to conceive of removing Indians to a place where they would be out of civilization's way, where they might have a chance to survive as savages, where they even might be brought to wished-for civilization. This was to be west of the Mississippi on land which no civilized man would ever covet. The conception seems to have been part of Jefferson's intention in arranging the Purchase. It was, in any case, an obvious solution to a worrisome problem and was hopefully entertained by both friends and enemies of the Indian, the former glad to have a means of keeping him out of harm's way, the latter glad to be rid of him. When the clash of Indian and white on the frontier finally demanded it, in the 1820's and 30's, the conception was realized formally as the government's policy of Removal, whereby Indians east of the Mississippi would trade lands needed by civilized men for western lands more suited to savage use.

[3] *American State Papers, Indian Affairs*, I, no. 4, 53.

First, beginning in 1825, Indians in the northwest country were maneuvered into ceding their lands and removing to the Indian Territory, west of the 95th meridian; the only violent resistance, that of Black Hawk and the Sauks and Foxes, was ruthlessly beaten down. Then in 1830 the southeastern Indians began moving west at the request of the government, and in ten years had almost all made new homes in the Territory. Of the southeastern Indians, only the eastern Cherokees, even then settled on farms and asking for citizenship, tried to assert their American rights. Their resistance was beaten down when in 1838 troops marched them from Georgia to their new home in the west; six months on the way, they lost by death on the march about one-tenth of their number. Such resistance and such an end to it made one thing clear: Indians could be considered only as charity cases, victims inevitably of the law of civilized progress.

President Jackson summed up the matter for his fellow Americans in his Second Annual Message, December 6, 1830:

> Humanity has often wept over the fate of the aborigines of this country, and Philanthropy has been long busily employed in devising means to avert it, but its progress has never for a moment been arrested, and one by one have many powerful tribes disappeared from the earth. To follow to the tomb the last of his race and to tread on the graves of extinct nations excite melancholy reflections. But true philanthropy reconciles the mind to these vicissitudes as it does to the extinction of one generation to make room for another . . . . Philanthropy could not wish to see this continent restored to the condition in which it was found by our forefathers. What good man would prefer a country covered with forests and ranged by a few thousand savages to our extensive Republic, studded with cities, towns, and prosperous farms, embellished with all the improvements which art can devise or industry execute, occupied by more than 12,000,000 happy people, and filled with all the blessings of liberty, civilization, and religion?
>
> The present policy of the Government is but a continuation of the same progressive change by a milder process . . . .[4]

[4] J. D. Richardson, ed., *A Compilation of the Messages and Papers of the Presidents, 1789-1897*, II, 520-21.

Thus mildly and progressively the Indian exchanged his home east of the Mississippi for one west and was forced out of American life into American history. What was left after Removal in the 1830's was border warfare, making the west itself safe for American civilization, and caring for those Indians who had been able to survive. With Removal, savagism no longer threatened civilized American life. Actually, we can see now that it never really had; it had threatened only individual American lives. The way to begin to know savagism, and through it civilization, was, simply enough, to destroy savages.

2

Concern for the Indian's sad state was as deep and as honest as certainty of his inevitable destruction. Jackson's and Knox's rhetoric amounts to formal public expression of American regret in the face of the tragic and triumphant meaning of the progress of civilization over savagism. For the Indian everywhere was known to be one of the lost.

Frontier accounts, to be sure, still reported him as one to be feared and hated. By 1800 the narrative of Indian captivity had become a staple source for thrilling and shocking details of frontier hardships. The Indian of the captivity narrative was the consummate villain, the beast who hatcheted fathers, smashed the skulls of infants, and carried off mothers to make them into squaws. This, the reader of a captivity narrative could assure himself, was the price one paid for living in the vanguard of civilization, for trying to be a peace-loving farmer in the presence of bloody savages. The narratives he was offered—*mélanges* of blood, thunder, torn flesh, and sensibility, of small fact and great fiction—were frenetic attempts to hold on to the crudest image of the triumphantly brutal Indian.[5] This Indian, and his counterpart in literature, excited American readers behind the frontier. But they knew he was fated to be something else.

[5] For an extended analysis of the captivity tradition at this period, see my "The Significances of the Captivity Narrative," *American Literature*, XIX (1947), 1-20.

For when they did see Indians, it was Indians drunken, diseased, and degraded; they were told that Indians beyond the frontier would sooner or later be in no better condition. As always in the two centuries before, liquor was seen to be the most effective agent in dissolving savage character. American and European travellers invariably reported scenes of debauchery and violence when Indians were given liquor; very often they registered the hope that something could be done about enforcing laws which prohibited the liquor traffic.[6] Some travellers, reporting frontier cruelty to Indians, made frontiersmen villainous and Indians crudely pathetic. Fortescue Cuming told in 1810 of a farmer on the Ohio, who, when asked if a small tribe of Miamis camped near him were any trouble, "replied with much sang froid . . . , 'We never permit them to be troublesome, for if any of them displease us, we take them out of doors and kick them a little, for they are like dogs, and so will love you the better for it.'" The farmer followed this with an account of a favorite pastime, getting Indians drunk and setting them to fighting among themselves.[7]

It was obvious that the frontiersman, whether he was farmer, trapper, or hunter, was involved in a simple fight for survival. This much of the message of captivity narratives and its kind could be accepted. By the same token, it was obvious that the frontiersman was an agent of cruel destruction. However necessary that destruction, its cruelty could not be overlooked. That it was at once inevitable and necessary, in fact, made it all the crueller. As the frontier advanced, the Indian came more and more to be celebrated as the pathetic victim of the frontiersman, and the

[6] Characteristic expressions—a few among many—in this vein are: John F. D. Smyth, *A Tour in the United States of America* (London, 1784), I, 186; C. F. Volney, *View of the Soil and Climate of the United States of America*, trans. C. B. Brown (Philadelphia, 1804), p. 354; DeWitt Clinton, "A Discourse," *New York Historical Society Collections*, II (1814), 83-84; Morris Birkbeck, *Letters from Illinois* (London, 1818), pp. 100-101; C. D. Arfwedsen, *The United States and Canada, in 1832, 1833, and 1834* (London, 1834), I, 431-33, II, 10-11, 23-35.

[7] Fortescue Cuming, *Sketches of a Tour to the Western Country* [1810], in R. G. Thwaites, ed., *Early Western Travels* (Cleveland, 1904), IV, 263.

frontiersman as the blind agent of civilized life. One had to go far west to see even the remnants of savage grandeur.[8]

The very pathos of the situation made for continual hope against hope that the condition of the Indian might be bettered and that somehow he might be brought to civilization. Official government policy operated on this hope, of course; and unofficial and semi-official organizations and individuals regularly advanced plans for amelioration and civilization. Generally, the plans involved removal, separation of Indians from whites, creation of a special Indian state, and education into a life of civilized farming. The main aim of the American Society for Promoting the Civilization and General Improvement of the Indian Tribes in the United States was, as indicated in 1824, in its first and only Annual Report:

> to secure for these tribes instruction in all branches of knowledge, suited to their capacities and condition; and for this purpose, to ascertain the character and strength of their moral and intellectual powers, and their dispositions to receive instruction; . . . to ascertain the number and names of the tribes, their places of residence, the extent, soil, and climate, of their respective territories, the stations where education families may be most advantageously located, and to suggest whatever means may be employed for their improvement.[9]

Such a plan would mean slowing down the American advance westward and forcing Americans in the west to observe treaty agreements. The organizer of the American Society, Jedediah Morse, knew this, having already made an official survey of Indian affairs for the government. Yet he had learned, as had other men close to Indian affairs in his time and before, that it was virtually impossible to slow down the advance of frontier civilization.[10]

[8] A characteristic statement, which I echo, is James Fenimore Cooper, *Notions of the Americans* (London, 1828), I, 328.

[9] *American Society for Promoting the Civilization and General Improvement of the Indian Tribes within the United States,* First Annual Report (New Haven, 1824), pp. 3-4.

[10] Jedediah Morse, *Report to the Secretary of War of the United States, on Indian Affairs* (New Haven, 1822), *passim.* See also Col. John Johnston, *Recollections of Sixty Years* [1846], ed. Charlotte C. Conover (Day-

Such hope against hope was the kind properly held by missionary organizations; for they had a spiritual basis for hope, one which was not tied entirely to worldly, empire-making considerations. The colonial impulse to missionary work lasted well into the nineteenth century. Missionary societies proliferated; for conversion of the heathen Indian seemed to be the only way to save him, Christianity being the one thing which civilization could give him and not take away. Not only was the New England missionary tradition carried on in the labors of the American Board of Commissioners for Foreign Missions, organized in 1810, but middle and southern Methodists and Baptists joined in.[11] The New England missionaries labored mainly in the south until, when their efforts were ended by Removal late in the 1830's, they followed their Indians west. Carrying on the tradition of Edwards, Brainerd, and Beatty, they strove for quick violent conversions as the only sure means to salvation and civilization.[12] Baptists and Methodists spread over the whole godless frontier and strove indiscriminately to evangelize both white men and red. And Quakers and Moravians continued, if on a smaller scale, the gentle yet firm work with the savages which they had begun before the Revolution. For all this, Indian missions, as their historian says, were a " virtual failure." [13]

There is abundant testimony to that failure. Learned religionists testified to it indirectly when they tried with fantastic scholarship from about 1815 on, once more to convince their readers and themselves that Indians were really Hebrews, descended from the

ton, Ohio, 1915); and Thomas McKenney, *Memoirs Official and Personal* (New York, 1846) for analogous accounts, the first by an Indian agent in the Ohio country from 1806 to 1853, the second by the head of the Bureau of Indian Affairs during the period of Removal.

[11] See Oliver W. Elsbree, *The Rise of the Missionary Spirit in America, 1790-1815* (Williamsport, Pennsylvania, 1928), pp. 25-83.

[12] See William W. Sweet, *Religion on the American Frontier*, III (Chicago, 1939), 43, f. n. 1.

[13] Elsbree, *Rise of the Missionary Spirit*, p. 48. The dreary detailing of abandoned missionary efforts in the mid-nineteenth-century *History of American Missions to the Heathen* (Worcester, 1840) implicitly confirms Elsbree's careful analysis.

Lost Ten Tribes.[14] This was, one must assume, part of a last-moment revivalist effort to find a secure place for the Indian in a civilized, Christian world. Americans, the argument went, would have to be loving and patient with these poor ignorant wandering Israelites.

Missionaries in the field testified to that failure directly when they reported, as optimistically as possible, on their prospects. In 1832 a Congregationalist missionary stationed in Oklahoma among the Osages wrote to the Board of Commissioners for Foreign Missions in Boston:

> . . . And certainly whatever obscurity rested on this subject [that of civilizing and Christianizing] eleven years ago has long since been removed by the history of these missions . . . . The Osages are as yet absolutely destitute of the motives which have ever been found necessary to inspire a people with any regard for letters. Still bound in chains of darkness, they have no religious objects to accomplish by a knowledge of the art of reading. Neither have they the motives which arise from business, and from prospects of improvement in their circumstances.[15]

Likewise, a Presbyterian missionary stationed among the Stockbridge Indians in Michigan Territory reported two years later:

> Nothing hardly is more to be deprecated in a temporal point of view than the removal of a tribe of Indians [;] it seems almost like transplanting aged trees, which, if not destroyed by so doing, hardly ever acquire sufficient thrift to rise above it and soon show marks of a premature old age. Altho' in watching the course of events respecting the Indians and seeing the evils of removal, I am sometimes almost ready to sink down into a state of despondency [,] still I am

[14] See, for example, Elias Boudinot, *A Star in the West* (Trenton, N. J., 1816); Ethan Smith, *View of the Hebrews* (Poultney, Vt., 1823); William Apes, *A Son of the Forest* (New York, 1829); Epaphoras Jones, *On the Ten Tribes of Israel, and the Aborigines of America* (New Albany, Indiana, 1831); Mordecai Noah, *Discourse on the Evidences of the American Indians Being the Descendants of the Lost Tribes of Israel* (New York, 1837).

[15] William Montgomery to the Board of Commissioners for Foreign Missions, August 27, 1832, in Sweet, *Religion on the Frontier*, III, 349.

upheld by the gracious promises[,] "Lo I am with you always," "And the wilderness and the solitary place shall be glad, and the desert rejoice and blossom as the rose." [16]

It was possible for men of religion to rationalize, or better, to spiritualize this failure in such a way as to fit their thinking into the progressivist pattern of pity and censure. In 1792, at the beginning of the period which culminated in Removal, John Heckewelder, the Moravian missionary and historian of the Delawares, reported a Baptist sermon which he had heard in the Ohio country:

In regard to the Indian war [the Baptist minister] said among the rest: "God has placed us here in order to be punished for our sins. For this purpose he makes use even of the heathen and as long as we do not change our course and become converted, this chastisement will continue." . . . He also said, "I certainly believe that we too are a scourge to the heathens because they do not ask after God." [17]

And in 1834, toward the end of that period, James Knowles, Professor of Pastoral Duties in the Newton Theological Institution, argued, as had New Englanders two centuries before him, that it had been part of God's inscrutable plan for America that the New England Indians should have been wiped out. For they would or could not obey "the great law of God" which "obliged them to become civilized, and to adopt those modes of life which would enable their territory to support the greatest possible number of inhabitants." What is left to do? Americans can fulfill their destiny "by saving from ruin the helpless descendants of the savage." [18]

The Indians who in the 1830's seemed most helpless and whose fate most deeply concerned Americans behind the frontier were the eastern Cherokees, the last large-scale victims of the government's

[16] Cutting Marsh to the Scottish Society for the Propagation of Christian Knowledge, February 1, 1834, *Wisconsin State Historical Society Collections,* XV (1900), 94.

[17] *Pennsylvania Magazine of History and Biography,* XII (1887), 48.

[18] James Knowles, *Memoir of Roger Williams* (Boston, 1834), pp. 95, 98.

Removal policy. The Cherokees were the most " civilized " of Indians, patently an agrarian people, settled, on their way to learning and literacy, hard-working, and brave. Georgians demanded their lands, insisting that they be moved west where they would be safe and where they could be educated safely into civilization, apart from the paradoxically evil influences of high civilization itself. Many Americans who in general favored the Removal policy did not favor it for the Cherokees, and even those who saw Removal as a necessity, denounced the government's actions. Yet the government went ahead, President Jackson in 1832 refused to carry out a Supreme Court order which would have safeguarded Cherokee lands, and Americans suddenly saw in the plight of the Cherokees the plight of all Indians. Denunciation of the federal government, of the state of Georgia, and of Georgians piled up in the eastern press; a one-sided pamphlet war resulted. Even young Ralph Waldo Emerson was shocked into making a speech and then writing a fierce letter to President Van Buren: " The soul of man, the justice, the mercy that is the heart's heart in all men, from Maine to Georgia, does abhor this business." [19] Still, no one thought to denounce American civilization. The point was that the Cherokees represented the certain hope that savages might become civilized. And even this certainty would not hold.

Americans thus were of two minds about the Indian whom they were destroying. They pitied his state but saw it as inevitable; they hoped to bring him to civilization but saw that civilization would kill him. Henry Marie Brackenridge recorded in his *Recollections of Persons and Places in the West* (1834) that he had

[19] The most effective pamphleteer was Jeremiah Evarts, writing under the penname " William Penn." See his *Essays on the Present Crisis in the Condition of the American Indians, First Published in the National Intelligencer* (Boston, 1829). Journalistic pieces are numerous, especially during the final years of Removal. See, for example: *New England Magazine,* I (1831), 545, IV (1833), 252: *National Enquirer,* II (1837), 75; *Jeffersonian,* I (1838), 52, 99, 158, 188, 263; *New Yorker,* V (1828), 78, 108, 254, 268. For Emerson's letter of April 23, 1838, see *Works,* Centenary Edition, XI, 89-96; and Ralph L. Rusk, *The Life of Ralph Waldo Emerson* (New York, 1949), pp. 266-67.

saved from hanging an Indian murderer by pleading that as an Indian he was "totally deficient on the very ground-work of our social order, in our state of civilization, exalted by Christianity." [20] Yet he had remarked many years before in a journal kept on a voyage up the Missouri that "the world would lose but little, if these people should disappear before civilized communities." [21] In 1839 travelling in "the Great Prairie Wilderness," Thomas Farnham, a Vermont lawyer, carefully surveyed the 135,000 Indians in the Territory and found hope that they would grow into civilization. Of the Choctaws removed from the south he wrote, "thus have the influences of our institutions begun to tame and change the savages of the western wilderness." And later he praised American efforts to "create and gratify" in "Indians those physical wants peculiar to the civilized state," thus to let them "enter at once, and with the fullest vigour into the immense harvests of knowledge and virtue which past ages and superior races have prepared for them." Yet he too was of another mind and was obliged to rhapsodize on the inevitable destruction of eastern Indians (in this case Sauks and Foxes) in the Territory:

> Like all the tribes, however, this also dwindles away at the approach of the whites. A melancholy fact. The Indians' bones must enrich the soil, before the plough of civilized man can open it. The noble heart, educated by the tempest to endure the last pang of departing life without a cringe of a muscle; that heart educated by his condition to love with all the powers of being, and to hate with the exasperated malignity of a demon; that heart, educated by the voice of its own existence—the sweet whisperings of the streams—the holy flowers of spring—to trust in, and adore the Great producing and sustaining Cause of itself, and the broad world and the lights of the upper skies, must fatten the corn hills of a more civilized race! The sturdy plant of the wilderness droops under the enervating culture of the garden. The Indian is buried with his arrows and bow.[22]

[20] Henry Marie Brackenridge, *Recollections of Persons and Places in the West* [1834], 2d ed. (Philadelphia, 1868), p. 251.

[21] Henry Marie Brackenridge, *Journal of a Voyage Up the River Missouri* [1816], in Thwaites, ed., *Early Western Travels*, VI, 128.

[22] Thomas Farnham, *Travels in the Great Western Prairies* [1843], in Thwaites, ed., *Early Western Travels*, XXVIII, 123-24, 142-43, 161.

The double-mindedness of a Brackenridge and a Farnham, of most Americans, indeed, resulted from a conflict of cultural theory with cultural actuality, of logic with reality. Americans had always felt that the process of acculturation, of throwing off one way of life for another, would be relatively simple. To be civilized the Indian would have merely to be made into a farmer; this was a matter of an education for a generation or two. Christianization would follow inevitably; perhaps Christianization itself was the way to civilization. But acculturation was not a simple process, as we know now, at least. For a culture is a delicately balanced system of attitudes, beliefs, valuations, conditions, and modes of behavior; the system does not change and reintegrate itself overnight, or in a generation or two. This is what those Americans who were trying to civilize the Indians inevitably discovered, although they did not know it precisely as this. Civilized, Christian life did not raise up all savages as it should have. Rather it lowered some savages and destroyed others. This was the melancholy fact which Americans understood as coming inevitably in the progress of civilization over savagism.

3

The basis of their understanding had long been part of the grand rationale of westward-moving colonialism. This was the tradition of the natural and divine superiority of a farming to a hunting culture. Universally Americans could see the Indian only as hunter. That his culture, at least the culture of the eastern Indians whom they knew best until the second quarter of the nineteenth century, was as much agrarian as hunting, they simply could not see. They forgot too, if they had ever known, that many of their own farming methods had been taken over directly from the Indians whom they were pushing westward. One can say only that their intellectual and cultural traditions, their idea of order, so informed their thoughts and their actions that they could see and conceive of nothing but the Indian who hunted.

Biblical injunction framed their belief; and on the frontier practical conditions supported it. The Indian with his known hunting ways needed many square miles on which to live, whereas the white farmer needed only a few acres. The latter way was obviously more economical and intelligent; it was essentially the civilized way. Therefore the Indian would have to move on to make way for a better and higher life. If the Indian's fate was a sad one and civilized men should be properly moved by it, still, in the long run, the prospects were exciting and ennobling. Thus an historian towards the end of the eighteenth century:

> The Savage has his day; and enjoys life according to the taste and habits he possesses; he casts his eyes abroad, over the extensive wilderness of his wild domain, and sighs at the apprehension that his nation and race must cease to exist, and that his mighty forests must finally bow to human strength; and that the hills and vallies, where he has enjoyed the chase, shall be covered with cities and cultivated fields of white men. His agonies, at first, seem to demand a tear from the eye of humanity; but when we reflect, that the extinction of his race, and the progress of the arts which give rise to his distressing apprehensions, are for the increase of mankind, and for the promotion of the world's glory and happiness; that five hundred rational animals may enjoy life in plenty, and comfort, where only one Savage drags out a hungry existence, we shall be pleased with the perspective into futurity.[23]

Yet belief in the glorious possibilities of a culture built out of cities and cultivated fields was based on something more than Biblical injunction and economic necessity. " Those who labor in the earth," Jefferson had written in 1784, " are the chosen people of God, if ever He had a chosen people. Whose breasts He has made His peculiar deposit for substantial and genuine virtue." [24] This is agrarian idealism, the belief that men, having a natural right to their land by occupation and labor, achieve status and dignity by exercising that right and becoming freeholding farmers.[25] It is a deep-rooted belief, whose theoretical ground derives

[23] James Sullivan, *History of the District of Maine* (Boston, 1795), p. 139.

[24] Thomas Jefferson, *Notes on the State of Virginia* [1784], *Works*, Memorial Edition, II, 229.

[25] See Chester Eisinger, " The Freehold Concept in Eighteenth Century

from the Lockean theory of the free individual and the metaphysics and sociology of his freedom. For Locke—and virtually all Americans were, in the most general sense, Lockeans—man achieved his highest humanity by taking something out of nature and converting it with his labor into part of himself. His private property, conceived of in terms of the close, personal relationships of an agrarian society, was his means to social maturity. It gave him stability, self-respect, privacy, and the basis for civilized society itself. For Americans the Lockean theory must have made savage society seem loose, immature, virtually anarchic, full of the false freedom of doing as one pleased; likewise, for Americans the theory now must have made it all the more possible to see how Indians could become truly rational animals. All, indeed, that an Indian would need to be on his way to civilization was, in the words of the Secretary of War in 1789, "a love for exclusive property."[26]

Through the end of the eighteenth century and well into the nineteenth, this theme was worked over by Americans who, trying to understand what was happening to the Indian, wanted to make sense of their feeling of pity and censure. The revolutionary General and political figure, Benjamin Lincoln, addressed a scholarly letter on the matter to the historian Jeremy Belknap, January 21, 1792. He laid down a general principle:

> Civilized and uncivilized people cannot live in the same territory, or even in the same neighborhood. Civilization directs us to remove as fast as possible that natural growth from the lands which is absolutely essential for the food and hiding-place of those beasts of the forests upon which the uncivilized principally depend for support.

Lincoln pleaded for fair and honest treatment of Indians who constituted the uncivilized of America. Yet, he had to conclude, ". . . the time will come when they will be either civilized or extinct."[27]

American Letters," *William and Mary Quarterly*, Ser. 2, XXVIII (1947), 42-59.

[26] *American State Papers, Indian Affairs*, I, no. 4, 53.

[27] *Massachusetts Historical Society Collections*, Ser. 6, XIV (1899), 512-15.

The matter was immediate and personal to Lincoln. Journeying to an Indian treaty at Detroit in 1793, he could see civilized agrarian power as divinely ordained. On July 14, on Lake Erie, he surveyed the landscape lovingly and rhapsodized in his journal:

> When I take a view of this extensive country, and contemplate the clemency of its seasons, the richness of its soil, see the saccharine, so grateful to our tastes, and necessary perhaps, from habit, to our happiness, flowing from the trees of the forest; and observe the fountains of salt water, and spots of earth impregnated with saline particles, called salt-licks, to which the beasts resort, from the former of which a full supply of salt can be drawn for all the inhabitants at a very moderate price, while their situation is so far inland as to make this article, important to the well-being of man and beast, too expensive to be obtained in any other way; when I farther consider the many natural advantages, if not peculiar to yet possessed by this country, and that it is capable of giving support to an hundred times as many inhabitants as now occupy it (for there is at present little more to be seen on the greatest proportion of the lands than here and there the footstep of the savage,) I cannot persuade myself that it will remain long in so uncultivated a state; especially, when I consider that to people fully this earth was in the original plan of the benevolent Deity. I am confident that sooner or later there will be a full accomplishment of the original system; and that no men will be suffered to live by hunting on lands capable of improvement, and which would support more people under a state of cultivation. So that if the savages cannot be civilized and quit their present pursuits, they will, in consequence of their stubbornness, dwindle and moulder away, from causes perhaps imperceptible to us, until the whole race shall become extinct, or they shall have reached those climes about the great lakes, where, from the rocks and the mountainous state, the footsteps of the husbandman will not be seen.[28]

As extinction of the Indian seemed more and more a likelihood, analyses like Lincoln's came more and more to furnish a basis for understanding what was happening. When the eastern Cherokees were praised in the 1830's, it was primarily because they were

[28] *Ibid.*, Ser. 3, V (1836), 138-39. Cf. the entry for August 2, pp. 151-53.

farmers and thus on the way to high civilization. For all explanations of the essential weaknesses of savage society had as a basic tenet the assumption that Indians were not farmers, and all plans for civilizing Indians assumed they needed to be farmers. Jefferson, a realist who believed that Indians would have to be crushed so long as they made trouble on the frontier, again and again advised his Indian subjects to accept the white man's farming ways, so to improve themselves. As he addressed the Potawatomis in 1802:

> [The] resources [of farming] are certain: they will never disappoint you: while those of hunting may fail, and expose your women and children to the miseries of hunger and cold. We will with pleasure furnish you with implements for the most necessary arts, and with persons who may instruct you how to make use of them.[29]

Even General Jackson, as a practicing Indian-hater, wrote President Monroe from his Tennessee headquarters, March 4, 1817, "Their existence and happiness now depend upon a change in their habits and customs . . . ."[30]

Much of the Congressional debate over the Removal policy in the 1820's and 30's centered on legalistic problems rising from the relationship between farming and hunting societies. The text for such debates most often was Vattel's classic *Law of Nations*, the standard American authority for international law. Vattel had considered the colonization of America and had written:

> The whole earth is destined to furnish sustenance for its inhabitants; but it can not do this unless it be cultivated. Every nation is therefore bound by the natural law to cultivate the land which has fallen to its share, and it has no right to extend its boundaries or to obtain help from other Nations except in so far as the land it inhabits can

[29] Jefferson, *Writings*, Memorial Edition, XVI, 391. For analogous remarks see *ibid.*, III, 489-94; X, 303; XII, 270-71. For Jefferson and the Indian problem on the frontier see *ibid.*, IV, 270-72, 280, 305; V, 413; VIII, 177-78; XI, 23-24; XIII, 160-61.

[30] *Correspondence of Andrew Jackson*, ed. John S. Bassett, II (Washington, 1927), 280.

not supply its needs. . . . Those who still pursue this idle [i. e., hunting] mode of life occupy more land than they would have need of under a system of honest labor, and they may not complain if other more industrious Nations, too confined at home, should come and occupy part of their lands. Thus, while the conquest of the civilized Empires of Peru and Mexico was a notorious usurpation, the establishment of various colonies upon the continent of North America might, if done within just limits, have been entirely lawful. The peoples of those vast tracts of land rather roamed over them than inhabited them.[31]

Seventeenth-century dependence upon Genesis had shifted to nineteenth-century dependence upon natural law. American progress could be rationalized and comprehended in predominantly naturalistic terms. The Indian's way and its fatal weakness could be placed in intelligible relationship to the white man's way and its glorious strength. Westward civilized destiny was clearly manifest even in the state of the savages who were about to die.

Thus the history of American relations with the Indians came to make orderly sense. For the law of nations might be squared with the civilized morality which developed out of the sense of private property, and these in turn with the facts of westward-moving American life. During the final years of the controversy over Removal, the western lawyer, journalist, and novelist, James Hall, set out to survey the history of " Intercourse of the American People with the Indians " in just such terms. His view is standard, even hackneyed.

The history of Indian-American relations is for Hall one of mistakes, misconceptions, and mistreatment. Indians, good in their simple fashion, had welcomed Europeans peaceably. Europeans had treated them as though they were sovereign nations but had not really believed that they were. There followed inevitably encroachment on Indian lands, Indian hatred, Indian retaliation,

[31] E. de Vattel, *Le Droit des Gens,* trans. Charles G. Fenwick (Washington, 1916), III, 37-38. On Vattel's importance for American political and legal thinking, see Fenwick's introduction, III, lviii-lix. On the use of Vattel in the debates over Removal, see Albert K. Weinberg, *Manifest Destiny* (Baltimore, 1935), pp. 77-99.

the barbarism and viciousness of savage warfare, and always Indian defeat. Proper treatment and a policy of separation would have meant gradual civilization and Christianization. But the terrible drive of Americans westward and their inability to keep themselves from taking over Indian lands had resulted only in converting Indian virtues into Indian vices and had necessitated Removal and its consequences of disease and degradation.

But, Hall argues, what is past is past. Indians are no longer simple and straightforward in their savage goodness, but degenerate. The question is now: "How shall we deal with a people, between whom and ourselves, there is no community of language, thought, or custom—no reciprocity of obligations—no common standard, by which to estimate our relative interests, claims and duties?" How, in short, shall we deal with a people with whom we have almost completely lost cultural contact? How shall we close the gap between savage life and civilized? Can it, in fact, be closed? Studying the record of Indian-white relations in America, Hall can pose his questions only in those terms which have made them, terms involving, above all, the theory of the hunting versus the farming culture and of the virtues of civilized systems of private land tenure.

Moreover, he can answer only in such terms. The savages are a "wandering horde" and have no sense of property, therefore no laws, therefore no government. It follows that they have not the rights which a properly integrated people or organized government could claim. Yet in this age of "liberal thought, free principles, and the dissemination of knowledge," Americans have a duty, as it were, to "create" rights for the savages. "To come at once to the point, we believe that it is the duty of our government, to take the Indians directly under its own control as subjects." Kept apart, forced into peaceful ways, they may be tutored into civilization, first into a pastoral, then into an agricultural state; they must, indeed, be tutored into a sense of private property. For ". . . the insecurity of property, or rather the entire absence of all ideas of property, is the chief cause of their barbarism." Thus "The chain of causes by which the condition of the unhappy race must, if at all, be ameliorated will be this: first, *personal security*, by the entire abolition of war among them, secondly, *permanent habitations*, and thirdly, *notions of property*."[32]

The hope of civilization is there, albeit dimly, as it was to be with Americans throughout their history. More important, there is a pitying, charitable awareness of the low state of the Indian and the inadequacy of his kind of life in the face of the life of civilized American society. Equally, there is confidence in the manifest destiny of that civilized life. The Indian, if he was to survive, would have to survive not as a savage but as a civilized man. The essence of his savagism was his life as a hunter. This was the master-key to the Indian problem: As hunter he must die; as hunter he was dying. For Hall's, and many another's, hope to civilize the Indian was being dashed by the onrush of civilization itself. And no man could, in the end, regret the onrush of civilization.

4

By the 1830's, with Removal accomplished, Americans had sufficiently mastered the Indian to search out his real meaning for them and their manifest destiny. The issues were clear, in a sense, because he who generated them was virtually dead. The problems generated by that virtual death continued into the century and beyond, and continue to our day. But that is a matter which is not immediately relevant to the American mastering of the Indian in practice and in theory and to the development in the American mind of the Indian as a symbol for all that over which civilization must triumph. The Indian who was important to Americans setting out to make their new society was not the person but the type, not the tribesman but the savage, not the individual but the symbol. The American conscience was troubled about the death of the individual. But it could make sense of his death only when it understood it as the death of the symbol.

Pity, censure, and their justification are the qualities we must distinguish in American thinking about the Indian between the

[32] James Hall, *Sketches of History, Life, and Manners in the West* (New York, 1835), I, 27-133.

Revolution and the period of Removal. We need not try to get directly at the psychological roots of such qualities. At best, knowing now what we know about our fundamental psychological nature as humans, we can only guess at such roots. We can say that the American, as the self-consciously civilized and civilizing man, could envision the possibilities of a life free from what he somehow felt to be the complexities of civilization. Envisioning that life, he might very well yearn for it. But seeing it, as he thought, in disturbing actuality to the west, he hated himself for his yearning. He was tempted, we might say; and he felt driven to destroy the temptation and likewise the tempters. He pitied the tempters, because in his yearning for a simpler life, he could identify with them. He censured them, because he was ashamed to be tempted, and he refused to deny his higher nature.

All this, perhaps, is too much to psychologize the situation and to ask too much of the evidence we have. I mean it only to suggest the possible roots of the pattern of pity and censure and to suggest that it derives from polarities deep in the American character, deep in all human character. It reflects the simple fact that the tensions of any way of life suggest to men that there is a simpler way, with fewer tensions, perhaps none, and that how men face up to the fact—and how they rationalize and symbolize their facing up to the fact—is an expression of the meaning that they at once find in and give to their situation in history. Our concern, however, is not with what their separate and collective unconscious made Americans be, but with what their conscious life and imagination told them they were.

What these nineteenth-century Americans were aware of was degradation and destruction of the Indian, Removal, desperate drives to civilize and to Christianize before it would be too late, abhorrence of the perverse cruelties of white man on the frontier, frightening glimpses of the Indian as the vanishing American. If they were to be borne, if men were to live with them, all these attitudes and inpulses had to be shown to be products of a civilizing process whose good finally negated the evil in them, even if it did not make that evil immediately less painful. When this came to pass, when the destiny of the savage was fully comprehended in its relationship to the destiny of the civilized man, the Indian had been mastered not only as individual but as symbol. The story of this mastering, of the development of an idea and its symbol and images, is the major burden of this study.

III

Character and Circumstance:

The Idea of Savagism

AMERICAN double-mindedness about the Indian issued rapidly into a theory of his life—an idea of savagism, as it was called. As all ideas should be, this one was for its time true. That is to say, it consisted of a set of interrelated propositions which held together and made logical sense of all that was known and felt about the Indian, and it made for understanding, belief, and action. As data about the Indian accumulated, the idea was first filled out, then modified, and finally broken through. By the time the idea could no longer contain the data—it was then the 1850's—psychological as well as physical Removal had been effected, and the Indian had become a creature of philanthropic agencies, scientific ethnology, and dime novels. Savagism no longer seemed to exist. At least, it no longer seemed seriously to threaten civilized existence.

We can distinguish two periods in the development of the idea of savagism: a period through, say, the first decade of the century—when reports from the Lewis and Clark expedition were coming in, in which little of empirical fact was known, in which scattered details involving a disappearing hunting society were given formal expression and found to be embodied in an actual person out of the actual American past; and a period through, say, 1851—the date of the publication of Morgan's *League of the Iroquois*, in which Americans began systematically to investigate their Indians, in which they fitted new facts to an old theory, until, as I have said, the theory itself would no longer contain the facts.

The two periods are to be distinguished only generally, as are all periods in the development of modes of belief. We can observe only trends, points of cumulation, intensities, since, as we must remind ourselves, the relation between a belief and the situation in which it develops is constant and dynamic, each reinforcing the other. Thus the separation of the materials in this study, cutting across chronological lines as it does, is made so that we can see analytically, in the large, the relationship between situation and belief. The American double-minded attitude toward the Indian, reduced to precise and formal terms and supported sometimes by investigation, more often by meditation, became the American idea of savagism. After that, the Indian became *sui generis* the American savage.

1

For Americans after the Revolution, study of the Indian and his nature was a pressing and personal need. The Indian was disappearing from America; once he had been *the* American. It was, in fact, an American duty to clear up European misconceptions of the Indian and to give him his savage due. Let the American writer, declared a Professor at the University of Pennsylvania in 1787,

> mark with attention the footsteps of civilization throughout the continent—let him learn the languages of the natives, compare them with those of the nations of the old world, and his labours will be amply rewarded.—It is thus only he can redeem the history of the origin of a people, some of whom have, probably, once made a distinguished figure on the theatre of the world, and who, at present, tinctured as they are with the vices of the Europeans, do not detract from the character of mankind.[1]

[1] Benjamin Smith Barton, *Observations on Some Parts of Natural History*, Part I [no more published] (London, 1787), pp. iv-v. Cf. Barton's "Observations and Conjectures . . . ," *American Philosophical Society Transactions*, IV [o. s.] (1799), 214-15; and his *A Discourse on Some of the Principal Desiderata in Natural History* (Philadelphia, 1807), pp. 16, 18-19. See also Jeremy Belknap, *A Discourse Intended to Commemorate the Discovery of America by Christopher Columbus* (Boston, 1792), p. 36; Jonathan Heart, "A Letter . . . to Benjamin Smith Barton," *American*

European writers on America, it was apparent, generally had failed to treat the Indian fairly, having either vilified his character or overpraised it. It became a kind of intellectual flourish for Americans writing on the Indian to refute Europeans at all possible points. The usual targets were the Scots, Robertson, Dunbar, and Lord Kames, and the Frenchmen, Lafitau, Raynal, and particularly De Pauw, with his picture of beardless Indian males with milk in their breasts. What was objected to was that they all, out of non-American ignorance, did what De Pauw had done—" [laid] down positions of [their] own construction, the weakness of which is equalled by nothing but by their frivolity and their fallacy." [2] American positions would be strong, because Americans might directly know the vanishing Indian. Americans would vindicate savage character even as they destroyed it.

Thus, as was proper for a people whose origins were colonial, Americans were committed to break through the limitations of their origins and learn the real truth about life in the new world. Yet, as we can see now, those very origins gave direction and impetus to their thinking. They asked the same questions about the Indian that Europeans had asked; but they asked them in their own way, adjusting questions to available evidence, and got their own answers.

They asked, for example, about the celebrated eloquence of the Indian, an eloquence which, for English and French authorities, had long seemed to be a significant point of difference between the savage and the civilized man. The formal talk at Indian treaties

Philosophical Society Transactions, III [o. s.] (1793), 220-21; Abiel Holmes, " Memoir of the Mohegan Indians," *Massachusetts Historical Society Collections,* Ser. 1, IX (1804), 75.

[2] See Thomas Jefferson, *Writings,* Memorial Edition, II, 81-93, V, 3-7, XIII, 156-57; Samuel Stanhope Smith, *An Essay on the Causes of the Variety of Complexion and Figure in the Human Species,* 2d ed. (New Brunswick, N. J., 1810), pp. 208-11; Hugh Williamson, *Observations on the Climate in Different Parts of America* (New York, 1811), pp. 2, 30-31, 66-67, 76-78. The statement on De Pauw is Barton's, *Observations on Some Parts of Natural History,* p. 53; cf. pp. 7-16, 22-24, and Barton's *Remarks on the Speech Attributed, by Mr. Jefferson, To an Indian Chief, Of the Name of Logan* (Philadelphia?, 1806?), pp. 10-11.

and the far-fabled death songs of noble savages—these had long been known to mark off the savage from the civilized, and had been readily interpretable as signs of the superiority of the savage to the civilized or, at the very least, as evidence of a kind of " original genius " forever lost to high civilization. The problem for Americans was to study even such limited superiority and, if it be found authentic, to show how it could be peculiarly characteristic of an inferior people.

In eighteenth- and nineteenth-century America this interest focussed particularly on the speech Chief Logan is said to have addressed to Lord Dunmore in 1774—a speech widely printed after 1775, but most celebrated in the version given in Jefferson's *Notes on the State of Virginia* (1784). As Jefferson gave it, it began like Matthew 25:35-36—" I appeal to any white man to say, if ever he entered Logan's cabin hungry, and he gave him not meat; if ever he came cold and naked, and he cloathed him not . . . ."—and it carried the feeling of authentic savage nobility. Although its genuineness was early questioned, for the most part it was accepted as savage gospel, even as late as the 1850's and 1860's when it had become one of the test pieces in McGuffey's Fourth and Fifth Readers.[3] The appeal of Logan's speech—and of myriad speeches and episodes like it regularly reported in newspapers, periodicals, and historical works—was to the sense of the simple greatness of the savage state. Yet the speech, and the tradition which it marked, could not be for Americans evidence of the absolute nobility of the savage. Rather for them it marked the inferior kind of nobility of the savage, a nobility which achieved its ends by emotion rather than by reason, by action rather than by thought, by custom rather than by law. (" What civilized nations enforce upon their subjects by compulsory measures, they effect by their eloquence," a close student of the Indian wrote in the 1790's.[4]) It was a kind of nobility which, paradoxically, had to be shown to have contributed to the death of the very people whom

[3] See Edward D. Seeber, " Critical Views on Logan's Speech," *Journal of American Folklore,* LX (1947), 130-46.

[4] Jedidiah Morse, *The American Geography* [1789], 3d ed. (Dublin, 1792), p. 18.

it characterized. Thus to account for savage eloquence was to be part of the specifically American task in working out an idea of savagism.

So too European interest in the mysteries of Indian language and European hypotheses concerning Indian origins and the Indian past became specifically American concerns, directed finally at specifically American ends. In the study of languages, the problem was taken to be one of collection and classification, in order to demonstrate the ultimate unity of mankind and to show how far the Indian had fallen from his proper humanity. Franklin,[5] Washington,[6] and Jefferson [7] encouraged the collection of Indian word-lists as part of an international project in comparative linguistics. Franklin and Washington both sent Lafayette word-lists which he requested for the German scholar P. S. Pallas, who was preparing a second edition of his gigantic world-wide comparative vocabulary. And it is Jefferson from whom our science of Indian linguistics primarily descends. He was particularly active, collecting Indian word-lists himself and encouraging others to do so, theorizing on the multiplicity of radical Indian languages, still projecting even after 1809 when his great collection of word-lists was lost. Jefferson's view was a minority one; as study of Indian languages developed toward the end of the eighteenth century and beyond, Americans could demonstrate that Indian languages were few, radically interrelated, and possibly of Asiatic origin.[8] There would yet come the problem of the relation of savage language to savage character.

To say the American Indian was ultimately Asiatic in origin

[5] Benjamin Franklin, *Writings,* ed. Smyth, VIII, 246-47, 304; IX, 571.

[6] George Washington, *Writings,* ed. Fitzpatrick, XXVII, 88; XXVIII, 88-89, 183-84, 191, 425, 525; XXIX, 369-70, 374-75; XXX, 64.

[7] Thomas Jefferson, *Writings,* Memorial Edition, II, 141; V, 390; VI, 231-32; VII, 267; XI, 79-81, 401-409; XII, 312-14; XIII, 157; XVI, 107-109.

[8] See, for example, William Dunbar, "On the Language of Signs among Certain North American Indians," *American Philosophical Society Transactions,* VI [o. s.] (1809), 1-18; and Benjamin Smith Barton, "Hints on the Etymology of Certain English Words . . . ," *ibid.*, VI [o. s.] (1809), 145-58.

was, of course, to say nothing new. Linguistic study was not making for a new theory; rather it was buttressing an old one. Yet what was important was that Americans were themselves finding new evidence for that theory. They might be worried about the mysteriously lost world of the mound-builders. They might continue to construct theories of Hebrew [9] and Welsh [10] origins; but mainly they held to the idea that Indians, as descendants of Noah, had come to America from the northern parts of Asia, with perhaps the exception of the Eskimos, who had come from Scandinavia. They concluded that the character of American savages showed basic affinities with that of northern Asiatic peoples; and they were thus able to classify and judge Indians virtually as northern Asiatic savages.

The recognized evidence for such a theory, according to a classroom lecture of 1816, was a "similarity of physiognomy and features," an "affinity of . . . languages," corresponding customs, and, incidentally, the "kindred nature" of Indian and Siberian dogs.[11] All this meant that Indians were part of the unity of mankind, yet somehow apart from it. Even if Indians were, say, of Hebrew origin, descended from the lost Ten Tribes, their relationship to the rest of humanity was one of a separated and isolated people. It was, indeed, their separateness and isolation which had primarily to be accounted for in theories of their origins. They were, in any case, as much colonials as had been Americans. The difference was that they had developed in desolate isolation. Originating as wanderers, they had lived as

[9] See above, pp. 61-62.

[10] See David Williams, "John Evans' Strange Journey," *American Historical Review,* LIV (1949), 277-95, 508-29.

[11] The classroom opinions of Samuel Latham Mitchel, "Professor of Natural History in the University of New-York," are reprinted in *American Antiquarian Society Transactions and Collections,* I (1820), 325-33, 338-44. Mitchel is an extremist in that at one point he thinks that perhaps northern Asia was populated by American Indians; equally, he can hold to the accepted view. For other examples of this accepted view see Jefferson, *Writings,* Memorial Edition, II, 127-42, XIII, 246-48; Samuel Stanhope Smith, *An Essay on the Causes of the Variety of Complexion and Figure in the Human Species,* pp. 181-83, 231-33.

wanderers, and were marked by the customs, habits and, in the long run, the fate of wanderers. They had been lost. Americans, who had found them and were failing to save them, needed, above all, to understand them before they should be gone forever.

2

In spite of the nationalism which forced its growth, the American understanding of the Indian depended on an idea of savagism whose main structure derived from European sources. American theorizing about the Indian owed its greatest debt to a group of eighteenth-century Scottish writers on man and society, to their historical method, and to the one of the group who wrote on the North American Indian. The group was the historians belonging to the Scottish school of common sense and moral sentiment; their method was that of the historical analysis of social process; and the one who wrote on the North American Indian was William Robertson, in his *History of America* (1777).

The grand intention of the eighteenth-century Scottish historians and writers on society—among them, Francis Hutcheson, Thomas Reid, Adam Ferguson, Lord Kames, and Robertson—was to construct a sociology of progress, a theory which would make comprehensible at once social stability and social growth, which would explain to Christians how they could originally have fallen and yet have come to such a high and noble state in their enlightened century. The Scots' thinking had evolved ultimately out of a Protestant theology in which the millennium had been rationalized from a certainty of the second coming of Christ into a certainty of the God-ordained, intelligent self-sufficiency of modern man to work out his own way with his common sense, his analytic reason, and his special moral sense. The Scots held that it might be conjectured back from empirical evidence how God was revealing His Word to modern man slowly but surely, how modern man was thus slowly but surely progressing to high civilization, how he had left behind him forever his savage, primitive state. This was the grand Christian, civilized Idea of Progress.[12]

[12] The best study of the Scots is Gladys Bryson, *Man and Society: The*

The Scots observed that man's " original nature " was unchanging, yet obeyed discernible laws of development intrinsic to itself and thus, in the words of a recent student of their thought, made for " the glory of the Creator, the satisfaction of the individual, and the greatest good of natural and civil society." Every human institution and custom was found to develop unilinearly and to furnish evidence for the laws of man's original nature. This development " was judged to be progressive, of the nature of a continuous movement with no breaks, as growth has no breaks, a movement directed by Nature." [13] Progress meant growth upward, growth for the better, because as man, his institutions, and his customs developed, they became, logically enough, more and more " social." Living fully in society—this was man's highest aim and the destiny toward which his self and his institutions and customs were evolving.[14] Social, technical, and moral progress were identical; the progress of the individual was to be measured in terms of the progress of the society which gave him his social being. The way into comprehension and evaluation of an individual was through analysis of his society; the way into comprehension and evaluation of a society, through analysis of its historical relation with other societies. The good life was absolutely good, the life of rich and complex society, through which alone could man's " original nature " mature. Any society—we should say any " culture "—was good insofar as it allowed for this good life. In the end, there was achieved a moral absolutism and something approximating cultural relativism.

Part of the empirical data which this idea of progress comprehended was that concerning primitive peoples, past and present. To this end, the Scots constructed what they called conjectural histories—their translation of *histoire raisonée*—and gave the

Scottish Inquiry of the Eighteenth Century (Princeton, 1945), which I generally follow here. On the larger significance of the Scottish inquiry for the development of the idea of progress, see Ernest Tuveson, *Millenium and Utopia* (Berkeley, 1950).

[13] Bryson, *Man and Society*, pp. 242-43.

[14] See, for example, Adam Ferguson, *Essay on the History of Civil Society* [1767] (Philadelphia, 1819), p. 8.

primitive his due, placing him in their past and present, as they felt, for good and for bad. A typical analysis,[15] that of Adam Ferguson's *Essay on the History of Civil Society*, begins with an attack on the notion that the state of nature was one of simple animality. Man, Ferguson insists, is by nature social. Civilization itself is natural to him; at every stage in his evolution he lives for a group; his is, in its fullest sense, the life of the family. Thus, Ferguson can conclude, every state is a state of nature, social nature, and man is limited only by the society in which he lives.

Such conclusions form a basis, at once morally absolute and culturally relativistic, for Ferguson's study "Of Rude Nations Prior to the Establishment of Property," in which conclusions are based on the writings of travellers and historians, some of whom have lived among savages. Ferguson finds the North American Indians, in whom he is particularly interested, to be hunters and fishers who have little or no sense of property ownership or of government. They own just what they need for day-to-day survival. The men value themselves for warlike policy, courage, and the like. Women, on the whole, are in base servitude. Finally, having little sense of property, the Indians have little need for social rank. Above all, they are egalitarian.

Ferguson evaluates such savage society for good and for bad; evaluation means for him historical and comparative analysis, based on a progressivist norm. He sees both the virtues and defects of savage society, and in his conclusion tries to take both into account:

> With all these infirmities, vices, or respectable qualities, belonging to the human species in its rudest state; the love of society, friendship, and public affection, penetration, eloquence, and courage, appear to have been its original properties, not the subsequent effects of device or invention. If mankind are qualified to improve their manners, the materials to be improved were furnished by nature; and the effect of this improvement is not to inspire the sentiments of tenderness and

[15] Analyses in the same vein are John Gregory, *A Comparative View of the State and Faculties of Man With Those of the Animal World* (London, 1765); and James Dunbar, *Essays on the History of Mankind in Rude and Cultivated Ages* (London, 1780).

generosity, nor to bestow the principal constituents of a respectable character, but to obviate the casual abuses of passion; and to prevent a mind, which feels the best dispositions in their greatest force, from being at times likewise the sport of brutal appetite, and of ungovernable violence.[16]

Ferguson finds primitive society potentially good; equally he finds it is only a high degree of civilization which will actualize that potentiality. As he writes later "Of The Separation of the Arts and Professions":

> It is evident, that, however urged by a sense of necessity, and a desire of convenience, or favoured by any advantage of situation and policy, a people can make no great progress in cultivating the arts of life, until they have separated, and committed to different persons, the several tasks which require a peculiar skill and attention. The savage, or barbarian, who must build and plant, and fabricate for himself, prefers, in the interval of great alarms and fatigues, the enjoyments of sloth to the improvement of his fortune: he is, perhaps, by the diversity of his wants, discouraged from industry; or, by his divided attention, prevented from acquiring skill in the management of any particular skill.[17]

Savage virtues are undeniably virtues, for they are incident to man's essential "sociality." Yet they need to be matured in rich, complex, civilized humanity. The primary means to this are private property and the division of labor, as these mark the end of human progress toward its goal of high civilization.

What generally emerges from Ferguson's *Essay*, and from others like it, is a simple and clear demonstration from conjectural history of a proposition which Americans, in their feelings of pity and censure over the fate of the Indians, needed desperately to believe: that men in becoming civilized had gained much more than they had lost; and that civilization, the act of civilizing, for all of its destruction of primitive virtues, put something higher and greater in their place. Americans could see this proposition demonstrated again and again. It was clear that primitive life

[16] Ferguson, *Essay*, pp. 171-72. [17] *Ibid.*, pp. 324-25.

carried with it concomitant virtues and defects, the products of the social form in which they were produced. Thus it was not a matter of mourning the destruction of primitive virtues. Rather, it was a matter of analyzing the virtues and defects, necessary in the very scheme of things, of a given stage of social evolution. As it happened, savage courage, fortitude, and freedom could all be developed only in a primitive society. But there were also more unfortunate products of that society—hardship, cruelty, warfare, lack of " social affections " and of refined religion, philosophy, and learning in general. Good qualities and bad were both part of a social whole which could not be broken down suddenly, but which should slowly evolve toward something better. Civilizers were agents of that evolution and that progress, and they should come to know that they were, even as they should be deeply and charitably moved by the fate of the savages over whom they were progressing. Scottish theory seemed to bear out American practice.

A special problem still existed, however. Why had American Indians not progressed to high civilization as had Europeans? What had happened to the historical line? The terms of the answer were simple: isolation and the overpowering effect of environment. The Scot who considered this problem in particular was the historian William Robertson, through whose lucubrations on the North American Indian the sociology of the Scots most often came to America. In Robertson, the Scots' historical method took on an environmentalist quality which made it immediately available for the analysis of contemporary primitive societies.

In his *History of America* (1777), Robertson considers the Indian first as an individual and as a member of society and concludes with a general estimate of Indian—that is, savage—virtues and vices. His view is much like Ferguson's. The Indian is essentially simple and undeveloped, living in an environment which demands that he concentrate all his energies on mere survival. (Robertson's word for environment is " climate," and it includes terrain, housing, plant and animal life, and the like.) He is " naturally " independent. His passions are not refined as they would be in a civilized society; rather they tend to the fierce and animal-like. He has little time or reason to think; his intellectual powers and attainments are few and limited.

The Indian as a cold, disaffected individual is, of course, the product of a rude social state necessitated by the exigencies of crude, isolated living. He must live in a small roaming group and survive by hunting; so he has little or no sense of property or wealth, little notion of government and civil organization, but has a " high sense of equality and independence." As a warrior—and his social state makes for continual warfare—he fights merely for the sake of fighting and glories in hardship, cruelty, and torture. Here he is especially to be noted for his passive fortitude and his ability to endure pain, which is due at once to his less sensitive constitution and to his tremendous passion for his honor as an individual.

Robertson proceeds to a discussion of Indian social forms and religion, and comes finally to an analysis of savage character. At the beginning, he insists that all men are born alike, that their development depends almost entirely on the stage of society in which they are born and on the environment in which that society finds itself. Hence the Indian's moral, political, and religious state can be wholly accounted for by referring to the hard life which he must lead. He has little need for political wisdom; he is a rover; his domestic feelings are unrefined. Since he is interested only in the arts of hunting and warfare, he overrefines them and thus becomes a crafty practicer of what are for Europeans artifice and duplicity.

Yet there are, along with savage vices, concomitant savage virtues: a devotion to freedom and independence; an unusual exuberance of speech and manner that makes for eloquence; perseverance, dignity, and implacability; heroism and bravery in war; and a devotion to the tribe, if only as an instrument of warfare and revenge. Hence in the end the glory of the Indian is the glory of savage life, and carries with it the misery of that life:

> The rude Americans, fond of their own pursuits, and satisfied with their own lot, are equally unable to comprehend the intention of the various accommodations, which in more polished society are deemed

essential to the comfort of life. Far from complaining of their own situation, or viewing that of men in a more improved state with admiration or envy, they regard themselves as the standard of excellence, as beings the best entitled, as well as the most perfectly qualified, to enjoy real happiness. Unaccustomed to any restraint upon their will or their actions, they behold with amazement the inequality of rank, and the subordination which takes place in civilized life, and consider the voluntary submission of one man to another as a renunciation, no less base than unaccountable, of the first distinctions of humanity. Void of foresight, as well as free from care themselves, they wonder at the anxious precautions, the unceasing industry, the complicated arrangements of Europeans, in guarding against distant evils, or providing for future wants; and they often exclaim against their preposterous folly, in thus multiplying the troubles and increasing the labour of life.[18]

This is at once indignant and envious. Robertson sees the savage as at once noble and ignoble—wanting in the end only his kind of life, and limited, for good and for bad, by that life. He is a savage living in a savage society and in a savage environment.

For Americans working to comprehend the Indian and his society, Scottish method and Scottish theory made for a major synthesis. Even if the relationship of American to Scottish philosophizing and historicizing is a complex one which we are only beginning to measure, we now know enough to see that the influence which I am tracing here is part of something larger and more general.[19] Eighteenth- and nineteenth-century Americans, trying to establish a prosperous new society out of a revolution, generally found that Scottish common-sense empiricism and intuitionism, the Scottish doctrine of the moral sense, and the Scottish idea of progress fitted into their own new-found need for order and stability of growth. In a word, as Americans read them, the Scots made rationalism, freedom, and individualism safe, even conserva-

[18] *Works* (London, 1824), IX, 94-95.

[19] See Merle Curti, *The Growth of American Thought* (New York, 1943), p. 236; Leon Howard, *The Connecticut Wits* (Chicago, 1943), *passim*; William Charvat, *The Origins of American Critical Thought* (Philadelphia, 1936), pp. 27-58.

tive. They made possible the interpretation of a revolution as a phase of social evolution. They assured progress and gave it a rationale. And so their thinking became American thinking. The Scots were taught as textbook gospel in the colleges; [20] they were printed and reprinted. They had succeeded in making common sense out of Locke, revolution, Christianity, and progress. For us what is important is that they had succeeded in making common sense out of savagism.

There developed, to be sure, a considerable debate over the accuracy and value of Robertson's opinions. In their nationalism and in their desire to give the Indian his full due, Americans were annoyed by Robertson's tendency to over-environmentalize, as one might say, and to make his Indians weaker than they seemed in reality—for example, beardless and undersexed. Thus he, and with him other Scots, could be accused of " laying down positions of his own construction." Jefferson's tendency to be of two minds over Robertson on the Indians is, as we shall see, characteristic of this American feeling. Yet Robertson was always taken as someone to conjure with, someone of importance [21]—so much so that in 1827 a man who, having been a long-time captive of the Shawnees, could have sketched Indian character first-hand, declined to do so because:

> Dr. Robertson, in the fourth book of his valuable History of America, has collected almost everything which, when his work was written, could be ascertained in relation to [the Indians.] Subsequent travellers and residents among them, have published facts and remarks, establishing the correctness of his general views. It may be questioned, whether any accession to those general views has been obtained, by later writers.[22]

[20] Bryson, *Man and Society*, p. 3.

[21] See, for example, John Davis, *Captain Smith and Princess Pocahontas* (Philadelphia, 1805), pp. 133-34; James McCulloh, *Researches on America*, 2d ed. (Baltimore, 1817), p. 20; Editorial Preface, *American Antiquarian Society Transactions and Collections*, I (1820), 4; " Address of the Rev. William Jenks, October 22, 1823," *American Antiquarian Society Proceedings*, I (1812-1849), 34-35.

[22] Charles Johnston, *A Narrative of Incidents Attending the Capture,*

This writer takes exception to Robertson only in matters of detail. His opinion, extreme as it is, points to the limitation that Americans were to set on Robertson's work. An American natural historian in 1811, objecting once more to Robertson's hairless, unmanly Indians, put the matter as fairly as he could and declared that Robertson should not be "criminated" where he depended for his data on the reports of "ignorant or dishonest travellers." [23] Robertson, and the Scots whose methods his work embodied, was to be corrected in fact, not in theory.

Still, significant as Robertson's work was for eighteenth- and nineteenth-century Americans, he was at most a carrier, at the least a symbol, of the influence of his fellows. The Scots had taken from Americans in the eighteenth century information concerning the existence of contemporary savages and had fitted it into a grand rationale of progress. Americans discovered the Indian as a fact of life, not of theory, and took back from the Scots the rationale and made it their own means of comprehending their relationship with him. Scottish theory was a point of departure, as is shown in the attitude of a young man of the 1830's out for what he calls a "romantic" adventure in the Rocky Mountains. When he wants to describe the Indians he sees, he must begin by quoting from "An old number of a Scotch paper that I have with me . . ." [24] Only then he can tell what he has seen.

This is what the Scots did for American students of the savage: enabled them both to see and to tell what they had seen; furnished a general theoretical frame which allowed them to bring empirical data together and gain an understanding of savagism. Yet, as they always must, the facts gradually modified the frame, then broke it and made for a new frame, a new theory. But then, as I have

Detention, and Ransom of Charles Johnston . . . , To Which Are Added, Sketches of Indian Character and Manners, With Illustrative Anecdotes (New York, 1827), p. 100.

[23] Hugh Williamson, *Observations on the Climate in Different Parts of America* (New York, 1811), p. 83.

[24] [James Hildreth,] *Dragoon Campaigns to the Rocky Mountains* (New York, 1836), p. 209. The "paper," which I haven't identified, gives a conventional analysis of the Indian as savage.

noted, it was the 1850's. The Indian was virtually dead, a creature on whom only scientific ethnology and anthropology could operate, one whom only philanthropy could bring alive. Our concern is with the Indian of the period before the 1850's, with the savagism in terms of which he was understood, and with Americans as they gained that understanding. Of the Scots and their influence we can say this: If they did not actually create the American understanding of savagism, they made its creation possible.

3

American pity and censure, American progressivist certainty of manifest destiny, American agrarian idealism and quasi-metaphysical faith in private property—each was authenticated by that understanding, as each contributed to its authentification. The Scottish theory of history and society was a rationale for Americans insofar as it made it possible for them to find a meaning in their experience with the Indian and to believe in that meaning. They had to find meaning in the hard facts of life. They had to include everything—the multifarious evidences of the Indian's past greatness and his present inferiority—and to make workable sense of it. At this point, with what we in our time know, we must avoid the temptation to second-guess. As students of our past, we must see it as it was, with only those empirical data available which were available. For men at their best see very little beyond what their timebound sensibilities will let them see. This, at least, is the way it was with Americans at the beginning of their national history. They could fully and honestly comprehend the Indian only in terms of that theoretical understanding of savagism which was possible to them in their time.

Thomas Jefferson, writing at length on the Indian in his *Notes on the State of Virginia* (1784), first outlined an American idea of savagism. The eleventh section, "*A description of the Indians established in that State*," is mainly factual and manifests Jefferson's tremendous interest in the Indians of North America and his desire that they should be studied closely and exactly. He gives an historical sketch of the Virginia Indians, locates them geographically and chronologically, and carefully sets down their numbers. He discusses the mounds of the Ohio country, origins (he inclines toward the theory of a northern Asiatic origin, but thinks it likely that the Eskimos are of Scandinavian stock), and problems in language and linguistics. He concludes with a table of "The nations and numbers of the Aborigines which still exist in a respectable and independent form."

This eleventh section of the *Notes* is primarily descriptive and statistical. Jefferson's more general interest in the savage is treated in the sixth section, "*A Notice of the mines and other subterraneous riches; its trees, plants, fruits, etc.*" Here he comes to a consideration of Buffon's theory that an inferior environment in America makes for inferior animals and men, witness the savage Indians. Jefferson, like so many others, has nothing but proper scorn for Buffon's picture of the Indian, sexually weak, practically hairless, unintelligent, cowardly, with little ardor of soul and none of the qualities that might make for the good life. In refuting Buffon, he outlines an American theory of the savage:

[Buffon's is] an afflicting picture, indeed, which for the honor of human nature, I am glad to believe has no original. Of the Indian of South America I know nothing; for I would not honor with the appelation of knowledge, what I derive from the fables published of them. These I believe to be just as true as the fables of Æsop. This belief is founded on what I have seen of man, white, red, and black, and what has been written of him by authors, enlightened themselves, and writing among an enlightened people. The Indian of North America being more within our reach, I can speak of him somewhat from my own knowledge, but more from the information of others better acquainted with him, and on whose truth and judgment I can rely. From these sources I am able to say, in contradiction to this representation, that he is neither more defective in ardor, nor more impotent with his female, than the white reduced to the same diet and exercise; that he is brave, when an enterprise depends on bravery; education with him making the point of honor consist in the destruction of an enemy by strategem, and in the preservation of his own person free from injury; or, perhaps, this is nature, while it is education which teaches us to honor force more than finesse;

that he will defend himself against a host of enemies, always choosing to be killed, rather than to surrender, though it be to the whites, who he knows will treat him well; that in other situations, also, he meets death with more deliberation, and endures tortures with a firmness unknown almost to religious enthusiasm with us; that he is affectionate to his children, careful of them, and indulgent in the extreme; that his affections comprehend his other connections, weakening, as with us, from circle to circle, as they recede from the center; that his friendships are strong and faithful to the uttermost extremity; that his sensibility is keen, even the warriors weeping most bitterly on the loss of their children, though in general they endeavor to appear superior to human events; that his vivacity and activity of mind is equal to ours in the same situation; hence his eagerness for hunting, and for games of chance. The women are submitted to unjust drudgery. This I believe is the case with every barbarous people. With such, force is law. The stronger sex imposes on the weaker. It is civilization alone which replaces women in the enjoyment of their natural equality. That first teaches us to subdue the selfish passions, and to respect those rights in others which we value in ourselves. Were we in equal barbarism, our females would be equal drudges. The man with them is less strong than with us, but their women stronger than ours; and both for the same obvious reason; because our man and their woman is habituated to labor, and formed by it. With both races the sex which is indulged with ease is the least athletic. An Indian man is small in the hand and wrist, for the same reason for which a sailor is large and strong in the arms and shoulders, and a porter in the legs and thighs. They raise fewer children than we do. The causes of this are to be found, not in a difference of nature, but of circumstance. The women very frequently attending the men in their parties of war and of hunting, child-bearing becomes extremely inconvenient to them . . . .[25]

In this vein Jefferson goes on, outlining generally the nature of the American Indian. The key concept is that of "circumstance." Further on in the same discussion, he puts it explicitly: ". . . to form a just estimate of their genius [i. e., special nature and talents] and mental powers, more facts are wanting, and great allowance to be made for those circumstances of their situation

[25] Thomas Jefferson, *Writings*, Memorial Edition, II, 81-85.

which call for a display of particular talents only." [26] He was to encourage officially and unofficially the search for facts and was himself always to see such facts as were available to him in the context of circumstances. Men were in essence everywhere the same, the Indian being " formed in mind as well as in body, on the same module with the 'Homo sapiens Europaeus.'" But circumstances, social structures, cultures, altered forms and expressions and achievements. To clinch his case, Jefferson concludes his *summa contra* Buffon with deep praise of a trait clearly produced by circumstances, that of Indian eloquence—savage oratory being best represented by the famous speech of Chief Logan.

In Jefferson's analysis there are the essential outlines of an American theory of savagism. He moves in the direction of cultural relativism, holds to a moral absolutism, and gives the savage his due as one whom circumstances, for good and for bad, have held in an early state of society. Yet neither in the *Notes* or elsewhere in his writing does he work out precisely the relationship between savage nature and savage circumstances; throughout the tendency is general. Still, as we shall see, for him one of the ways to social criticism was through a comparison of savage and civilized life in Europe and America.[27]

Finally, there is to be noted the unity of Jefferson's thinking on the Indian with his thinking on man in general and its debt to the Scots. He may or may not have consciously indebted himself to Robertson; for although he objected violently to Robertson when the latter followed Buffon, he placed Robertson's *History of America* high on a list of required reading for a young man studying for the law.[28] A particular influence, however, would matter little. Certainly Jefferson knew the work of the Scottish school in general; and Robertson's *History* was, of course, only one product of what amounted to a cooperative enterprise. Jefferson was writing specifically in terms of Scottish moral sense philosophy when he

[26] *Ibid.*, II, 87.

[27] See below, p. 153.

[28] Letter to Chastellux, June 17, 1785, *Writings,* Memorial Edition, V, 3-7; and letter to John Garland Jefferson, June 11, 1790, *Writings,* ed. Ford, V, 179-82.

said of Indian government (in a passage added to editions of the *Notes* after 1787): " Their only controls are their manners, and that moral sense of right and wrong, which, like the sense of tasting and feeling in every man, makes a part of his nature." [29] In the 1780's, in his own copy of Lord Kames' *Principles of Morality and Natural Religion* (1751), he underscored and commented approvingly on Kames' statement that the form of the moral sense varies with the nature of man and is refined as human nature is refined; further, he underscored Kames' remarks on the moral sense of savages.[30] And, in 1814 he wrote of all men what he had written earlier of the Indian:

> Men living in different countries, under different circumstances, different habits and regimens, may have different utilities; the same act, therefore, may be useful, and consequently virtuous in one country which is injurious and vicious in another differently circumstanced. I sincerely, then, believe . . . in the general existence of a moral instinct.[31]

The Scots gave to Jefferson a way of bringing into focus and relationship all that he could discover of the Indian. The theory of moral sense, which interested him particularly in the 1780's when he was putting together the *Notes on the State of Virginia*, explained the savage's essential humanity. The theory of the progressive stages of history and of the relationship of character to circumstance explained the savage's essential inferiority, the final inferiority of even his savage virtues. Certainly Jefferson had noted that humanity and that inferiority independent of his reading of the Scots. Certainly what is most important is the content and quality of his understanding of savagism and not its genesis. Yet for the historical record we must note that as the American theory of the savage takes its clearest and most definite

[29] *Writings, Memorial Edition*, II, 128.

[30] Adrienne Koch, *The Philosophy of Thomas Jefferson* (New York, 1943), pp. 15-39. Miss Koch here analyses Jefferson's large general indebtedness to the Scots, particularly in the 1780's.

[31] Letter to Thomas Law, June 13, 1814, *Writings*, Memorial Edition, XIV, 143.

origins in Jefferson's thinking, so it takes its form and unity, however amorphous, from the thinking of the Scots whom Jefferson knew well.

Anxious to know as many facts as possible, Jefferson had been cautious in making large-scale pronouncements about the Indian. Other writers thought enough facts were available and so made definitive pronouncements, rushing in triumphantly where Jefferson would not tread. Their opinions have that form and unity which mark the establishment and consolidation of a way of belief.

In the first volume (1790) of the American edition of the *Encyclopaedia*, there is a lengthy essay on the Indian, part of the clergyman-historian Jedidiah Morse's much-reprinted article on "America."[32] Frank to acknowledge at once his indebtedness and objections to Robertson and other foreign authorities, concerned to vindicate the savage in the eyes of the world, Morse writes an account specifically in the historical and environmentalist pattern set by the Scots who at the time dominated the thinking of his New England. At the outset of a section on "Customs and dispositions of [the] North Americans," he sets his theme: "The character of the Indians is altogether founded upon their circumstances and way of life." Since the Indian must fight and hunt to survive, he has neither time nor occasion for gaiety and high spirits. Essentially he is an individualist, rising among his fellows only through "superiority in personal qualities of body or mind." He is ruled, if it may be called being ruled, by persuasion, not coercion. He is most a social being when he is at war; for war—"if we except hunting and fishing"—is his whole life. His social virtues, then, are warlike virtues.

There follows a disquisition on Indian warfare: ceremonies, dances, ensigns, the sort of strategy which is demanded by social

[32] *Encyclopaedia*, I (Philadelphia, 1790), 541-47. The whole article was reprinted separately as *The History of America* (Philadelphia, 1790) and often after that. The section on the Indian was reprinted verbatim in John Lendrum, *A Concise and Impartial History of the American Revolution* (Boston, 1795), I, 15-98. Morse anticipates the *Encyclopaedia* account in brief in his *American Geography* (Elizabethtown, 1789).

circumstance and individualism (itself a product of social circumstance), the practice of adopting or torturing prisoners, with special emphasis on the stoicism of those tortured and their heroic death songs. "But," Morse adds, "neither the intrepidity, on one side, nor the inflexibility, on the other, are among themselves matters of astonishment: for vengeance, and fortitude, in the midst of torment, are duties which they consider as sacred; they are the effects of their earliest education, and depend upon principles instilled into them from their infancy."

Morse writes at length, with particular instances, of Indian hospitality, of burial customs, of superstitions, of cruel treatment of women, of marriage customs, of Indian eloquence, and even of the "Peculiar manners of different nations." In sum, he finds that the Indian is everywhere essentially the same, as he is everywhere the savage living in savage society. He concludes his essay with a lengthy defence of the Indian against the charges of Buffon and De Pauw. Indians are not cowardly, perfidious, stupid, vain, effeminate, or in any way degenerate.

> . . . such partial and detached views . . . were they even free from misrepresentation, are not the just ground upon which to form an estimate of their character. Their qualities, good and bad (for they certainly possess both), and their way of life, the state of society among them, with all the circumstances of their condition, ought to be considered in connection, and in regard to their mutual influences.

Such became more and more clearly the standard opinion. By 1810 it could be formalized in a long essay by Samuel Stanhope Smith, clergyman and President of the College of New Jersey. Smith's "Of the Natural Bravery and Fortitude of the American Indians" is appended to the second edition of his *Essay on the Causes of the Variety of Complexion and Figure in the Human Species* (1810). The essay, coming from the head of the American institution where the Scottish philosophy was gospel, aims to correct the extremist notion of one of the Scots, Lord Kames, that there had been more than a single creation of mankind; its purpose is "to establish the unity of the human species." Smith would account for all racial and cultural differences in terms that are primarily environmental, and he would account for differences among individuals in terms of differences in their cultures. Toward the end of the *Essay*, he summarizes his procedure thus:

> . . . when the whole human race is known to compose only one species, this confusion and uncertainty [as to national and local traits] is removed, and the science of human nature, in all its relations, becomes susceptible of system. The principles of morals rest on sure and immutable foundations.—Its unity I have endeavoured to confirm by explaining the causes of its variety. Of these, the first I have shewn to be *climate*, by which is meant, not so much the latitude of a country from the equator, as the degree of heat or cold, which often depends on a great variety of other circumstances. The next is *the state of society*, which may augment or correct the influence of climate, and is itself a separate and independent cause of many conspicuous distinctions among mankind. These causes may be infinitely varied in degree; and their effects may likewise be diversified by various combinations. And, in the continual migrations of mankind, these effects may be still further modified, by changes which have antecedently taken place in a prior climate, and a prior state of society.[33]

It is the implications of such a position that have led Smith before this to explain Indian character in terms of Indian society and Indian society in terms of its isolation in a wild environment.[34] And it is the implications of such a position that have led him to make a general statement on the problem of understanding and judging savage character:

> The exaggerated representations which we sometime receive of the superior ingenuity of men in savage life, are usually the result of inconsideration. Savages are the subjects of eulogy for the same reason that we admire a monkey,—that is, a certain resemblance of the actions of men in civilized society which was not expected from the rudeness of their condition. There are doubtless degrees of genius among savages as well as among civilized nations: but the comparison should be made of savages among themselves, and not of the genius of a savage, with that of a polished, people.[35]

[33] Samuel Stanhope Smith, *An Essay on the Causes of the Variety of Complexion and Figure in the Human Species*, 2d. ed., p. 244.

[34] See, for example, *ibid.*, pp. 197-204. [35] *Ibid.*, f. n. 1, pp. 193-94.

This is perhaps crueller than Smith intends, for in his appendix on the " Natural Bravery and Fortitude of the American Indians " he intends as much to praise savagism as to condemn it.

Specifically, he intends to expatiate upon Kames' remarks (unusual for one of the Scots)[36] concerning savage warfare as an indication of the natural cowardice, pusillanimity, and cruelty of the Indian. Actually, so Smith tries to prove, both the strategy of the Indians' wars and their hard custom of torturing prisoners " result from their state of society, and the peculiar situation of their small hordes, and from certain habits and opinions existing among them which have originated, in a great measure, from the same causes." [37] For the savage such customs amount to natural virtues.

Having originated among Tartar tribes in northern Asia, and having emigrated to North America, the Indian, surrendering to his environment, gradually abandoned all traces of civilization. He is " . . . man completely savage, but obliged by the nature of the forest which he inhabits, and the variable temperature of the heaven under which he lives, as well as by enemies with which he is surrounded, to employ both courage and address, for his subsistence, and defence. He is of savages, therefore, the most noble, in whom the unaided powers of human nature appear with greater dignity than among those rude tribes who either approach nearer to the equator, or are farther removed towards the poles." Warfare is almost his entire life. " If the passions of such uncultivated minds are often atrocious, they sometimes display such heroic, and even sublime efforts of courage, and unconquerable firmness of soul, as justly excite our wonder, and command our admiration." [38]

Smith's description of the causes and conduct of Indian warfare is as bloodily detailed as he can make it. Wars occur often because Indians are individualistic to a fault, because they have no way to determine ownership of tribal domains, because they have no proper machinery for settling disputes. From Indian individualism follows the conduct of wars—modes of attack, the love of surprise

[36] See my " The Eighteenth-Century Scottish Primitivists: Some Reconsiderations," *ELH*, XII (1945), 203-20.

[37] *Essay*, pp. 354-55.

[38] *Ibid.*, pp. 357-58.

and secrecy, merciless butchery with the tomahawk, and afterward torture and heroic defiance of torture.

At the end of his account, Smith discusses in detail the significance of the Indian's unmilitary use of concealment and surprise in fighting, his practice of adopting prisoners, his practice of torturing prisoners, and his ability to bear pain and torture. All are explained in terms of savage life and its milieu. First: The Indian must fight as he does in order to adapt himself to the sort of country in which he lives; witness his success against Braddock. Second: An Indian woman can take a new husband, or a family can adopt a new son in this sort of society, where there is no civilization to make for " refined " domestic sensibilities and emotional ties; and on the other hand, a prisoner will easily accede to being adopted into another tribe because, dishonored as a prisoner, he is dead to his own people. Third: " Refined and polished nations correct the extreme violence of the passions by the improvements of reason. The education of a savage is intended not to correct, but to give full and unrestrained scope to them." [39] The desire and the need for vengeance negate the possibility of any human kindness. Fourth: The Indian, like the Spartan, is trained of necessity to be only a warrior and to endure the hardships of warfare. This is the only good life for him. " An energetic *will*, created by sublime sentiments, by strong passions, or even induced by the habit of conflicting with dangers and sufferings, imparts to the soul a strength which suspends, in a great measure, the sensation of pain, and wholly deprives it of those additional terrors with which a timid imagination invests it." [40] In short, these four qualities evolve naturally and by certain universal, necessary moral and physical laws in savage society itself. If human nature is essentially the same, circumstances alter cases and place the Indian with his savage virtues and vices, in his proper place below civilized man. Indians, Smith says early in his *Essay*, are not far from the " primitive and absolute savagism " which civilized men have escaped. Circumstances make the human past part of the human present.

[39] *Ibid.*, p. 399.

[40] *Ibid.*, pp. 407-408.

3

Jefferson's, Morse's, and Smith's accounts represent primary stages in the evolution of an American idea of savagism. They are, however, only three accounts among many. And although they represent that theoretical writing which gave way after 1810 to writing nominally more descriptive, still we can trace their influence deep into the new century. Later accounts of this theoretical kind are myriad, and are significant only as echoings and reechoings of their antecedents.

Such accounts occur in contexts various enough to indicate the proliferating and deep-cutting significance of the idea which they embody. They occur in collections of Indian "anecdotes," collections which continue a journalistic tradition going back into the middle of the eighteenth century;[41] in pamphlets and essays considering the Indian "problem";[42] in works on Indian origins, even when their authors do not subscribe to the orthodox opinion of northern asiatic origins;[43] in popular descriptions of Indian "traits";[44] in investigations into Indian religion;[45] and, most of

[41] George Turner, *Traits of Indian Character*, 2 vols. (Philadelphia, 1836); [John Farmer?], *A Collection of Indian Anecdotes* (Concord, N. H., 1837); [John L. Blake?], *Anecdotes of the American Indians* (Philadelphia, 1843).

[42] Ezra Stiles, *The United States Elevated to Glory and Honor* (New Haven, 1783); [Silas Wood], *Thoughts on the State of the American Indians* (New York, 1794); "On the causes of the depopulation of the American Indians," *Analectic Magazine*, VII (1816), 323-327.

[43] James McCulloh, *Researches on America* (Baltimore, 1816—reprinted, expanded, under varying titles, 1817 and 1829); Elias Boudinot, *A Star in the West* (Trenton, 1816). McCulloh propounds a theory of separate Indian origin, related somehow to the existence of Atlantis; Boudinot is one of the strong proponents of the theory of a Hebrew origin.

[44] Benjamin Rush, "An Account of the Vices Peculiar to the Indian of North America," *Essays, Literary, Moral and Philosophical* [1798] (Philadelphia, 1806), pp. 256-260; Hugh Williamson, *Observations on the Climate in Different Parts of America* (New York, 1811); Washington Irving, "Philip of Pokanoket" and "Traits of Indian Character," *The Sketch Book* [1819], *Works* (New York, 1880), II, 389-405, 406-30; John Treat Irving, *Indian Sketches*, 2 vols. (Philadelphia, 1835); Job. R. Tyson,

all, in works on the history of the Indian and his wars with civilized men.[46] The concern everywhere is to comprehend; and comprehension is in terms of savagism and of the nature and limitations of its virtues. As the author of one of these treatises, printed in 1812 and reprinted in 1828, put it:

> The savage state has, no doubt, its advantages. It promotes bodily activity. Few among them are sickly, feeble or deformed. Their minds possess an astonishing degree of fortitude and passive courage.

Discourse on the Surviving Remnant of the Indian Race in the United States (Philadelphia, 1836). A curiosity is the fake captivity narrative, *Memoirs of Charles Dennis Rusoe D'Eres* (Exeter, 1800), which has appended to it a long account of Indian traits, pp. 97-157.

[45] Samuel Jarvis, "A Discourse on the Religion of the Indian Tribes of North America" [delivered December 20, 1819], *New York Historical Society Collections,* III (1821), 181-268; William Apes, *A Son of the Forest* (New York, 1829); Job Durfee, "The Idea of the Supernatural Among the Indians" [lecture delivered January 1838], *The Complete Works of Job Durfee* (Providence, 1849), pp. 249-71.

[46] [Henry Trumbull,] *History of the Discovery of America* (Brooklyn, 1802, and often thereafter), pp. 66-86; De Witt Clinton, "A Discourse Delivered Before the New-York Historical Society" [December 6, 1811], *New York Historical Society Collections,* II (1814), [39]-116; Daniel Clarke Sanders, *A History of the Indian Wars with the First Settlers of the United States* [1812] (Rochester, 1893, reprinted from ed. 1828), Chaps. XVIII-XXVIII; Epapharas Hoyt, *Antiquarian Researches* (Greenfield, Mass., 1824); Joseph Doddridge, *Notes on the Settlement and Indian Wars of the Western Parts of Virginia and Pennsylvania* (Wellsburg, Va., 1824); Alexander Withers, *Chronicles of Border Warfare* (Clarksburg, Va., 1831); Timothy Flint, *Indian Wars of the West* (Cincinnati, 1833); Harvey Newcomb, *The North American Indians,* 2 vols. (Pittsburgh, 1835); *Chronicles of the North American Savages* (a periodical which lasted the year 1835); John Winter, "A Brief Sketch of Indian Origins, Character, Religion, Government, &c.," Chapter VIII of *A Narrative of the Sufferings of Massy Harbison,* 4th ed. (Beaver, Pennsylvania, 1836); [John Frost], *Indian Wars of the United States* (Philadelphia, 1840, and often thereafter); *Events in Indian History* (Lancaster, Pennsylvania, 1841); [Samuel Goodrich], *Lives of Celebrated American Indians* (Boston, 1843); [Goodrich], *History of the Indians of North and South America* (Boston, 1844); [Goodrich], *The Manners, Customs, and Antiquities of the Indians of North and South America* (Boston, 1844).

Their political talents are not inferior; and some of their speeches would not dishonor an European parliament. Their love of country burns with a pure, ardent and inextinguishable flame. They rush up to the cannon's mouth and throw themselves on the weapons of certain death, if their last efforts can leave their tribe safe and free. All they do is for the common weal, and private interest scarcely finds any place to enter.

The disadvantages of the savage state are more than a balance. Intellectual improvement will be out of the question. The mind will remain a subject too invisible to be noticed. Absolute want, not rational culture, will be the topic of conversation, when they meet. They will have virtues indeed, but they will be few; and these not founded on ethical principles, discovering the reasons of their duty, carried to any sufficient extent.[47]

5

Operating from a moral absolute—that involved in the theory of man's social destiny—Americans were able to achieve a satisfactory kind of cultural relativity. Before one judges the Indian, so their argument went, one must understand him. And when one understands, one will see that judgment of the savage as being noble or ignoble is precluded. Savage life and civilized life are realms apart, separated by centuries of cultural history, or by entirely different environmental situations, most likely by both. Hence what is good for a savage is not necessarily good for a civilized man. The ideals of a savage society are built around the hunt and warfare; and its members can develop no further, no higher, than their life will let them. To follow up a favorite example, in an Indian society women must do all the manual labor, because in order for that society to survive, the men must be occupied with nothing but the basic problem of feeding and defending it. The Indian is not a beast because he treats his women as he does; our saying that he is, is tantamount to our judging behavior in a savage society in terms of behavior in a civilized society. Even as what seem to us to be the Indian's

[47] [Daniel Clarke Sanders,] *A History of the Indian Wars With the First Settlers of the United States*, pp. 143-44.

inferior traits are the products of his immature and inhibited society, so are his superior traits. American writers noted again and again that the Indian's ability to bear tremendous physical pain stoically makes him neither better nor worse than the civilized man, but rather is simply a characteristic result of the natural ideals and aims of a warrior-dominated society in which all men must expect to do just that, grow used to doing just that. Savage virtues, then, like savage vices, are uniquely savage.

The simplest way to describe the Indian would be to say that he was uncivilized. The simplest way to evaluate him would be to say that his virtues and vices, his bravery and cruelty, were products of his being uncivilized. One would thus be evaluating not so much the qualities of an individual as those of a society; and one would be placing that society in relation to one's own in such a way that history, and the idea of progress which gave meaning to history, would solve the problem of evaluation. The idea of history as progress made it possible fully to comprehend the culturally earlier as the morally inferior, even as an environmentalist analysis of societies made it possible to account for the contemporaneity of that which should have been part of the past. Savagism could be known only in terms of the civilization to which, by the law of nature, it had to give way.

The idea of savagism had explained the Indian. In the second decade of the nineteenth century and beyond, Americans were constrained to learn if the Indian, and all the rich details of his life which poured in from the reports of travellers and explorers, would explain savagism.

IV

The Zero of Human Society:

The Idea of the Savage

THE IDEA of savagism was at best an hypothesis which called for proof. Proof required first-hand observation and then close analysis, classification, and summing-up of what had been observed. Facts were collected first-hand, recorded, analysed, and conclusions come to. In the end the hypothesis was proved in fact; the savage proved savagism; a symbol bodied forth an idea.

Yet we can look back at American studies of the Indian and see, in a century-long perspective, how the facts belie those conclusions. For we may work with hypotheses which do not press us to see primitive cultures as at once historically anterior and morally inferior to ours. Indeed, we feel committed to avoid such historicizing and moralizing, and rigorously to separate anthropology from philosophy, description from evaluation. But then, the Indian is no great personal issue to us. Hence, to understand the situation of Americans whose thinking we are now tracing, we must remind ourselves how certain of our hypotheses inevitably press us to conclusions and assurances which justify our way of life as exclusively and as certainly as the idea of savagism justified theirs. We simply have to remind ourselves, for example, how hard it is for us to find a place in our world for societies which achieve their ends in ways which seem to deny the fundamental moral, social, and political hypotheses of our society. Thus forewarned, perhaps, we can proceed to see how, in a nineteenth-century milieu, the savage, as known in stern fact, could and did prove savagism, progress, and the manifest destiny of American civilization.

1

Everywhere the facts of Indian life were being gathered and disseminated, formally and informally, officially and unofficially. John Adams, always skeptical, felt the need for fact-gathering when, in the 1790's, he wrote an indignant note in the margin of his copy of Rousseau's *Discourse on Inequality*, itself embodying praise for the agrarian over the savage, hunting way of life:

> Reasonings from a State of Nature are fallacious, because hypothetical. We have not facts. Experiments are wanting. Reasonings from Savage Life do not much better. Every writer affirms what he pleases. We have not facts to be depended on.[1]

It was Adams' great friend, Thomas Jefferson, who encouraged Americans to go systematically after the facts. In 1803, with the advice of his learned friends, he classified the kinds of information to be collected by Lewis and Clark in their exploration of the western country:

> The extent and limits of their possessions;
> Their relation with other tribes or nations;
> Their language, traditions, and monuments;
> Their ordinary occupations in agriculture, fishing, hunting, war, etc. and the implements for these;
> Their food, clothing, and domestic accommodations;
> The diseases prevalent among them, and the remedies they use;
> Moral and physical circumstances which distingish them from the tribes we know;
> Peculiarities of their laws, customs, and dispositions;
> Any articles of commerce they may need or furnish, and to what extent.

[1] "John Adams on Rousseau," *More Books*, I (1926), 61; the dating of the entry is my guess. On Rousseau and progress, see A. O. Lovejoy, "The Supposed Primitivism of Rousseau's *Discourse on Inequality*," *Essays in the History of Ideas* (Baltimore, 1948), pp. 14-37.

And, considering the interest which every nation has in extending and strengthening the authority of reason and justice among the people around them, it will be useful to acquire what knowledge you can of the state of morality, religion, and information among them; as it may better enable those who may endeavor to civilize and instruct them, to adapt their measures to the existing notions and practices of those on whom they are to operate.[2]

Such categorization of data marks most formal, official attempts to collect information on the Indian. Indian Agents were instructed to gather under orderly headings as much material as they could.[3] Western exploring parties, sent out by the government, given instructions like those of Jefferson to Lewis and Clark, almost always numbered scientists among their members.

Reports of such parties supplied rich details of Mississippi Valley, plains, and far western Indian life, details generally unabsorbed into any formally exposited whole but colored nonetheless by the prejudices of men who were looking to see savages. Biddle's writing-up of the Lewis and Clark expedition (1814),

[2] Nicholas Biddle, *History of the Expedition Under the Command of Lewis and Clark* [1814], ed. E. Coues (New York, 1893), I, xxvii-xxviii. On February 28, 1803 Jefferson asked Benjamin Rush's advice on preparing such a questionnaire; Rush wrote out a list of questions for "Merryweather Lewis before he went up the Missouri"; see *The Autobiography of Benjamin Rush*, ed. G. W. Corner (Princeton, 1948), pp. 265-66.

[3] See, for example, the questionnaire prepared by Lewis Cass, Governor of Michigan Territory, *Inquiries, Respecting the History, Traditions, Languages, Manners, Customs, Religion, &c. of the Indians, Living within the United States* (Detroit, 1823); the report prepared (January 15, 1827) for William Clark, then Superintendent of Indian Affairs at St. Louis, by Thomas Forsyth, a subagent, "An Account of the Manners and Customs of the Sauk and Fox Nations of Indians," printed from MS. in Emma Blair, ed., *The Indian Tribes of the Upper Mississippi Valley and Region of the Great Lakes* (Cleveland, 1911), II, 183-245; and the official instructions given Captain Bonneville for his Rocky Mountain journey, as Washington Irving records them in the Appendix to his *Adventures of Captain Bonneville* (1837). Cf. generally the attempts at such analytic categorization by Schoolcraft (who was in the Indian Service), discussed below, pp. 124-25.

James' of the Long expedition (1823), and Keating's of his own (1824)—each testifies to the opinion of a man who, however careful he might be to record the complexities of Indian life, could most readily conceive of it in the simple pattern of savagism. For example, after showing that to hunting and warfare are to be traced the qualities of Indian life, Keating writes of a Sauk chief:

[His observations] breathe throughout a wisdom which would have done honour to the philosophers of old, and a morality of which no Christian need have blushed. Indeed they speak strongly in favour of the doctrine, that wisdom and morality are the spontaneous growth of the human heart, the seeds of which have been implanted by the Great Creator himself; that civilization does not produce them; that the real benefit which results from it is, that, in some instances, it may curb the passions which would otherwise impede their growth. The Indian appears to us to possess ideas of virtue and morality, which are fully as valuable as those that are supposed by some philosophers to be the exclusive appanage of civilization. True, they are, perhaps, but too frequently checked in their growth by the uncontrolled sway which his evil propensities exercise over him . . . .[4]

Keating's account is built from close observation of Potowatamis, Sauks, Foxes, Winnebagoes, and Sioux; Biddle's and James' (following journals of first-hand observation), of Sioux, Pawnees, Arapahoes, Cheyennes, and others. The details are set down carefully enough for use by twentieth-century ethnologists, and most often go uninterpreted. Yet even uninterpreted details are categorized and classified, in terms of the radical difference between farming-civilized and hunting-savage societies, to point toward conclusions such as Keating's.

Unofficial, private travellers, writing more personal and informal accounts, interpret their observations in much the same manner, even as they try to set down as much first-hand detail as possible.[5] They see, for example, that Plains Indians are not

[4] William H. Keating, *Narrative of an Expedition to the Source of St. Peter's River* [1824] (London, 1825), I, 238.

[5] I speak here of travel narratives such as these: Henry M. Brackenridge, *Journal of a Voyage Up the River Missouri*, 2d ed. enlarged (Balti-

Eastern Woodland Indians. Yet, ironically enough, the predominantly hunting culture of the Plains Indians supports their notion that Eastern Indians—in general, as much agrarian as hunting peoples—are almost exclusively hunters. They can even distinguish clearly among tribes and types. By the 1840's and 50's they had come to know Osages, Chickasaws, Choctaws, Crees, Chippewas, Blackfeet, Shoshones, Comanches, Sioux, Pawnees, and many others. Still, they all conclude that the Indian is everywhere essentially the same, the savage of their idea of savagism. The traveller must cap his descriptions with this, on Indians as chronologically true primitives, in 1831:

In their manners, the aborigines of the North West, resemble the people of the earliest ages of the world.[6]

Or this, a Virgilian tag, on Indians as unhappy hunters, in 1833:

> Oh happy—if he knew his happy state,
> The man, who, free from turmoil and debate,
> Receives his wholesome food from Nature's hand,
> The just return of *cultivated* land.[7]

Or this, on Indians as pitiable savages, in 1846, from one who, unlike most of his fellows, had come to praise them:

more, 1815); Thomas Nuttall, *A Journal of Travels into the Arkansas Territory* (Philadelphia, 1821); Daniel Harmon, *A Journal of Voyages and Travels* (Andover, 1820); Caleb Atwater, *Remarks Made on a Tour to Prairie du Chien* (Columbus, 1831); James Pattie, *The Personal Narrative,* ed. Timothy Flint (Cincinnati, 1833); John B. Wyeth, *Oregon* (Cambridge, 1833); [Robert Baird], *View of the Valley of the Mississippi* (Philadelphia, 1832); [James Hildreth], *Dragoon Campaigns to the Rocky Mountains* (New York, 1836); Washington Irving, *A Tour on the Prairies* (published as the first volume of the *Crayon Miscellanies* [Philadelphia, 1835]), *Astoria* (Philadelphia, 1836); John K. Townsend, *Narrative of a Journey across the Rocky Mountains* (Philadelphia, 1839); Josiah Gregg, *Commerce of the Prairies* (New York, 1844); Rufus Sage, *Western Scenes and Adventures* (Philadelphia, 1846).

[6] Caleb Atwater, *Remarks Made on a Tour to Prairie du Chien,* p. 101.

[7] John B. Wyeth, *Oregon,* p. 106.

> [The Indian] has a heart instinctive of more genuine good feeling than his white neighbor—a soul of more firm integrity—a spirit of more unyielding independence. Place the white man in his condition, divested of all the restraints of law, and unacquainted with the learning and arts of civilized life—surrounded by all the associations of the savage state—and the Indian, by comparison, will then exhibit, in a more striking light, that innate superiority he in reality possesses.
>
> No: The Indian should not be despised. He holds weighty claims upon our pity, our compassion, and our respect,—but never should he be despised.[8]

Even if he went so far as to envy the Indian, the traveller would have in the end to pity him because he was not civilized.

Men who could not journey to see Indians in person could see them pictured in numerous collections of Indian sketches and portraits.[9] Where eighteenth-century grand-style painters like Charles Wilson Peale, Benjamin West (he who exclaimed, upon first seeing the Apollo Belvedere, " My God, a Mohawk! "), and Gilbert Stuart were interested in primitive heroic types, later painters were mainly illustrators working in the tradition of the picturesque, concerned to record particulars and details. James O. Lewis, who published nine crude portfolios of portraits and landscapes in 1835 and 1836, had accompanied the Indian officials Lewis Cass and Thomas McKenney to get to the Indians of the northwest. Before Removal, Charles Bird King painted Indians visiting Washington for an official Indian Gallery, assembled under the direction of McKenney. John Mix Stanley, who had travelled and painted in the northwest and in the southwest from the 1830's through the 1850's also contributed, as did Lewis. (Although the gallery, coming eventually to the Smithsonian

[8] Rufus Sage, *Western Scenes and Adventures*, 3d ed. (Philadelphia, 1855), p. 86.

[9] See H. Chadwick Hunter, " The American Indian in Painting," *Art and Archaeology*, VIII (1919), 81-97; Benjamin Draper, " John Mix Stanley," *Antiques*, XLI (1942), 180-82; and Bernard De Voto, " The First Illustrators of the West," *Across the Wide Missouri* (Boston, 1947), pp. 391-415.

Institution, was destroyed by fire in 1865, much of its contents was preserved and given wide popularity in McKenney's *History of the Indian Tribes of North America*, published in three folio volumes in 1836, 1838, and 1844, and republished in smaller format three times soon thereafter.) Alfred Jacob Miller, first and best painter of the Rocky Mountain West and its people, was taken on the expedition of Captain William Drummond Stewart in 1837. Seth Eastman, who supplied portraits to Henry Rowe Schoolcraft, was a soldier on western frontier duty in the 30's and 40's. George Winter began in 1837 to paint Indiana Indians; 1837 was the year they were being removed, and Winter explicitly felt himself, so his journals indicate, to be a kind of historian.[10] But then, all these men were willy-nilly historians and painting as such.

We have one contemporary artist's lengthy and repetitious testimony to the significance of his work for the history of savage and civilized man in America. It is that of George Catlin, the self-fabling and widely travelled Pennsylvanian who first taught Americans to look at their west.[11] (Miller had preceded Catlin west, but his paintings have only recently been rediscovered and made available.) In his *Letters and Notes on the Manners, Customs, and Condition of the North American Indians* (1841), Catlin insists that he has aimed to preserve in portraits and scenes the true Indian; he has gone as far west as possible to see the Indian as he really is, as he really was before the coming of the white man. For Catlin, Plains Indians are natural men, savage men, living according to standards which are perfectly adequate for savages. If the Sioux are poor by civilized standards, by savage standards they are not; scalping is by civilized standards a barbarous custom, but it is related to " the necessities of Indian life." Towards the end of the *Letters and Notes*, he records in a long meditation what his travels have meant to him. He has seen the west, its wilds, its sublimity, its frighteningly primitive freedom, its bound-

[10] See the Introduction to a catalog of Winter's paintings, *George Winter, Pioneer Artist of Indiana* (Indianapolis, 1939).

[11] See DeVoto, as cited above.

lessness, and, above all, its people—" the valiant and the brave, whose deeds of chivalry and honour have passed away like themselves, unembalmed and untold." He has " viewed man in the artless and innocent simplicity of nature, in the full enjoyment of the luxuries which God has bestowed upon him." He has seen civilization come " *with all its vices*, like the *dead of night* . . . ," hunting lands plowed, savage graves desecrated, " this splendid Juggernaut rolling on . . . ." He has " stood amidst these unsophisticated people, and contemplated with feelings of deepest regret, the certain approach of this overwhelming system, which will inevitably march on and prosper, until reluctant tears shall have watered every rod of this fair land. . . ." And so on, until: " All this is *certain*. Man's increase, and the march of human improvements in this New World, are as true and irresistable as the laws of nature. . . ." Finally, he envisions the race of Americans settling in the west, half-way between " *literal democracy* and *aristocracy*." [12]

Materials for the study of Indian life were thus plentifully available. The pressing need for a means to bring them together was satisfied in the organization, from the 1790's onward, of societies devoted to the investigation and interpretation of the national past. The aim of the Massachusetts Historical Society, founded in 1791, was to assemble materials " to mark the genius, delineate the manners, and trace the progress of society in the United States. . . ." [13] The Society published in the first volume of its *Collections* (1792), among other things, Gookin's seventeenth-century *Historical Collections of the Indians in New-England,* and in a prefatory note in the second volume asked for American gentlemen of science to collect information on the aborigines. In early volumes of the *Collections* of the New York Historical Society (incorporated 1809) there were printed essays on Iroquois history and on savage religion; in early volumes of

[12] George Catlin, *North American Indians* [1841] (Edinburgh, 1926). I quote from I, 269; II, 176-81.

[13] *Massachusetts Historical Society Collections,* Ser. 1, I (1792), 1.

the *Transactions and Collections* of the American Antiquarian Society (incorporated 1812), descriptions of Indian antiquities, discourses on Indian origins, Gallatin's great *Synopsis* of Indian languages, and (from the seventeenth-century manuscript) Gookin's *Historical Account of the Doings and Sufferings of the Christian Indians of New England*; in the first volume of the *Collections* of the New Hampshire Historical Society (incorporated 1823), a scholarly edition of Samuel Penhallow's eighteenth-century *History of the Wars of New England with the Eastern Indians* and a note on the Indians of New Hampshire; in early volumes of the *Collections* of the Maine Historical Society (incorporated in 1822), oddments of Indian history and Indian antiquities.

The end of such publication was historical, therefore "philosophical" and moral. Thus a prefatory note to the first volume (1831) of the Maine Historical Society *Collections* urges Americans to write down the life of the Indian who, in his unprecedented resistance to and corruption by civilization, is soon to disappear entirely:

> The causes which have made the natives of this country an exception to all the other experiences of the world, are well worthy the inquiries of curious and philosophical minds, and will be likely to excite a higher interest as they recede more and more from future ages. They seem to imply a difference, if not an inferiority of nature. Everything therefore which can serve to illustrate their character, whether in their primitive and natural state, or in their decline and degenerate condition under the deleterious influence of their civilized conquerors, must always be regarded with great interest.[14]

The matter had already been urgent enough for the American Academy of Arts and Sciences to announce in June 1824 a prize to be awarded for the best essay on the history of the Indians of

[14] *Maine Historical Society Collections,* I (1831), unpaged preliminary material. For an analogous observation in an analogous context, see "Address of Isaac Goodwin, August 24, 1820," *American Antiquarian Society Proceedings* (1812-1849), pp. 160-61.

North America.[15] Materials were abundant, but the time alloted to savagism was running out.

The history, life, and manners of the savage, then, as well as his fate and its meaning could prove savagism. The task that lay before Americans after 1815 was to fill in details of the proof. The basic details were readily available: antiquities had been searched out; [16] languages had been classified; [17] explorers and travellers had observed and recorded contemporary facts; antiquarians and historians had dug up old records of the Indian's clash with the white man. What was needed, in the words of Lewis Cass, who knew the northwest Indians at first-hand, was fuller knowledge of " the moral character and feelings of the Indians, of their mental discipline, of their peculiar opinions, mythological and religious, and of all that is most valuable to man in the history of man." [18] What we must sketch out now are the final episodes in the triumph of the idea of savagism as it became the idea of the savage.

2

Essentially that triumph was, we must remember, the triumph of a method, a mode of historical and moral understanding. It was a method which came to be applied not only to the savage and his fate but to the whole of American life. Thus Edward Everett explained, in his Phi Beta Kappa oration at Harvard in 1824, " The Circumstances Favorable to the Progress of Literature in America ":

But as, in the formation of the individual character, there are

[15] *United States Literary Gazette*, I (June 15, 1824), 76. I have not been able to learn if the award was ever made.

[16] Chiefly in the first volume of the *American Antiquarian Society Transactions and Collections* (1820).

[17] Chiefly in Albert Gallatin's *Synopsis of the Indian Tribes, ibid.*, II (1836), 1-422, which definitively synthesized official and unofficial word-listing in its own time.

[18] *North American Review*, XXII (1826), 55. Cass, of course, felt that Americans were ignorant in these matters; but the way he categorizes their ignorance shows that he felt it to be an ignorance to be easily remedied.

causes of undisputed and powerful operation, so, in national character, there are causes, equally certain, of growth and excellence on the one hand, and of degeneracy and ruin on the other. It belongs to the philosophy of history to investigate these causes; and, if possible, to point out the circumstances, which, as furnishing the motives, and giving the direction, to intellectual effort in different nations, have had a chief agency in making them what they were, or are. Where it is done judiciously, it is in the highest degree curious thus to trace physical or political facts into moral and intellectual consequences, and great historical results; and to show how climate, geographical position, local relations, institutions, single events, and the influence of individuals, have fixed the characters and decided the destiny of nations.[19]

This is the method of the Scots naturalized, completely absorbed into American thinking. The method cut two ways, comprehending at once American civilization and American savagism by placing them one after another in the long line of the progress of man and society.

Those who had lived with the Indian and knew him well could comprehend him thus. Even the Moravian missionary John Heckewelder, held to his Delawares by a tie of warm Christian charity, living very close to them, writing for love, not scholarship, published in 1818 a treatise in which the Indian is in the end the particular and concrete embodiment, the symbol, of the idea of the savage. Heckewelder's *Account of the History, Manners, and Customs, of the Indian Nations, Who Once Inhabited Pennsylvania and the Neighboring States* is intended as an objective record of savage life which will defend the Delawares against the vilifications of Indian-haters. His objectivity is that of a missionary who is sure that his Indians can be brought to the glory of Christian civilization if non-Christian civilization does not destroy them first. The core of Indian life, for him, is its hunting culture; and the quality of that life is pathetically simple. Explicitly, he maintains that he is not, as we should say, a primitivist;

[19] Joseph Blau, ed. *American Philosophic Addresses, 1700-1900* (New York, 1946), p. 65.

but feeling that he must give the Indian his due, he defends him on strictly Christian, humanitarian grounds. What he assumes is that a savage true to the best of savagism is superior to a civilized man corrupted by the vices of civilization.[20]

His analysis of the Indian character follows closely from such an assumption. His interest is in the Indian before he was corrupted, and he is frank to say that he is writing the "history of early times." [21] His Indians, as he summarizes their "General Character," [22] are communists, sharing all things alike from the Great Spirit; hospitable, civil, and friendly; innately just and driven by their sense of justice to wild heroic deeds. Still,

> . . . we must . . . look to the other side of the picture. It cannot but be acknowledged that the Indians are in general revengeful and cruel to their enemies. That even after the battle is over, they wreak their deliberate revenge on their defenceless prisoners; that in their wars, they are indifferent about the means which they pursue for the annoyance and destruction of their adversaries, and that surprise and stratagem are as often employed by them as open force. This is all true.

He has a simple explanation for this awful truth:

> Deprived by the light of the only true Christian Religion, unchecked by the precepts and unswayed by the example of the God of peace, they indulge too much, sometimes, the violence of their passions, and commit actions which force the tear from the eye of humanity. . . .[23]

This is, if we consider it closely, a crude form of the argument from progress, as we have seen it develop. Hence the contemporary approval of Heckewelder's *Account*, in spite of its author's tendency (all unconsciously) to identify himself with his Dela-

[20] John Heckewelder, *Account* (Philadelphia, 1818), p. 254. The *Account* constituted the first volume of *American Philosophical Society Transactions*. Cf. a whole chapter in which Indians and whites are compared, pp. 327-45.

[21] *Ibid.*, p. 8.

[22] *Ibid.*, pp. 83-91.

[23] *Ibid.*, p. 91.

wares and to rhapsodize over their lives.[24] For Heckewelder, in his own Moravian way, was proving what all were proving—what, in fact, all were committed to prove.

Others who had lived with the Indians reported on their lives in much the same terms. Charles Johnston, as we have seen, felt bound to make explicit his indebtedness to the Scottish tradition when, in 1827, he added to the story of his captivity " Sketches of Indian Character and Manners." His thesis is simple enough: " In all ages, and in all countries, savage man displays the same general traits of character and of manners. These depend, essentially on the state of society in which he exists. . . ." [25] Edwin James, who had written the narrative of Long's exploration, put together his *Narrative of the Captivity and Adventures of John Tanner . . . During Thirty Years Residence Among the Indians in the Interior of North America* (1830) to show, simply enough, how, living among savages under the conditions of savagism, a white man had become nothing but a savage, for good and for bad.[26] In 1850 Lewis Garrard set down his " romantic " adventures of 1846 and 1847, when he had gone west and lived with the Cheyennes, shared intimately in their life, and even danced the scalp-dance with them. He admitted that he envied their " free and happy life," yet qualified his envy with, " to them, who know no other joys than those of the untaught savage, *such* a life must be the acme of happiness. . . ." He was obliged to congratulate himself that he lived " in an age of progressive civilization " and to characterize his dear Cheyennes as " a wofully degenerate set." [27] And in 1850 too the terribly sentimental Mrs. Mary Eastman, living among the Sioux, compiled three volumes of brave, wild sketches of Indian life, two to accompany Indian portraits by her husband

[24] See the anonymous review of the *Account, North American Review,* IX (1819), 155-78.

[25] *A Narrative of the Incidents Attending the Capture, Detention, and Ransom of Charles Johnston* (New York, 1827), p. 102. On Johnston and the Scots, see above, p. 89.

[26] Edwin James, *Narrative* (New York, 1830), especially pp. 3-4.

[27] Lewis H. Garrard, *Wah-To-Yah and the Taos Trail* [1850], ed. R. L. Bieber (Glendale, California, 1938), pp. 83, 108, 121.

Col. Seth Eastman, and concluded in one of them: "The Indian, delighting in war and in glorious deeds, is yet ignorant of the greatest victory of which man is capable—the conquering of one's self. His sorrows are not sanctified in him; he does not come from them holy and great." [28] The means to this victory would be, obviously enough, Christian civilization.

The assurance of such a victory was fully in the minds of men who strove to do up the Indian encyclopedically. Scholarly antiquarians and collectors like Samuel Gardner Drake and Benjamin Thatcher compiled and wrote books which public demand encouraged them continually to expand, revise, and republish. Drake's *Biography and History of the Indians of North America*, for example, reached its eleventh edition in 1857; and Thatcher's *Indian Biography*, in great part depending on (stealing from, Drake claimed [29]) Drake's book, reached its fourteenth edition in 1860.[30] Both had first appeared in 1832 and both let the historical record exposit the idea of savagism.[31] But their work, for all its popularity, was not as ambitious as the most celebrated of the kind, Thomas McKenney's and James Hall's "monumental" *History of the Indian Tribes of North America.*[32]

[28] *The American Aboriginal Portfolio* (Philadelphia, 1853), pp. iii-iv. Cf. Mrs. Eastman's comments, *passim*, in *Dahcotah, or, Life and Legends of the Sioux around Fort Snelling* (New York, 1849); and in her *Chicora* (Philadelphia, 1854), also published as *The American Annual* (Philadelphia, 1855?).

[29] See the prefatory notes to the *Book of the Indians* (Boston, 1833), this the second form of the *Biography and History*; and to the *Indian Captivities* (Boston, 1839).

[30] Drake was also a pioneering editor of books on Indian history. He published Church's *History of King Philip's War* in 1825, The *Old Indian Chronicle* (a collection of tracts on King Philip's War) in 1836, Increase Mather's two histories of New England Indian troubles in 1862 and 1864, and Hubbard's *History* in 1865.

[31] The idea is implicit throughout their writings and gives them form. Drake, however, is explicit in at least two places, his introductions to Increase Mather, *The Early History of New England* [1677] (Boston, 1864), pp. xi-xvi, and to the *Indian Captivities* (Boston, 1839), pp. vi-vii.

[32] This judgment is Bernard De Voto's, *Across the Wide Missouri*, p. 399.

McKenney had begun the commissioning and collecting of Indian portraits in 1821 when he was Superintendant of Indian Trade; he had published a description of the Chippewas in 1827 in his *Sketches of a Tour to the Lakes*; and as chief of the Bureau of Indian Affairs in the later 1820's, he had been able to add to his collection of portraits. Out of office in 1830, deeply concerned with the problem of Removal, he planned to collect the portraits and to offer Americans at long last a true picture of the Indian. Hall, celebrated as a western lawyer, editor, and author, joined McKenney to help in the writing. Failing in an attempt to induce George Catlin to let them use his drawings too, they nonetheless published what they had in three folio volumes, 1836, 1838, and 1844. The first two volumes consist of about 125 portraits of Indians and a few "scenes" of Indian life, accompanied by biographical, historical, and explanatory comments, presumably McKenney's. The third volume has, first, a "History of the Indian Tribes in North America," which is for the most part a survey of the state and distribution of Indians in the 1830's and which also seems likely to be McKenney's, and second, an "Essay on the History of the North American Indians," signed by Hall. The volumes were intended to be definitive, with first an encyclopedic survey and then an interpretation of what had been surveyed.

From the point of view of the twentieth-century anthropologist, the *History* splits in two, with the "Essay" finding little or no support from either the portraits, McKenney's comments on them, or his historical survey.[33] From the point of view of the mid-nineteenth-century American and from the point of view of the historian of that American's mind, whatever wholeness the work has derives from the integrating force of the "Essay." For it is the "Essay" which, in this perspective, makes sense out of the magnificent wild portraits and McKenney's reiterated descriptions

[33] Cf. the comment by H. J. Braunholtz, who edits the third volume of the modern edition of the *History*: ". . . . [Hall's] general conclusions, which seem to have been partly influenced by a desire for rhetorical effect, are not entirely consistent with the more detailed circumstances which they themselves describe." (*The Indian Tribes of North America* [Edinburgh, 1933], III, xiii.)

of Indians who cannot long defend themselves from white civilization. Hall explains that McKenney's Indians are savages and barbarians, hunters and wanderers, having not that sense of permanence which comes from private property and settled government and which makes for high civilization. His key terms are: "roaming from place to place," "want of a home," "the absence of property," and "the habit of invading without scruple the lands of others." [34] These are the usual terms and they make Hall's Indians, if not McKenney's, the usual Indians.

3

As it came to be the idea of the savage, the idea of savagism culminated in the work of Henry Rowe Schoolcraft, an Indian agent who loved his charges, who had married one of them, and who devoted a good part of his life to making them known to others. What concerned him most was the structure of Indian thought and of the savage mind ("savage mentality," he called it most often) as they related to the structure of Indian life. Most writers on the Indian before him had ended their work by considering the savage mind; but he began with that mind and worked outward. One of his contemporaries, Samuel Morton, had suggested that a combination of what amounted to physical anthropology and phrenology would be the means to analysis of the Indians; [35] but Schoolcraft went far beyond this, studied Indian myths, and related them to the conditions of Indian life.

[34] *Ibid.*, III, 235.

[35] Samuel Morton, *Crania Americana* (Philadelphia, 1839), especially pp. 1, 62-83, 269-91. Thomas Farnham offers a phrenological analysis of a college-educated Rocky Mountain noble savage in his *Travels* (1843); he finds the Indian's "high points" to be "Causality, Comparison, Eventuality, Locality (superb!), Benevolence, Wonder, Ideality, Secretiveness, Destructiveness, Adhesiveness, Combativeness, Self-Esteem, Hope"; other points (those marking civilized qualities) are "low"—Thwaites, ed., *Early Western Travels* (Cleveland, 1904), XXVIII, 161. And Lydia Maria Child, in her *Letters from New York* (New York, 1843), pp. 247-57, describes phrenologically fifteen Indians she saw at the American Museum; she finds them to exhibit all sorts of near-animal qualities.

He published volume after volume on this general theme: his *Algic Researches* (1839) four times under three different titles; his *Onéota* (1844-1845) nine times under five titles; his *Notes on the Iroquois* (1846) twice; and his *Historical and Statistical Information* (1851-1857) twice under different titles.[36] The theme builds up and becomes more complex in the later volumes of this series, yet remains essentially the same: What holds the Indians to savagism is the wildness of their life; what makes that wildness meaningful to them are their myths and their religion; what makes these myths and that wildness possible is their "mental characteristics"; what makes for those mental characteristics is their savagism. As a government official and a humanitarian, Schoolcraft always hoped to civilize the savages. As a scientist (of a sort) he always insisted on seeing the savage objectively. If it is his objectivity which interests us here, we must nonetheless remember that it takes its quality from his hopes.

In his *Algic Researches* (1830) Schoolcraft gets at the Indian mind—the Algonquin mind, of course—through its beliefs as expressed in a collection of mythological tales. (It was a later version of *Algic Researches* which furnished Longfellow the materials for *Hiawatha.*) He begins by describing the Algic race and its culture at the time of the coming of white men: "They existed so completely in the hunter state as to have no relish for any other kind of labour, looking with an inward and deep contempt on the arts of husbandry and mechanics." Such conditions made for their "mental Character":

They were formal, and inclined to stateliness in their councils and public intercourse, and very acute and expert in the arrangement and discussion of minor matters, but failed in comprehensive views, deep-reaching foresight, and powers of generalization. Hence they were liable to be called cunning rather than wise. They were, emphatically, men of impulse, capable of extraordinary exertions on the instant,

[36] I follow the bibliographical data in Chase and Stellanova Osborn, *Schoolcraft-Longfellow-Hiawatha* (Lancaster, Pennsylvania, 1942), pp. 562-72. Contents of the volumes vary somewhat, of course. But for the purposes of my analysis here, such variations are not significant.

but could not endure the tension, mental and physical, of long-continued exertions. Action appeared to be always rather the consequence of nervous, than of intellectual excitement. Above all, they were characterized by habits of sloth, which led them utterly to despise the value of time; and this has appeared so constant a trait, under every vicissitude of their history, that it may be regarded as the probable effect of a luxurious effeminacy, produced upon the race under a climate more adverse to personal activity.

And he adds, hard upon this last,

It should be borne in mind, that the character first drawn of the Algic race is essentially that which has been attributed to the whole of the North American tribes, although it is not minutely applicable to some of the interior nations.[37]

There is here the whole complex of savagism: the picture of men who, living under wild circumstances apart from civilization, have developed specifically noncivilized virtues. For Schoolcraft the Algic race had none of the arts of civilization. He explains:

And this was perfectly natural. Of what use were these arts to a comparatively sparse population, who occupied vast regions, and lived, very well, by hunting the flesh and wearing the skins of animals? To such men a mere subsistence was happiness, and the killing of a few men in war glory. It may be doubted whether the very fact of the immensity of an unoccupied country, spread out before a civilized or half civilized people, with all its allurements of wild game and personal independence, would not be sufficient, in the lapse of a few centuries, to throw them back into a complete state of barbarism.[38]

Schoolcraft brings to his Algics a view of savagism which they will have to support.

Therefore, in the " Preliminary Observations on the Tales " he points out that the tales, with their terror, wildness, superstition, " style of narration," polytheism, and use of metamorphoses and personifications, clearly exhibit the character of the Indian mind:

[37] Henry Rowe Schoolcraft, *Algic Researches* (New York, 1839), I, 18-20.

[38] *Ibid.*, I, 25-26.

its emphasis upon the immediate and particular; its inability to abstract; its practical, hardheaded morality. Here is the essence of Indian religion, in which, for example, the nearest thing to an incarnation is to be found in the legend of Manibozho (whom Longfellow cleaned up for his appearance in Hiawatha); and he is more "a monstrosity than a deity," being everything good and bad for everyone—athletic, warlike, sexually gross, a trickster, a hero—in all ways, a truly savage god.[39] The two volumes of tales which Schoolcraft prints (the Chippewa Manibozho tale is the chief of these) fully bear him out. They are not civilized tales.

Onéota (first published serially in 1844-1845) in its various versions (its later title was regularly *The Indian in His Wigwam*) is an *omnium gatherum* of the facts of Indian life.[40] Preliminary essays on the "Character of the Red Man in America" and "Domestic Conditions of the Tribes and Constitution of the Indian Family" point out that the Indian is basically like all men, deriving his particular qualities from the conditions of his life. The heart of that life, Schoolcraft finds, is Indian religion. What follows is an encyclopedic collection of legends, myths, biographical sketches, songs and poems, captivity narratives, notes on antiquities, and essays on the Indian problem.

Notes on the Iroquois (1846) is an official report to the government on the possibilities of civilizing the Iroquois. In the face of facts which depress all others, Schoolcraft is full of high hope that these Indians may be once and for all leaving hunting for farming. (Curiously enough, he maintains that the cultivation of corn is indigenous to Iroquois culture, but he still insists that they are hunters only now emerging from an "absolute barbaric state.") He finds the Iroquois increasing in numbers, stabilizing the organization of their society, and improving as individuals. Of the Cayugas he writes:

Thus it appears that the energies once devoted by their ancestors

[39] *Ibid.*, I, 31-35.

[40] I have used the edition printed as *The Indian in His Wigwam* (Buffalo, 1848).

to war and hunting, are in good earnest now directed to husbandry and the arts; and there is every encouragement to hope, and reason to believe, that by a continuance in the best measures, they will be wholly reclaimed and added to the numbers of useful, intelligent and moral citizens. In viewing the condition of such a people, hardy, well formed and active, and pressing forward, as they are, in the great experiment of civilization, humanity consoles itself with the hope, that the energy and firmness of purpose which once carried them, in pursuit of warlike glory, far and wide, will develop itself, as it has already signally commenced to do, in the labors of the field and the workshop. . . .[41]

A fading hope for civilization, a feeling of absolute need for it, informs Schoolcraft's masterwork, *Historical and Statistical Information Respecting the History, Condition, and Prospects of the Indian Tribes of the United States* (1851-1857). This is a collaborative work, really, which Schoolcraft began in 1847 to get together at the direction of the Secretary of War. He was commissioned "to collect and digest such statistics and materials as may illustrate the history, the present conditions, and future prospects of the Indian tribes of the United States." He drew up a huge questionnaire (with some 348 main topics, ranging from origin to language) which the government circulated among Indian agents, missionaries, and travellers—all, in fact, who might supply useful information. He prepared his six-hundred page folio volumes, with hundreds of plates, issuing them year by year, apparently as the information came to him; the immense amount of material hardly digested; the arrangement shifting from volume to volume; the mass of the data being, as we can see it now, beyond Schoolcraft's encompassing.

Yet he was sure he had encompassed it. The received idea of savage society, though he did not know it, supplied him, just as it had supplied others before him, with categories into which to fit data. The questions he had his informants ask virtually supplied their own answers. The informants were to find out *how* the Indians whom they knew hunted and warred; *how* loosely their society was organized; *how* brave, simple, cruel, incapable of

[41] *Notes on the Iroquois* (New York, 1846), pp. 65-66.

systematic thinking they were; *how much* they clung to the immediacies of life about them; *how little* sense of progress they had.[42] Moreover, as Schoolcraft tried to bring the mass of data together and to comment on it, he had an analytic method which would guide him in studying and so help him and his assistants encompass it. This was essentially the historical-environmentalist method of the eighteenth-century Scots, which is the methodological basis for an essay contributed to the fourth volume of the work by the scientist Samuel Forrey. In his "Distinctive Characteristics of the American Aboriginal Tribes," Forrey follows the work of an English intellectual descendant of the Scots, James Prichard, who had laid it down as law in his *Natural History of Man* (1843) that "instincts, habits, and powers of perception and intellect" vary and are to be understood with situation and circumstances.[43]

At bottom, it is Schoolcraft's feeling of his civilized relationship to the uncivilized which holds his masterwork together. His prefatory note does no more than echo the prefatory note to the *Algic Researches*, twelve years before it:

> With all their defects of character, the Indian tribes are entitled to the peculiar notice of a people who have succeeded to the occupancy of territories which once belonged to them. They constitute a branch of the human race whose history is lost in the early and wild mutations of men. We perceive in them many noble and disinterested traits. The simplicity of their eloquence has challenged admiration. Higher principles of devotion to what they believe to be cardinal virtues no people ever evinced . . . .

[42] The questionnaire was first printed in 1847 as *Inquiries Respecting the History, Present Condition, and Future Prospects of the Indian Tribes of the United States.* I have seen the edition of Philadelphia, 1851, printed to accompany the final six-volume report.

[43] *Historical . . . Information* (Philadelphia, 1851–1857), IV, 365. Forrey is here quoting from Prichard, ed. (London, 1848), pp. 74-75. Prichard in his earlier *Researches into the Physical History of Man* (London, 1813, p. 41, n.) had acknowledged the influence of Samuel Stanhope Smith's notion of the selective influence of cultural standards in human evolution. Clearly, then, there was a kind of international give-and-take among Anglo-American thinkers of the Scottish School.

Mistaken in his belief in a system of gods of the elements—misconceiving the whole plan of industrial prosperity and happiness—wrong in his conceptions of the social duties of life, and doubly wrong in his notions of death and eternity, he yet approves himself to the best sensibilities of the human heart, by the strong exhibition of those ties which bind a father to his children, and link whole forest communities in the indissoluble bonds of brotherhood.[44]

In his chaotic masterwork itself, Schoolcraft comes back again and again to his basic understanding of the savage mind and the savage character. The first volume is focused on a survey of Indian prehistory and of the contemporary Indian in general. Treating of the Indian's "Intellectual Capacity," Schoolcraft remarks animism and resulting polytheism; these so order Indian life—so confuse it, really—that progress is blocked.[45] From the second volume on, he begins more and more to deal with particular tribes. Yet in the second volume he expatiates on the ruinous effect of hunting on human happiness. For him the Indian's state explicitly represents a fall from a God-ordained agrarian state; he envisages Indians who came as wanderers to America where ". . . the continent itself presented features which were calculated to lead the mind from the intellectual, the mechanical, and the industrial, to the erratic, physical, and gross."[46] Filling out the volume with facts and figures, he yet ends it with an essay on the "Importance of the Pastoral State to the Races of Men," in which he concludes, "Labor, law, and arts, must triumph, and they have triumphed in America as in Europe."[47] The third, fourth, and fifth volumes are organized in the pattern of the second. They are full of facts and figures relating to specific tribes, with general commentary to bring them into the plan of the whole. And in the sixth volume, a synoptic history of the Indians of North America, in a chapter called "The Indian Viewed as a Man Out of Society," he formally sets a general theme for the whole. He admits eleven long years after the optimism of the *Notes on the Iroquois* that the Indian has failed to become civilized. He has

[44] *Ibid.*, I, ix-x.
[45] See especially *ibid.*, I, 15, 29-42.
[46] *Ibid.*, II, 46-47.
[47] *Ibid.*, II, 520.

not been asked to do too much, Schoolcraft insists, only to give up his hunting ways. The Indian is to be pitied, and to be censured; for

> Man was created, not a savage, a hunter, or warrior, but a horticulturist and a raiser of grain, and a keeper of cattle—a smith, a musician—a worshipper, not of the sun, moon, and stars, but of God. The savage condition is a declension from this high type; Greece and Rome were in error on this point. The civil and social state was the original type of society for man, and it was just, therefore, to require a return to it.[48]

In Schoolcraft's last thinking savagism has become so abhorrent as to be abolished from human history. This is perhaps the logical end to the process we have been observing. First the savage was put back in history; then he was put out of it. For the eighteenth-century Scots and the Americans who had followed them, savagism (or barbarism) was the first and lowest state of society; it was, in the most technical sense, precivilization. For Schoolcraft, savagism has become simply noncivilization. If pity will do no good, then little but censure is left. And the Indian must die, since noncivilization is not life.

For us, the materials of Schoolcraft's masterwork must belie its theme of simple noncivilization. The complexity of Indian customs and traits, the richness of Indian legend and belief, the stubborn self-sufficiency of Indian cultures, are embodied in his six volumes, as they are, if one looks hard enough for them, in most earlier works on the Indian. In the *Historical and Statistical Information*, we can see how data deny conclusions—how, for example, Schoolcraft's Indians do find in their religions meanings and rewards, motives for living and dying, which he cannot be satisfied with and so cannot see for what they are. The chaos of the work is perhaps a product of a tension between recalcitrant human data which will simply not be brought into proper focus and a mind which is sure that it has brought them into focus. Bringing them into focus was for Schoolcraft a mode of belief in

[48] *Ibid.*, VI, 27.

himself, his work, and the people whom he was trying to save. For him, his masterwork must have at most moments made triumphant sense; for him it must have been glorious all-inclusive proof of the triumph of civilization over savagism.

He did have some small doubts as to his accuracy in matters of fact, especially the facts of Indian religion. The complexity of the legends which he had collected disturbed him. Even as he doubted, however, he could say that it was precisely this complexity which made the Indian harder and harder to civilize and thus intrinsically less and less worthwhile.[49] But he had no doubts as to matters of meaning; here he was certain. This certainty marks, perhaps, the culmination of a tradition, the culminating episode in the history of a mode of belief. It is useful to note that even if Schoolcraft's masterwork was intended to help clear the way for saving the Indian, still the cover of the first edition was decorated with a gold-stamped picture of a prostrate settler—a ferocious Indian standing over him, ready to flee, with a knife in his right hand and the settler's scalp in his left. Even by Schoolcraft's time obviously it was civilization which was still being saved.

4

After Schoolcraft, not much in this kind could be said about the Indian and his savage nature. Indeed, with the Indian virtually disposed of in fact as well as in theory, not much more needed to be said. Soon there would be only the newer kind of frontier, the farming frontier, with Indian raids becoming more and more matters only for wild, woolly, far-western tales. Progress would be a matter of what had to be—the converting of lands into farms and cities, and the elevating of men on those farms and in those cities into American freemen. The Indian, in fact and in theory, had shown that he could have none of this. Yet there were still such voluminous materials as Schoolcraft had; and there were new materials, new data, new facts, and new evidences which were steadily accumulating. What could Americans do with them?

[49] *Ibid.*, I, vii-viii.

They could, of course, continue to do as Schoolcraft had done. Some few writers continued explicitly to do so.[50] Most often, however, men as serious about this matter of the Indian as Schoolcraft had been, were forced by the sheer weight of evidence and by the self-contradictions in his work to try to go beyond him. They could, they felt, only begin once more at the beginning. Their feeling was expressed by one of them, who in 1868, looking back at Schoolcraft's masterwork, wrote: "The government work on the Indians . . . . was unfortunate in its editor. It is a monument of American extravagance and superficiality. Mr. Schoolcraft was a man of deficient education and narrow prejudices, pompous in style, and inaccurate in statement. The information from the original observers it contains is often of real value, but the general views in aboriginal history and religion are shallow."[51] The need was to be increasingly objective and to work deep. In the 1850's and after, one could be objective about the Indian as one could not have been ten, twenty, or thirty years before; one could be objective about a creature who had been reduced to the status of a specimen picked up on field trips. One could move toward scientific analysis and away from pity and censure.

With the beginnings of such a move, we can see, if dimly, the beginnings of the end of the idea of savagism and of the Indian as savage.

The Indian, becoming the province of learned groups especially organized to study him, soon was a scholarly field in himself, just like a dead language. When the American Ethnological Society was organized in 1842, its members set up a series of *Transactions* to treat scientifically of the Indian. When the Smithsonian Institution was organized in 1846, its scientists were specifically bidden to gather information on the Indian, including " particular history,

[50] See for example, John DeForest, *History of the Indians of Connecticut* [1851] (Hartford, 1852), Chapter 1; Minnie Myrtle, *The Iroquois; or, The Bright Side of Indian Character* (New York, 1855); Col. R. B. Marcy, *Thirty Years of Army Life on the Border* (New York, 1866).

[51] Daniel G. Brinton, *The Myths of the New World* [1868] (New York, 1876), p. 41.

comparative philology, &c." and to prepare it in *Reports*.[52] And in 1879 when the Bureau of Ethnology was organized under the great John Wesley Powell, its work was combined with that of the Smithsonian Institution, and a corps of specialists was set to work on specific tasks. American anthropology and ethnology, as we know them now, were firmly begun. Emphasis in the work of these organizations was self-consciously descriptive. Under Powell, the Bureau of Ethnology began to publish its *Annual Reports*, volumes which collected and organized what were intended to be (and most often were) facts as facts.

Yet even while scientists moved towards the modern study of the Indian as a normally complex and difficult human who possessed a tolerably respectable civilization of his own, they continued to think of him literally as a primitive, as one whose way of life was somehow earlier than their own. They continued to try to comprehend that way of life historically, in its relation to the long evolution of man toward high civilization. It is not within the scope of this study to treat fully of this continuity and of the transformation of the idea of the savage into the idea of the primitive. Still we must note at least how and why the evolutionary emphasis of the new, scientific theory of the primitive followed so easily from the historical-moral emphasis of the theory of the savage which had preceded it.

The early work of Lewis Henry Morgan shows both this continuity and this transformation. In *The League of the Iroquois* (1851), which his contemporaries proclaimed " the first scientific account of an Indian ever given to the world," [53] Morgan describes a people who have " the highest position among the Indian races of the continent living in the hunter state." Assuming that the progress of a people is in " exact proportion to the wisdom of the institutions under which their minds were developed," he is sure that he can completely comprehend these Iroquois. In spite of his close observation of Iroquois agriculture, he insists that a

[52] *Smithsonian Institution Contributions*, I (1848), vi.

[53] The words are Powell's. See Panchanan Mitra, *A History of American Anthropology* (Calcutta, 1933), p. 111.

hunting culture has "enchained" them to savagery and that the need for communal lands to be hunted has kept them from accumulating private property and from organizing the progressive society which private property would have made possible. The League which the Iroquois organized had offset this tendency, but not sufficiently and not in time to let them develop a civilization which could long survive the coming of the white man.[54]

Morgan's main interest in *The League of the Iroquois* is, as the title indicates, Iroquois government. This he treats as an institution which at once limited Iroquois culture and made for its achievement. Assuming that forms of government evolve from the monarchical, to the oligarchical, and then to the democratic, Morgan points out that the Iroquois, as the most advanced of hunters in America, had reached the second stage when the white man came. Then he evaluates their society:

> The institutions which would be expected to exist under such a political system as that of the Iroquois, would necessarily be simple. Their mode of life and limited wants, the absence of property in a comparative sense, and the infrequency of crime dispensed with a vast amount of the legislation and machinery incident to the protection of civilized society. While, therefore, it would be unreasonable to seek those high qualities of mind which result from ages of cultivation, in such a rude state of existence, it would be equally irrational to regard the Indian character as devoid of all those higher characteristics which ennoble the human race. If he has never contributed a page to science, nor a discovery to art; if he loses in the progress of generations as much as he gains; still there are certain qualities of his mind which shine forth in all the lustre of natural perfection. His simple integrity, his generosity, his unbounded hospitality, his love of truth, and, above all, his unshaken fidelity—a sentiment inborn, and standing out so conspicuously in his character, that it has not untruthfully become its characteristic: all these are adornments of hu-

[54] Lewis Henry Morgan, *League of the Ho-Dé-No-Sau-Nee, or Iroquois* (Rochester, 1851), pp. 54-59. On Morgan's insistence on the fact that the Iroquois' was a hunting culture in spite of their patent agricultural life, see Bernhard Stern, *Lewis Henry Morgan, Social Evolutionist* (Chicago, 1931), p. 64.

manity, which no art of education can instill, nor refinement of civilization can bestow. If they exist at all, it is because the gifts of the Deity have never been perverted.

There was, however, a fatal deficiency in Indian society, in the non-existence of a progressive spirit. The same rounds of amusement, of business, of warfare, of the chase, and of domestic intercourse continued from generation to generation. There was neither progress nor invention, nor increase of political wisdom. Old forms were preserved, old customs adhered to. Whatever they gained upon one point they lost upon another, leaving the second generation but little wiser than the first. The Iroquois, in some respects, were in advance of their red neighbors. They had attempted the establishment of their institutions upon a broader basis, and already men of high capacity had sprung up among them, as their political system unfolded. If their Indian empire had been suffered to work out its own results, it is still problematical whether the vast power they would have accumulated, and the intellect which would have been developed by their diversified affairs, would not, altogether, have been sufficiently potent to draw the people from the hunter state into the agricultural state. The hunter state is the zero of human society, and while the red man was bound by its spell, there was no hope of his elevation.[55]

To be sure, *The League of the Iroquois* is devoted mainly not to this sort of analysis and evaluation but rather to a full description of Iroquois society and its workings. Morgan's value as ethnologist lies much more in that description than in this analysis and evaluation. And much of what he says here of the Iroquois he could say later (in his *Ancient Society*, 1877) of all "early" cultures. Still, in the perspective within which we are viewing him, we must see what he brings with him from the past. In this passage, it is the idea of savagism stated with comparative sophistication and complexity, but in the end essentially that of the writers who have come before him. Morgan is able to give the Iroquois their due, to put forth pity and censure, because he is

[55] *League*, pp. 141-43. Cf. pp. 347-48 where Morgan discusses Iroquois religion in the same fashion.

able to give them their due as savages and properly to relate their savagism to his own civilization.

As he continued to investigate Indian and other primitive societies, Morgan strove more and more to interpret primitive people in their own terms, not his; he strove for the fullest objectivity, for descriptions of interrelated wholes, not of parts evaluated out of context.[56] The method of Darwinian evolution (as interpreted by Herbert Spencer) freed him, moreover, from some of the normative tendencies of those earlier writers whose work he seems surely to echo. He saw, for example, no reason to subscribe to that part of Christian theology which accounted for savage cultures as the result of postlapsarian degradation [57]—in Schoolcraft's words, as the " declension from [a] high type." He opposed such a view explicitly and thus removed an essential prop from under the earlier tradition which identified historical analysis with moral-theological evaluation. Yet he took the very results of that earlier analysis and evaluation and supported them by objective description and by comparative evolutionary theory. And for all his striving for objectivity, he could never manage, in the words of a latter-day critic, " that sympathetic projection into alien mentality which anthropology is supposed to foster." [58] This could be because he thought in a tradition which again and again celebrated its own freedom from that savage mentality.

What remains of Morgan's work for ethnographers and anthropologists are his brilliant descriptions of Iroquois culture. What remains for sociologists are his comparative, institutional analyses of the evolution of culture. What remains for us, however, is the fact that he took to his descriptions and analyses the idea of savagism and all that idea implied. The difference between his work and that of his predecessors is this: whereas for him the

[56] Stern, *Lewis Henry Morgan*, p. 65.

[57] This was in his *Ancient Society* (New York, 1877). See Leslie A. White, " Lewis Henry Morgan: Pioneer in the Theory of Social Evolution," *An Introduction to the History of Sociology*, ed. Harry Elmer Barnes (Chicago, 1948), p. 140.

[58] Robert Lowie, " Evolution in Cultural Anthropology," *American Anthropologist*, XLVIII (1946), 225.

Indian in the end furnishes only some of the evidence for a general evolutionary theory of progress, for them the Indian *is* that evidence. The difference is between a man who possesses his belief and men who are possessed by it. Morgan's work can well be cleared of its infusion of savagism. The work of his predecessors, as we have seen it, cannot.

5

Eighteen-fifty-one, then, is as good a date as any on which to mark the death of the idea of savagism and of the American savage. For in 1851 were printed the first volume of Schoolcraft's *Historical and Statistical Information*, in which savages and savagism can hardly live in the presence of facts which deny their existence, and Morgan's *League of the Iroquois*, in which savages and savagism are so completely absorbed into a universal theory of progress as to lose their separate identity and their separate meaning.

V

An Impassable Gulf: *The Social and Historical Image*

EVEN as all American thinking about the Indian was based, at the very least, on an implicit comparison of savage and civilized life, a great deal of his thinking about himself was based on explicit comparison of the two. For the American before 1850—a new man, as he felt, making a new world—was obsessed to know who and what he was and where he was going, to evaluate the special society in which he lived and to know its past and its future. One means to this end was to compare himself with the Indian who, as a savage, had all past and no future. The final result was an image of the Indian as man out of society and out of history.

As a man sprung from western European stock, the American had inherited a notion, faint but clear, that the simpler life of the savage was a good devoutly to be wished for. As a civilized man face to face with savages, he tested this notion in theory and practice and found it sometimes inviting, sometimes amusing, more often puzzling. Evaluating the savage's role in his good society, he could in the end only define and redefine that society and himself as he might flourish in it. The repetitiousness of his arguments is important to us, because it marks a growth towards the certainty which made for American self-knowledge, so for American self-confidence, so for the westward course of empire.

1

In its origins the American's need to compare himself with the Indians whom he knew is as deep and basic as his humanity. A major western European intellectual and imaginative tradition was that of primitivism—the belief that other, simpler societies were somehow happier than one's own. Believing thus, one would be concerned to search for and find such a society and the men who lived in it; that is to say, one would be concerned to find noble savages. The discovery of America furnished savages in abundance. The question was: How noble were they? On the one side there was set in motion a current of strongly antiprimitivistic thinking. This current directly fed that American thinking about the Indian which issued into the idea of savagism. On the other side, there was set in motion a current of primitivistic thinking which swept the Indian into the work of European critics of society. Since this Indian was that noble savage who theoretically embodied all that good men should be, for primitivists in the seventeenth and eighteenth centuries what he *actually* was came less and less to be a serious issue. What mattered was what Europeans should be. The need was to recover that portion of the primitive self which civilization had corrupted and, in the process, to lay bare the faults of civilization.

Thus a primitivistic mode of social criticism came to America fully developed and virtually innocent of actual study of actual primitives. The trick for Americans was to preserve the mode in the face of primitive actuality. The trick soon became merely humorous; or it simply failed. Writers who tried it seriously only confused themselves. When this had come to pass, however, actual primitives were well enough known as savages to furnish in themselves the foundation for a new critical mode, and there developed an antiprimitivistic criticism which could only affirm the glories of American civilization and American progress westward. For the forces which informed the idea of savagism at one and the same time destroyed the idea of the noble savage and made isolated radicals of those who would believe in it.

In eighteenth-century literary periodicals, themselves imitations of their English betters, there first began to appear the noble savage as critic of American society. One example among many such will suffice:[1] the "Letter from an Indian Chief to his Friend in the state of New York," printed in the *American Museum* in 1789.[2] Here the chief considers the relative happiness of civilized men and Indians. Having been educated among the whites, he feels that he knows their ways well. Among them, "the happiness of the people is constantly sacrificed to the splendor of empire; hence your code of civil and criminal laws have had their origin; and hence your dungeons and prisons." The Indian needs no code of laws; he simply obeys what the Great Spirit has written on the heart of every rational creature. His society thus has no courts of law, no "splendid villains," and no idle rich. Its members do not have the artificial wants and fears created by civilization. And the chief concludes:

> Cease then, while these practices continue among you, to call yourselves christians, lest you publish to the world your hypocrisy. Cease to call other nations savage, while you are tenfold more the children of cruelty, than they.

[1] For example, "Instances of Indian Fidelity," *Massachusetts Magazine*, III (1791), 230, reprinted in *American Museum*, X (1791), 27-28; "A Dialogue Betwixt Mercury, an English Duellist, and a North-American Savage," *New-York Magazine*, III (1792), 175-77; "The Savage and the Civilized State Compared," *South-Carolina Weekly Museum*, I (1797), 456-59. One or more of these may be reprintings of pieces from English periodicals. I have been unable to run down any origins for them; but I must admit that I didn't think it worthwhile to search very hard. In any case, it is difficult to distinguish them from their English equivalents. (On the latter see Benjamin H. Bissell, *The American Indian in English Literature of the Eighteenth Century*, Yale Studies in English, LXVIII [New Haven, 1925], especially pp. 37-77; and Hoxie Neale Fairchild, *The Noble Savage* [New York, 1928], especially pp. 23-171.) An example of an English equivalent directly available to American readers and imitators is Dr. Johnson's "An Indian Speech" (*Idler* No. 81), reprinted in the *Lady's Magazine and Repository of Useful Knowledge*, III (1793), 268-269.

[2] *American Museum*, VI (1789), 226-27, reprinted in the *Weekly Magazine*, III (1789-1790), 50-51.

The object of this primitivistic critique, as of others in the tradition which it carried on, was to make man live up to his truly civilized nature. "Truly civilized" had come to mean simpler, less sophisticated, rationally self-controlled, enlightened. Out of theory, wishful thinking, and reading in the theorizing and wishful thinking of travellers, there had been conceived the image of the Indian as the paradoxical man who was civilized because he was uncorrupted by civilization. This was the tradition and the convention of the noble savage.

In America such convention and tradition had to be set against what were taken as the facts of savage life and its corruption by civilization. Certainly such facts were themselves the product of another kind of theorizing and wishful thinking, but they were nonetheless consented to. If an American wanted to be a primitivist, he would have somehow to avoid those facts.

One way was to make primitivism into a game and to play at it for sport. Only thus could Benjamin Franklin take the noble savage's side against civilization's. When it came to practical problems of westward expansion, Franklin, to be sure, could be as pitying, honest, and hard-headed as the next man. Summing up his long experience in Indian affairs, he wrote to the Governor of Georgia in 1787:

> During the Course of a long Life in which I have made Observations on public Affairs, it has appear'd to me that almost every War between the Indians and Whites has been occasion'd by some Injustice of the latter towards the former. It is indeed extreamly imprudent in us to quarrel with them for their Lands, as they are generally willing to sell, and sell such good Bargains: And a War with them is so mischievous to us, in unsettling frequently a great Part of our Frontier, & reducing the Inhabitants to Poverty and Distress, and is besides so expensive that it is much cheaper as well as honester, to buy their Lands than to take them by Force.[8]

[8] Benjamin Franklin, *Writings*, ed. Smyth, IX, 625-26. It seems to me that this letter well sums up Franklin's general attitude towards the Indian problem. But see, for an extensive study which takes another view, Julian

Here he was as free to recognize white injustice to the Indian as he was to foresee the Indian's doom. Further, in *A Narrative of the Late Massacres in Lancaster County* (1764), he attacked the inhumanity and barbarousness of Pennsylvania frontiersmen who butchered simple-minded, peace-loving Christian Indians. And in his Swiftian "Supplement to the Boston *Independent Chronicle*" (1782), a gruesome invoice of scalps which the English enemy are said to require their Indian allies to send them in exchange for supplies, he made Europeans share equally with Indians in inhumanity and barbarousness. This was to recognize the facts of savage life and to regret, but not to deny, its weakness.

Nonetheless Franklin could avoid the facts and, in the finest primitivistic fashion, use the Indian to criticize the excesses, and possible excesses, of his own civilized society. In his *Remarks Concerning the Savages of North America* (1782) he politely mocked the stylish society of Paris and Passy. "Savages we call them, because their Manners differ from ours, which we think the Perfection of Civility; they think the same of theirs." He begins thus and so continues, constructing a conventional eulogy of Indian politeness, Indian "Conversation," Indian religion, and Indian hospitality and honor.[4] None of it is to be taken seriously; patently it is a game, a case of good old Ben Franklin, fur cap and all, speaking as he knew his French ladies would like to have him speak, and suggesting that, after all, things with high society are perhaps not quite as fine as they might seem. What we should remark here, after having noted Franklin's honesty, pity, and hard-headedness, is his primitivistic playfulness. Those Indians with whom one might well deal cheaply as well as honestly and those Indians who are victims of civilized inhumanity are not in this primitivistic bagatelle, as they are not supposed to be.

Hector St. Jean de Crèvecoeur, a man who dreamed as Franklin refused to, could not simply play at primitivism. Searching for

Boyd, "Dr. Franklin: Friend of the Indian," *Journal of the Franklin Institute*, CCXXXIV (July-August, 1942), 311-330.

[4] *Writings*, ed. Smyth, X, 97-104. On the complicated origin of the piece, see A. O. Aldridge, "Franklin's Deistical Indians," *American Philosophical Society Proceedings*, XIV (1950), 398-410.

Utopia, he would be serious; not finding it among civilized men, he would say that he found it among men uncivilized. So in his *Letters from an American Farmer* (1782) he was obliged to create an Indian unlike the one he really knew.[5] Which is to say, he was obliged to create a noble savage. The good life, as he first pictures it in his *Letters* is that of the simple, hardy, honest free farmer and Nantucket fisherman. Life for such as these before the Revolution is " modern, peaceful, and benign " ; men in America are " strangers to those feudal institutions which [had] enslaved so many." [6] The Indian forms part of this healthy, clean-smelling country and coast life only as he is superior to those crude frontiersmen whom the Farmer encounters and as he is one to be pitied in his degradation. In all, he is at this point simply a good neighbor. Yet when the War comes and the Farmer finds himself, a little man, caught in a quarrel which is not of his making, he thinks that he must compromise with the Indian's way:

I will [he decides] revert into a state approaching nearer to that of nature, unencumbered either with voluminous laws, or contradictory codes, often galling the very necks of those whom they protect; and at the same time sufficiently remote from the brutality of unconnected savage nature.[7]

He will take his family with him and somehow hold on to the best of both civilized and savage life. At one point he is sure that he does not want his children to become "perfectly Indianised"; at another point he is not so sure:

There must be something more congenial to our native dispositions [in Indian life], than [in] the fictitious society in which we live; or else why should children, and even grown persons, become in a short time so invincibly attached to it.[8]

[5] See Howard Rice, *Le Cultivateur Américain* (Paris, 1933), pp. 125-26; and Ralph H. Gabriel, " Crèvecoeur and His Times," in Crèvecoeur, *Sketches of Eighteenth-Century America* (New Haven, 1925), pp. 1-2.

[6] Hector St. John de Crèvecoeur, *Letters from an American Farmer* [1782] Everyman's Library Edition, p. 11.

[7] *Ibid.*, p. 211.

[8] *Ibid.*, p. 215.

The Indian of the forest becomes, in short, nature's "undefiled offspring." So the Farmer comes, virtually in spite of himself, to idealize the savage. We can watch Crèvecoeur force himself into the idealizing.

The Farmer's predicament is, as we know now, precisely Crèvecoeur's. He wrote the *Letters* primarily for European readers and published them at a time when America, her society, and her future were international ideological issues; he wanted to naturalize and to simplify the American according to the European dream. Indeed, in the French versions of the *Letters* (1784-1787) the savages are even more ennobled, so that it becomes more and more logical for the Farmer to go to them.[9] Moreover, in putting together the *Letters* for their English publication, Crèvecoeur omitted certain portions which, although they do not present the Indian in an wholly unfavorable light, make it clear just how unfortunate it would be for the Farmer's children to become "perfectly Indianised."[10] Some of the omitted sketches, only recently made available, make the Indian into an ignorant barbarian. In one of them, a Moravian minister comments on the virtual impossibility of bringing the Indian to civilization; and in others there are stories of frontier killing and of a captivity, all told in considerable and sometimes violent detail. And on the other side of the ledger, there are sketches in which Crèvecoeur blames whites for encouraging Indian cruelty on the frontier and in which he shows how childlike and honest the Indian really is.[11] This Indian is not the one whom Crèvecoeur, riding a primitivistic thesis hard, wanted to let his English and American readers see.

[9] Rice, *Le Cultivateur Amèricain*, pp. 2-5, 130-36.

[10] Henri L. Bourdin and Stanley T. Williams, eds., "Crèvecoeur on the Susquehanna, 1774-1776," *Yale Review*, XIV (1925), 552-84; and Henri L. Bourdin, Ralph H. Gabriel, and Stanley T. Williams, eds., *Sketches of Eighteenth-Century America* (New Haven, 1925). Most of these sketches were reprinted, somewhat softened, in the French versions of the *Letters* (1784, 1787).

[11] "Crèvecoeur on the Susquehanna," *Yale Review*, XIV (1925), 582; *Sketches of Eighteenth-Century America*, pp. 132-34, 192-206, 207-20, 221-27.

Certainly, he knew that savage life really was not worthwhile; and in 1801 he could say so explicitly in his *Voyage dans la haute Pennsylvanie.*[12] But earlier, in order to condemn civilized life, he has been forced into a confused and confusing primitivism. For the serious primitivists—and Crèvecoeur's seriousness forced him into primitivism—the problem was one of finding a symbol for primitive good which would sustain any critique in which it carried the burden of meaning. And the American Indian had to be forced to be what the out-and-out primitivist like Crèvecoeur wanted him to be. (Reading Crèvecoeur, Thomas Jefferson concluded that American Indians really were not "precisely as Mr. de Crevecoeur . . . depictured them."[13]) It was a desperate and not very successful trick.

A Quaker exotic like William Bartram found it to be no trick at all. A radical of sorts, he was sustained by a Quaker romantic naturalism, a firm belief that what is closest to God's earth is best. Besides, the southeastern Indians among whom he travelled in 1773-1777 were so clearly an agrarian people that he might well discover in their culture all the virtues missing in his own as he saw it moving away from the life of the plain farmer. What he found in his Indians, as he recalled them in his *Travels* (1792), was evidence that when they needed moral guidance, they received it from "a more divine and powerful preceptor, who, on these occasions, instantly inspires them, and as with a ray of divine light, points out to them at once the dignity, propriety, and beauty of virtue." [14] What he found, that is to say, was a people in whom

[12] He says, for example (*Voyage dans la haute Pennsylvanie* [Paris, 1801], I, 14-15): "C'est donc seulement à l'époque où l'homme est devenu granivore, qu'il a pu connoitre la commiseration et la pitié: que ses moeurs sauvages et farouches ont été remplacé par des affections plus douces, et que ses voisins sont devenus ses amis."

[13] Letter to Volney, November 17, 1796, in Gilbert Chinard, ed., *Volney et L'Amérique* (Baltimore, 1923), p. 51.

[14] *The Travels of William Bartram*, ed. Mark Van Doren (New York, 1928), p. 46. Cf. p. 111, where the same idea is expressed in much the same language. (The edition cited here, it should be noted, is a reprint of the edition of London, 1792, the first edition having been printed at Philadelphia in 1791. Differences between the two editions are small,

the Inner Light glowed with a freshness and intensity which could not be dimmed.

Bartram everywhere endows his Indians with an idyllic freshness with which to contrast the decadence of white men. Cherokee hospitality moves him to an apostrophe: " O divine simplicity and truth, friendship without fallacy or guile, hospitality disinterested, native, undefiled by artificial refinements." [15] He tells how, encountering some " Cherokee virgins " gathering fruit, he broke in on a " sylvan scene of primitive innocence " and went chasing playfully after the " gay assembly of hamadryades "; together they had picknicked in " Elysian fields." [16] In Part IV of the travels he constructs a richly detailed " Description of the Characters, Customs and Persons of the American Aborigines." The account is aimed towards one conclusion: " As moral men [the Indians] certainly stand in no need of European civilization." [17] In his " Description " he can only marvel at how the southeastern Indians have held on to their integrity in the face of civilized corruption and temptations to corruption, and must conclude that Indians are closer to God and God's Nature than are civilized men. He makes a recommendation: " Do we want wisdom and virtue? let our youth then repair to the venerable council of the Muscogulges [i. e., Creeks]." [18] Bartram himself wanted soft, luxuriant, primitive wisdom, and he thought civilized men needed it. To convince civilized men, and to convince himself, he had to find it somewhere. So he went to the noble savage, who, of course, was there waiting for him.

Philip Freneau, a stronger and more direct thinker than Bartram but like him a radical of sorts, was in much the same predicament. He attempted in his *Tomo-Cheeki, the Creek Indian in Philadelphia* (1790-1795, first collected in 1795) to naturalize that primitivistic mode in which a simple and wise foreign visitor was at once critic of the bad society and standard for the good. Tomo-Cheeki was meant to be, like Goldsmith's Lien-Chi-Altangi,

being confined to matters of usage. See N. B. Fagin, " Bartram's Travels," *Modern Language Notes*, XLVI [1931], 289-291.)

[15] *Travels*, p. 284.

[16] *Ibid.*, pp. 289-90.

[17] *Ibid.*, p. 385.

[18] *Ibid.*, p. 387.

the rational sage criticizing the absurdities of civilization. Yet circumstances would not let him be. He turned out to be not urbane but violent; and the conditions of his own life could not be taken to make for the good. In the end, Freneau found that he could not go all the way and posit an Indian society to which whites should go to school. Unhappy in a Federalist America, however, he still would be a primitivist, and so he invented a primitivism beyond primitivism, a dream-vision of the simple good.

In the second essay of the series,[19] Tomo-Cheeki pictures the ideal life of the savage as contrasted with that of the civilized man, dreary and cooped up in Philadelphia.

> In the morning early we rise from the bed of skins to hail the first dawn of the sun. We seize our bows and arrows—we fly hastily through the dews of the forest—we attack the deer, the stag, or the buffaloe, and return with abundance of food for the whole family. Wherever we run it is amidst the luxuriant vegetation of Nature, the delectable regale of flowers and blossoms, and beneath trees bending with plump and joyous fruits.

". . . carried along upon the great wheel of things," the Indian is content.[20] The civilized man is never content. In successive essays Tomo-Cheeki pictures him as acquisitive, warlike, given to useless study, vain, a slave to his desire for ease and luxury. Most important, he is represented as having foully mistreated the Indian, driving him westward, corrupting him with liquor, and killing him with disease.

So Freneau comes up against the problem of the ignobled savage as vehicle and symbol in a primitivistic critique. And he must dispose even of Tomo-Cheeki as such. In the second essay,

[19] I follow the numbering of the essays as published in the *Time-Piece*, March 15–June 16, 1797, where they were collected for the second time. They were first published in collected form in the *Jersey Chronicle*, May 23–October 31, 1795. For bibliographical data see Lewis Leary, *That Rascal Freneau* (New Brunswick, N. J., 1941), pp. 448-49, 457, 459-61, 462-64, 473.

[20] II, *Time-Piece*, March 20, 1797.

that with the picture of the life of the noble savage, Tomo-Cheeki declares that he would like to leave the ugly city for his home, but that he must stay until he has obtained the blankets, looking-glasses, and brandy which his tribesmen have sent him for. And in the seventh essay, " A short talk on Drunkenness," he praises the man who can lose himself in drink, who can be made magnanimous and valorous because he is drunk, and damns him " who was never known to transgress the bounds of strict sobriety in drinking." This is the Tomo-Cheeki whom Freneau had pictured in an essay of 1788, a sot who is kept from suicide only by the opportunity to drink more of " the celestial beverage." [21] This Tomo-Cheeki is corruptible, and no proper standard for a proper primitivist.

Yet Freneau was bound to discover the good life through one who had at least known it in the past. In the eighth essay he makes Tomo-Cheeki fall asleep while contemplating the sad history of man. The unhappy Indian sage dreams that the genius of the earth had decided to do away with all men—Indian and white, savage and civilized—and, having been unsuccessful in deciding which of the " inferior " animals was to rule hereafter, had created a new being, outwardly like men but yet one whose " main spring shall be Benevolence." These new creatures, so Tomo-Cheeki says in recounting his dream, lived the right life.

> They built no towns; they seemed to have no idea of war or contention: the spirit of justice, benevolence, and every amiable virtue was prevalent within them; they walked on the margin of the ocean; they dwelt on the green banks of the rivers, but discovered no propensity to build ships, or seek for other continents; they made or retained no slaves of their own or of the inferior species: a constant summer reigned: nor could I perceive that the harmony of Nature was at all disturbed on the ocean, in the woods, or in the elements above.[22]

This is desperately radical thinking. We must remark its circumstances and Freneau's predicament. When the primitivistic

[21] *Miscellaneous Works* (Philadelphia, 1788), pp. 122-28.

[22] VIII, *Time-Piece*, April 28, 1797.

mode failed him, he resorted to one even more deeply and regressively primitive, that of dream-work. And Freneau's once noble savage is so much corrupted by civilization that even he can only dream of primitive nobility.

The dead end of this primitivistic tradition is reached in such an incoherent fantasy as *The Savage*, published anonymously in 1810 by one John Robinson and republished twice after his death, in 1833 and 1838. In *The Savage*, a series of essays in the usual mode, the Indian Piomingo ("A Headman and Warrior in the Muscogulgee Nation") defends this radical thesis:

> Civilization is a forced state: it is not natural for one man to bend, cringe, and creep to another. A noble spirit, a spirit that is inspired by the proud dignity of virtue, will bear every evil—sickness, pain, confinement, death—rather than have recourse to the mean arts of the sycophant . . . .[23]

He discusses Truth, The Effects of Civilization, Old Age, Language, Titles, Slavery, The Devil, The Schoolmaster, and so on to The State of the Nation—corrupt, commercial, decadent. Everything civilized is evil; all evil stems from a fear of the natural; the age of natural men, the true Golden Age, is in the savage past. As Robinson gets into his hodgepodge critique, he forgets who the nominal critic is. But no matter. What is important is that someone says everything that has to be said and that civilization is shown up for what it really is. Thus Piomingo is hardly an Indian, exhibiting, as he does, explicit acquaintance (and disgust) with Joe Miller, Fanny Hill, and others like them, talking learnedly in the very language and manner he attacks. He is as incoherent, as confused, and as inconsistent as the doctrine which Robinson makes him preach. Primitivism, insofar as it exists, has become not a desperate trick but a neurosis.

2

We must remember that at bottom primitivistic thinking in America was always radical. It protested social injustice and

[23] John Robinson, *The Savage* [1810] (Knoxville, Tenn., 1833), p. 97.

imbalance, and it feared the excesses which any society, as a society, was exposed to. Thus it was just in purpose, as all radical thinking is just. Yet, when it was cast in primitivistic terms, it was fatally weak. For it was tied to a simplistic fantasy which confused and corrupted its radicalism. Try hard as he might, the American primitivist who chose to image the Indian as noble savage could not fully escape the confusions and vitiation his choice of subject and vehicle made him liable to. And he could think of the Indian in no way which would not confuse and vitiate.

Even intellectuals as independent as the Transcendentalists were so limited. They constructed analyses in which they tried to move from the idea of a past savage perfection to one of a future civilized perfection. The latter was to be analogous to but not identical with the former. They failed in this latter-day primitivism; for the savage could not be made a proper starting point for such analyses, even as earlier he could not be made into a vehicle for them.

Emerson, for example, could accept the passing of the Indian as inevitable, yet wanted still to hold on to something of the natural life of the savage. He felt that life about him in names, relics, the very past as it grew into the present; he felt that life as one item in the All of Nature. He felt it in the Indian with whom Henry Thoreau hunted: "An Indian has his knowledge for use, and it only appears in use. Most white men that we know have theirs for talking purposes." [24] This passage in his journal for 1857, which he developed into a portion of "Country Life," a lecture delivered first in December 1857, constitutes a primitivistic variation on the doctrine of "Experience." What Emerson was after was knowledge which would be for use in civilization. He got nowhere looking to the noble savage for examples; for noble savages did not exist. Of the Indian, Emerson had to write late in his life, in an essay called, judiciously enough,

[24] Ralph Waldo Emerson, *Journals*, IX, 111. Cf. an entry for 1843, *ibid.*, VII, 23.

"Civilization": "He is overpowered by the gaze of the white, and his eye sinks." [25]

Another transcendentally radical thinker, Margaret Fuller, travelled among northwestern Indians in 1843 and came later to confuse her deep and genuine feeling about their sadly and defiantly ennobled state with her deeper dissatisfactions with the society which nurtured her. For her there was a lesson in the Indian's condition:

As man has two natures—one like that of the plants and animals, adapted to the uses and enjoyments of this planet, another which presages and demands a higher sphere—he is constantly breaking bounds, in proportion as the mental gets the better of the mere instinctive existence. As yet, he loses in harmony of being what he gains in height and extension; the civilized man is a larger mind but a more imperfect nature than the savage.[26]

What interested her was not primitivity as such, or even the Indian as perfected primitive, but rather the danger civilized men should run if they could not achieve in their civilization something of the wholeness of primitivity. Yet she could make her Indians exhibit harmony of being only by sentimentalizing them. This is a form of fantasy, which in the end vitiated this much of her radical critique of civilization.

Finally, Henry Thoreau studied savage wholeness and harmony and even prepared to write a great book on it.

The charm of the Indian to me [he noted in his journal in April 1841] is that he stands free and unconstrained in Nature, is her inhabitant and not her guest, and wears her easily and gracefully. But the civilized man has the habits of the house. His house is a prison, in which he finds himself oppressed and confined, not sheltered and protected . . . .[27]

[25] Ralph Waldo Emerson, *Works,* Centenary Edition, VII, 20. Cf. an analogous statement of 1835, *ibid.*, XI, 50-62.

[26] Margaret Fuller, *Writings,* ed. Mason Wade (New York, 1941). This is from the posthumous *At Home and Abroad* (1856). Cf. *Writings,* pp. 57-58, 60-62, 74-92.

[27] Henry Thoreau, *Writings*, Manuscript Edition, VII, 253.

It was not that Thoreau wanted to do away with civilization, but rather that he wanted civilized men to have that integrity he found in savages. However much he envied savage simplicity, as such it was not for him. He could not conceive of civilizing the savages; for, as he had decided by 1858, "Individuals accept their fate and live according to it, as the Indian does." Yet this is only the first part of an entry which concludes: "The fact is, the history of the white man is a history of improvement, that of the red man a history of fixed habits of stagnation." [28] Thoreau's problem was to see the Indian for what he was and to accept and learn from him all he could. Hence he explored the Indian as he explored all natural things. His journals are full of detailed accounts and descriptions. He spent his dying days compiling from published essays and his journals *The Maine Woods*, itself largely devoted to the story of his hero, the Indian guide Joe Polis. And during the last ten years of his life he filled some 2800 pages with notes on the American Indian, for the most part bits copied down from sources ranging from the *Jesuit Relations* to Schoolcraft.[29] He was searching, one assumes, for the means to demonstrate savage harmony and wholeness to American readers and to set up an example for them.

In his own way, Thoreau came clearly to understand the fate of the Indian. He had outlined it, in 1849, in *A Week on the Concord and Merrimack Rivers*:

The white man comes, pale as the dawn, with a load of thought, with a slumbering intelligence as a fire raked up, knowing well what he knows, not guessing but calculating; strong in community, yielding obedience to authority; of experienced race; of wonderful, wonderful common sense; dull but capable, slow but persevering, severe but just, of little humor but genuine; a laboring man, despising game and sport; building a house that endures, a framed house. He buys the

[28] *Ibid.*, XVI, 251-52.

[29] On Thoreau's Indian notebook, see Albert Keiser, "Thoreau's Manuscript on the Indians," *Journal of English and Germanic Philology*, XXVII (1928), 183-99; and Keiser's discussion of Thoreau in his *Indian in American Literature* (New York, 1933), pp. 209-32.

Indian's moccasins and baskets, then buys his hunting-grounds, and at length forgets where he is buried and plows up his bones . . . .[80]

He wanted to let the Indian live as he pleased; that failing, he wanted to study the Indian so closely as to know the very principle of his existence. Thus he tried hard during his later years to come to know that principle. As nearly as he could put it down it was this, in the words of the last entry in his journal concerning Indians:

> It is the spirit of humanity, that which animates both so-called savages and civilized nations, working through a man, and not the man expressing himself, that interests us most. The thought of a so-called savage tribe is generally far more just than that of a single civilized man.[31]

Savages, in their humanity and their thought, in their harmony and their wholeness, might guide men into the happiness proper to civilization. This seems to be the direction in which Thoreau was moving, although we can never be sure. Everything in him was left incomplete. The report is that the last word he said before he died was "Indians."[32]

Emerson, Margaret Fuller, and Thoreau wanted to demonstrate the perfectibility of civilized men in America. They thought that they might see in the Indian a creature whose being would authenticate the possibility of perfection. His was savage perfection, different in kind, but not in function, from civilized perfection. So they looked hard at the Indian, not to find noble savages, but to establish the possibility of noble civilized men. Yet even if they avoided the primitivistic fantasies of Crèvecoeur, Freneau, and their kind, they could not know enough about Indian harmony and wholeness to make them seem in any way desirable to most Americans. For most Americans, civilization could learn nothing from the savagism over which, according to the Law of Nature and Nature's God, it had triumphed.

[80] *Writings*, Manuscript Edition, I, 52-53.

[81] February 3, 1859, *ibid.*, XVII, 438.

[82] Keiser, *The Indian in American Literature*, p. 209.

3

From the time of the Revolution onward, Americans tried to place the Indian in their lives, to place him as he really was—a warrior and hunter, his life, his achievements, and his virtues sharply limited by his warring and hunting. Being out-and-out progressivists, they could agree with John Adams in his misreading of Rousseau: "I am not . . . of Rousseau's Opinion. His Notions of the purity of Morals in savage Nations and the earliest Ages of civilized Nations are mere Chimeras." [33] But feeling personally involved with the Indian, as Adams did not, they were obliged to give him his due and to learn a lesson in social values from that involvement. Benjamin Smith Barton wrote in 1799:

> It is a mortifying circumstance, that in proportion as we extend our acquaintance with the features or manners of rude nations, we are collecting materials for an history of human superstitions, and of mental miseries. If, in the progress of our researches, we discover that instinct, reason, the light of nature, has taught to these nations the existence of some great superintending being, the source of life and good: if we discover among them the unequivocal acknowledgment of a future state of existence, in which the warrior and the hunter, and the virtuous of either sex, are thought to repose from all their cares, and to taste, in fulness, unmixed physical pleasures (for the savage mind asks no more), still we discover them under the pressure of that superstitious fabric, which is founded upon the innumerable follies and weaknesses of men.[34]

American double-mindedness about the Indian, American pity and censure, was to find expression in confident essays on the good life in America.

[33] Letter to Benjamin Waterhouse, February 26, 1817, in *Statesman and Friend, Correspondence of John Adams with Benjamin Waterhouse, 1784-1823*, ed. W. C. Ford (Boston, 1927), p. 123. Cf. "Letter XXXII," *Letters to John Taylor* [1814?], Adams, *Works*, ed. C. F. Adams, VI, 518-19.

[34] "Observations and Conjectures," *American Philosophical Society Transactions*, IV [o. s.] (1799), 212. Cf. the Preface to Barton's *New Views on the Origin of the Tribes and Nations of America*, 2d ed. (Philadelphia, 1798), p. vi.

An oration of Benjamin Rush's, delivered before the American Philosophical Society in 1774, demonstrates what the life of the Indian can teach the civilized man. In his "Inquiry Into the Natural History of Medicine Among the Indians of North-America," [35] Rush compares the health of savages and civilized men and concludes that diseases among the Indians are few and simply treated, for the hard life of the savage is conducive to good health. If the progress of medicine among them has not reached that among civilized men, it is because they have no real need for such progress. It is just "in those branches of knowledge which relate to hunting and war, that the Indians have acquired a degree of perfection that has not been equalled by civilized nations." Civilization, there is no doubt, brings with it a multiplicity of diseases:

> I am not one of those modern philosophers, who derive the vices of mankind from the influence of civilization; but I am safe in asserting, that their number and malignity increase with the refinements of polished life.

As men become more civilized, they become more subject to disease; there are for them more ways of dying. Medical researches cannot keep up with the development of disease among them.

Thus Rush is led from medicine to sociology. He asks, "Do the blessings of civilization compensate for the sacrifice we make of natural health, as well as of natural liberty?" The answer, of course, is yes; civilized men must accept what they have, even though they have often paid too high a price for it. Now they must use artificial means, perhaps, to regain a physical and spiritual well-being that once was theirs by nature. Moreover, civilized men do not have to be savages to live naturally; simplicity is still held on to in some civilized countries. In Switzerland, Denmark, Norway, and Sweden, in some parts of frontier New England and Pennsylvania, there is living evidence that the blessings of civilization were not "*originally* purchased at the expense of

[35] Benjamin Rush, *Medical Inquiries and Observations*, 2d ed. (Philadelphia, 1794), pp. 9-77.

health." Civilized morality, bravery, and beauty do not have to be attended by civilized disease. There is an ideal society: one in which children are educated "in a manner more agreeable to nature"; in which the liquor trade is controlled; in which only healthful manufactures are allowed. It is, most important, a predominantly agricultural society. There is, then, a middle way between savagism and decadent civilization. It is the way of agrarian idealism, the way of American society before Jackson.

Rush's argument, certainly, needed for support only the simplest version of the idea of savagism, that involving the causative difference between a hunting and an agrarian society. The rest followed. It followed with equal simplicity for others in Rush's time too. In a travel note of 1788 Jefferson condemned farmer-peasant European society because its kind of degradation did not even allow for the freedoms of hunter-savage society; in America, by the same token, civilized men were beyond both peasantry and savagism.[36] Tom Paine, not so primitivistically minded in 1795 as he had earlier been, could best begin his argument for public ownership of the land by outlining the limits and the advantages of the Indian's natural society:

> To understand what the state of society ought to be, it is necessary to have some idea of the natural and primitive state of man; such as it is at this day among the Indians of North America. There is not, in that state, any of those spectacles of human misery which poverty and want present to our eyes in all the towns and streets in Europe.
>
> Poverty, therefore, is a thing created by that which is called civilized life. It exists not in the natural state. On the other hand, the natural state is without those advantages which flow from agriculture, arts, science, and manufactures.
>
> The life of an Indian is a continual holiday, compared with the poor of Europe; and, on the other hand it appears to be abject when compared to the rich. Civilization, therefore, or that which is so called, has operated two ways: to make one part of society more

[36] Thomas Jefferson, "Memorandums of a Tour," [1788] *Writings*, Memorial Edition, XVII, 280; letter to Edward Carrington, January 16, 1787, *ibid.*, VI, 55-59.

affluent, and the other more wretched, than would have been the lot of either in a natural state.

It is always possible to go from the natural to the civilized state, but it is never possible to go from the civilized to the natural state. . . .[37]

The possibilities of the most happily civilized life, it followed, were in America. A writer in the *American Museum* in 1792 had made all this explicit in "The Savage and the Civilized Man, an European and an American Picture." [38] First, in parallel columns, he compared the savage with the European: The savage, "the being, whose destiny we lament, is cheerful, alert, courageous by nature, lives contentedly, and dies without regret, because he conceives he shall soon revive"; the European, "the being, whose lot we boast of, bears in his emaciated and furrowed visage, the traces of misery, is never sure of to-morrow, and dies in the midst of troubles, fears, and uncertainty." Then he compared the savage to the American: the life of the savage is beastly hard, and insecure, so that old age is dreary and unhappy; the American "preserves, by temperance, the vigour of youth, till an advanced period; his declining years are crowned with respect and veneration; and his last repose is in the arms of filial affection." The social significance of this savage, we must remark, is negative. He shows what Americans are not, thus what they are, thus what all men might be. By the turn of the century, the primitivistic fantasy was irrelevant to men who thought as these did.

The Indian's significance for American life, then, came to be explicitly negative. One of the triumphs of the idea of savagism lay in its isolating the Indian so as to prove that he had isolated himself. To this creature, generated by the idea which comprehended him, writers on American society looked only for a tragic (or pathetic) example and a warning. They called him momen-

[37] Tom Paine, *Complete Writings*, ed. Foner, I, 610. See V. E. Gibbens, "Tom Paine and the Idea of Progress," *Pennsylvania Magazine of History and Biography*, LXVI (1942), 191-204.

[38] *American Museum*, XI (1792), 212-14.

tarily to mind and dismissed him forthwith—so completely did the idea comprehend him, so completely did he demonstrate the idea.

Looking at the Indian in his relation to the whole of their society, Americans could see manifest the law of civilized progress. Late in life, Jefferson wrote to a friend:

Let a philosophic observer commence a journey from the savages of the Rocky Mountains, eastwardly towards our sea-coast. These he would observe in the earliest stage of association living under no law but that of nature, subsisting and covering themselves with the flesh and skins of wild beasts. He would next find those on our frontiers in the pastoral state, raising domestic animals to supply the defects of hunting. Then succeed our own semi-barbarous citizens, the pioneers of the advance of civilization, and so in his progress he would meet the gradual shades of improving man until he would reach his, as yet, most improved state in our seaport towns. This, in fact, is equivalent to a survey, in time, of the progress of man from the infancy of creation to the present day.[39]

Other philosophic observers saw what Jefferson had seen, and could outline it in much the same terms.[40] They could learn of

[39] To William Ludlow, September 6, 1824, *Writings*, Memorial Edition, XVI, 74-75.

[40] See, for example, Caleb Atwater, "Descriptions of the Antiquities Discovered in the State of Ohio and Other Western States," *American Antiquarian Society Transactions and Collections*, I (1820), 221-22; Frederick Grimké, *Considerations Upon the Nature and Tendency of Free Institutions* (Cincinnati, 1848), *passim*. That such an analysis was almost universally accepted is indicated by the tone of Joel Poinsett's opposition to it in his *Inquiry into the Received Opinions of Philosophers and Historians on the Natural Progress of the Human Race from Barbarism to Civilization* (Charleston, S. C., 1834). Poinsett insists that Indians are savages, but insists equally that their savagism is fixed, has been so from the beginning, and will be so forever; his feeling that they are doomed is, of course, all the more certain because of his minority opinion on the idea of progress. Finally, it might be noted in passing, that the fine distinction between the savage and the barbarous, although it was held by more and more writers through the 1850's, was never much used in differentiating among kinds of Indians and is thus not particularly germane to my analysis here.

the law of progress from any number of learned authorities, especially from those Scots who were so influential in their thinking and from those French social theorists who built upon and verified the works of the Scots.[41] American experience with the Indian could only authenticate the fact that there were natural and necessary uniformities in the growth of men and their societies.

Progress seemed to most nineteenth-century Americans a fact at once hard, pragmatic, and commonsensical; and if we are to understand the nature and fate of the nineteenth-century savage, we must attend closely to the feeling of hardness, pragmatics, and common sense. It is abundantly evident, for example, in a celebrated lecture which John Quincy Adams delivered in 1840, "The Progress of Society from the Hunter State to that of Civilization." We have a newspaper report of the lecture and can follow it as an approving journalist did.[42]

Of all animals only man, Adams said, is social, not simply gregarious; and his social nature makes him "a being of progression." He is first a hunter, with "individuality . . . stamped upon [his] mind," with "no fixed habitation." In this state he indulges "now in the wild excitement of the chase, now in indolent indulgence." His wife is only his slave. "His abode, the forest, with its intricate mazes and dark caverns, his mind [is] but a reflection of his outward condition." Gradually, however, he discovers that some animals may be domesticated and his condition eased. So he becomes a shepherd; his wandering is regularized, his life more ordered, his vision of the world and himself perpetually enlarged. There develops for him a polytheistic religion centered on the worship of natural phenomena. The shepherd's

[41] On the Scots, see above, Chapter Three. On the French, see Charles and Mary Beard, *The Rise of American Civilization,* IV: *The American Spirit* (New York, 1942), pp. 73-83; and Henry Nash Smith, *Virgin Land, The American West as Symbol and Myth* (Cambridge, 1950), p. 218.

[42] Baltimore *Sun,* December 3, 1840. The lecture was delivered on December 1. It was delivered also the same year in Boston, New York, and Brooklyn. See Charles and Mary Beard, *The Rise of American Civilization,* pp. 153-154.

wife is no longer a slave, but still merely an " object of sensual pleasure." Polygamy develops, and man is one step closer to true monogamous, conjugal love. So man progresses and becomes a " tiller of the soil." He obtains " a fixed habitation." " His vision of his world and himself further enlarged, he [begins] to abandon the errors of polytheism and polygamy." " In this state of husbandman, he [possesses] the three essential conditions of happiness; a unity and fixedness of habitation, a unity of conjugal affection, and a unity of worship." Thus there is now " an approximation towards the state denominated civilized." Division of labor, barter, trade, financing, technical enterprise, the " mechanic arts," more and more complex government develop. And so one reaches modern man.

The report of Adams' lecture tantalizes one into desiring to see the whole work. But even an outline indicates where Adams stood on the question of savagism and civilization. There is, to be sure, no specific mention of Indians or of writers on Indians. Still, in 1802 Adams had declared in an oration that both heaven's physical and moral laws destined lands held by the savages of North America for civilized men and civilized use. And in 1825 he had declared that he still found " unanswerable " his argument of 1802.[43] Others had found the argument unanswerable too and had proved in theory and in practice how and why it was unanswerable. One finally differentiates Adams on progress from Hall, Schoolcraft, and Morgan on savagism only as they chose different ways to express their devotion to civilization.

Clearly, the triumph of civilization over savagism was culminating in nineteenth-century America. The antiquarian Alexander Bradford made it out to be all the greater when he pointed out that, if Indians were ultimately orientals, their destruction was that of oriental civilization by Anglo-European Christian civilization. He concluded in 1841:

The old system,—its moral and social elements,—its capacity for

[43] John Quincy Adams, *An Oration Delivered at Plymouth, December 22, 1802* (Boston, 1802), especially pp. 23-24; autobiographical note, which W. C. Ford dates 1825, *Writings*, ed. Ford, III, 10-11.

self-improvement,—had thus been fairly tried and tested; and the time had arrived when a new race, and the Christian religion, were appointed to take possession of this soil.[44]

Scientifically more orthodox than Bradford, the Swiss-American scholar, Arnold Guyot, in his enormously popular Lowell lectures of 1849, demonstrated that civilized man was born in Asia, reached his youth in Europe, and his manhood in America. He made the Indian " indigenous " to America, a creature of the forests, with a " vegetative nature," a being melancholy, cold, insensitive, and stoical, " the lowest grade on the scale of civilization." Europeans would triumph over him because, unlike him, they would not surrender to nature:

> Man himself, the one being preëminently free, is liable to [nature's] influence, in proportion as he neglects the exertion of those superior faculties wherewith he is endowed for the conquest and subjugation of that nature which was intended, not to govern, but to serve him.[45]

Europeans, then, had developed to the point where they could conquer American nature and so themselves develop further. The savage was savage by virtue of his being unable to develop so. God's intention was to let Old World man take over.

In an American milieu, this Old World man was refining the institutions of civilization to an hitherto unknown degree. As he did so, he was constantly reminded that his institutions were not only superior to those of his European forebears but also to those of his Indian contemporaries. For the Indian had failed to exploit American nature exactly as the white man was succeeding and was to succeed. There had been made possible a new dimension of civilized freedom. William Ellery Channing, discoursing in 1830 on the nature of a national letters, was bound to argue the significance of freedom for that letters, of American institutions

[44] Alexander W. Bradford, *American Antiquities and Researches into the Origin and History of the Red Race* (New York, 1841), pp. 434-35.

[45] Arnold Guyot, *The Earth and Man,* trans. C. Felton [1849] (Boston, 1873), pp. 216-218. On the popularity of Guyot's lectures, see Smith, *Virgin Land,* pp. 41-43.

for that freedom, and of the failure of savagism for the success of those institutions:

The only freedom worth possessing is that which gives enlargement to a people's energy, intellect, and virtues. The savage makes his boast of freedom. But what is it worth? Free as he is, he continues for ages in the same ignorance, leads the same comfortless life, sees the same untamed wilderness spread around him. He is indeed free from what he calls the yoke of civil institutions. But other and worse chains bind him. The very privation of civil government is in effect a chain; for, by withholding protection from property, it virtually shackles the arm of industry, and forbids exertion for the melioration of his lot. Progress, the growth of power, is the end and boon of liberty; and, without this, a people may have the name, but want the substance and spirit of freedom.

Here the savage has become an image for the negative of progress and civilization.[46]

As such an image, small but useful, the Indian was coming to figure in works devoted to the scholarly study of American institutions.

In 1833, in a college textbook, *Principles of Government*, Nathaniel Chipman began with an orthodox version of savagism (from "observation of real life and manners . . .") and concluded that the Indian society lacked all that American society offered—a sense of community, of law, of right and liberties, and of private property.[47] In 1836 in another textbook, *Elements of Political Economy*, Samuel Newman expatiated on the capacity of civilized men for developing "natural aids to production" and of savage men to waste them.[48] In 1838, surveying *The American Democrat*, James Fenimore Cooper, who had already celebrated the Indian in literature, analysed the growth of the sense of prop-

[46] William Ellery Channing, "Remarks on National Literature," [1823] *Works* (Boston, 1882), p. 125.

[47] Nathaniel Chipman, *Principles of Government: A Treatise on Free Institutions* (Burlington, Vt., 1833), especially pp. 1-15.

[48] Samuel Newman, *Elements of Political Economy* (Andover, Mass., 1835), pp. 65-68.

erty in terms of the growth of society from the savage to the civilized.[49] In 1831-1838, arguing in his *Opinions on Various Subjects* for a kind of socialism, William Maclure hoped to rescue men whom civilization had mistreated from the temptations of savagism.[50] In 1838 and 1839, in his *Manual of Political Ethics*, and in 1841, in his *Essays on Property and Labour* Francis Lieber argued the significance of the sense of property negatively in terms of savages who lacked it.[51] And in 1848 and 1858, in his *The Past, The Present, and The Future* and his *Principles of Social Science*, Henry Carey, attacking the "pessimistic" theories of Ricardo and Malthus, pointed out that land was badly used by savages, not by properly civilized men—that is, not by Americans.[52] Such declarations as these are by no means central in the treatises in which they occur. They mark only a casual, incidental mode of analysis; further they mark an antiprimitivistic assumption so deeply certain as not to need developing. But then, they result ultimately from an idea of the savage which had demonstrated that he was in no way central in American life.

4

The Indian belonged in the American past and was socially and morally significant only as part of that past. Coming to understand their past as the crucial modern working out of the law of progress, Americans were able to put him in his place. He belonged in American prehistory, or in the non-American history of North America. This they could be sure of; this their researches showed them. So early it became proper to preface histories of

49 James Fenimore Cooper, *The American Democrat* [1838], ed. H. L. Mencken (New York, 1931), pp. 127-133.

50 William Maclure, *Opinions on Various Subjects . . .* , 3 vols. (New Harmony, Indiana, 1831-1838), I, 165-68, 470-72; II, 442-43.

51 Francis Lieber, *Manual of Political Ethics*, 2 vols. (Boston, 1838-1839), I, 135, 142-48; *Essays on Property and Labour* (New York, 1841), pp. 47-77.

52 Henry C. Carey, *The Past, the Present, and the Future* [1848] (Philadelphia, 1859), pp. 247-48, 262, 274, 346-47; *Principles of Social Science*, 3 vols. (Philadelphia, 1858-1859), I, 94-101, 198-207.

America with a survey of the nature and fate of the aborigines. Morse's *Encyclopaedia* account functions thus; and so do, for example, those of Jeremy Belknap in his *History of New Hampshire* (1784-1792), of Samuel Williams in his *Natural and Civil History of Vermont* (1794), of Robert Proud in his *History of Pennsylvania* (1797-1798), and of Ezekiel Sanford in his *History of the United States Before the Revolution* (1819).[53] The surveys of the Indian in these histories amount to statements and restatements of the idea of savagism; perhaps one should consider them as independent variations on that idea. Still, their intention is explicitly historical and only implicitly moral; whereas accounts like those which I have surveyed in Chapters III and IV are explicitly moral (the science of society being considered a moral science) and only implicitly historical. What we should note once more is the recto-verso relationship of history and morality. We may look to Samuel Williams for typical testimony to this. Having discoursed in the regular manner on Indian virtues and Indian vices, he concludes:

> Such were the disadvantages attending the savage state. They appear to have been inseparably connected with it: And of such a nature, as to prevent the improvement, progress, or increase of society. We need not hesitate to pronounce, that these disadvantages far exceeded any advantages that could attend it; and operated with a certain and fatal tendency, to continue man in a state of infancy, weakness, and the greatest imperfection. The freedom to which it led, was its greatest blessing; but the independence of which the savage was so fond, was never designed for man: And it is only in the improvements of civil society, that the human race can find the greatest increase of their numbers, knowledge, safety, and happiness.[54]

The history of Vermont follows.

[53] Jeremy Belknap, *The History of New Hampshire, 1784-1792* (Boston, 1813), I, 100-103; Samuel Williams, *Natural and Civil History of Vermont* [1793] (Burlington, 1809), I, 160-250, 493-503; Robert Proud, *History of Pennsylvania* (Philadelphia, 1797-1798), I, 292-326; Ezekiel Sanford, *History of the United States Before The Revolution* (Philadelphia, 1819), pp. ix-cxcii.

[54] Williams, *Natural and Civil History of Vermont* I, 224.

The history of the whole of America followed too. In the second quarter of the nineteenth century, the great progressivist historians could say much more about the Indians but still could only conclude what their antiquarian forebears had concluded. In the third volume of his *History of the United States* (1839), George Bancroft devotes almost seventy pages to "The Aborigines East of the Mississippi." His sources are all-inclusive; his analysis of savagism is relatively complex and sophisticated. It is carried even to the study of primitivity in language (he notes "The absence of all reflective consciousness, and of all logical analysis of ideas") and religion (he notes that Indian religions were those in which "manitou" was present in all things, that there was in them "no conception of an absolute substance, of a self-existent being"). He can conclude only:

> . . . equalling the white man in the sagacity of the senses, and in judgments resting on them, [the Indian] is inferior in reason and the moral qualities. Nor is this inferiority simply attached to the individual; it is connected with organization, and is the characteristic of the race.[55]

Thus he is free to return to a theme which he had set down in his first volume (1834) in a chapter on "New England and Its Red Men": that the Indian fought civilization and was killed by it because he "could not change [his] habits."[56]

Bancroft's version of savagism and the place he gives it in his *History* must be referred back to his explicit progressivism.[57] So must that of Richard Hildreth in the first volume of his *History of the United States of America* (1849), a picture of "human society under its simplest and most inartificial [i. e., "natural"] forms . . . ."[58] So must that of a popularizer like Marcius Will-

[55] George Bancroft, *History of the United States*, 19th Edition (Boston, 1866), III, 302. The whole account occurs on pp. 235-318.

[56] *Ibid.*, I, 382.

[57] See *ibid.*, II, 269-70 for a typically explicit statement. Bancroft's philosophy of history, a transcendentalist, nationalistic version of the eighteenth-century idea of progress, is closely analyzed by Russel Nye, *George Bancroft, Brahmin Rebel* (New York, 1944), 99-101.

[58] (New York, 1882), I, 51-70.

son in his *American History* (1847).[59] So, above all, must that of the prime historian of the victory of civilization over savagism, Francis Parkman.

In the first of his histories, *The Conspiracy of Pontiac* (1851), Parkman put down what was for his generation the greatest record of that victory. The greatness of the record derived from the greatness of the victory. For it was a victory which had made life in America possible; and Parkman, as his journals eloquently testify, was determined to know it as only a historian of civilization could. In the long run, he wrote in the preface to his history, it was the conquest of Canada in the eighteenth century which made possible an "ordered democracy" in America. If that conquest spelled hope and a high future for the American colonists, it spelled doom for the Indians, who had allied themselves with the French in order to hold the British off and who had found themselves deserted, friendless, about to be despoiled of the lands which had sustained them.

> Thenceforth [Parkman wrote] they were destined to melt and vanish before the advancing waves of Anglo-American power, which now rolled westward unchecked and unopposed. They saw the danger, and, led by a great and daring champion, struggled fiercely to avert it. The history of that epoch, crowded as it is with scenes of tragic interest, with marvels of suffering and vicissitude, of heroism and endurance, has been, as yet, unwritten, buried in the archives of governments, or among the obscurer records of private adventure. To rescue it from oblivion is the object of the following work. It aims to portray the American forest and the American Indian at the period when both received their final doom.[60]

Final doom was Parkman's subject. The historical progress of civilization over savagism gave it meaning and order and made its pain into tragedy.

Parkman had prepared himself well to treat of his subject. In 1846 he had gone west and had seen the actuality of American progress. The experiences of this journey he had written up from

[59] (New York, 1856), pp. 55-62.

[60] Francis Parkman, *Works,* Centenary Edition, X, ix-x.

his journal as *The Oregon Trail* (1847), midway in which he declared, "I had come into the country chiefly with a view to observing the Indian character." He had to work very hard to make his observations; bad luck in choosing travelling companions, bad timing, illness, even what seems to us a naturally aristocratic propensity to refuse to throw himself wholeheartedly into the venture—such were the hazards of the trail. But he finally got to his Indians, although he never got to see them warring, as he had hoped to. He lived and travelled with a large group of Sioux and came to know them well, as savages virtually untouched by civilization. (Of one he was even able to echo Benjamin West's remark on seeing the Apollo Belvedere, "My God, a Mohawk!") What he saw was a people whose "mental features" were like those of their brethren in the east, however different might be their manner of living. He saw that they lived monotonous, unvaried lives and thus needed something as violent as warfare to give meaning to their existence; that they were intellectually and emotionally simple; that they were, in sum, at once heroic and childlike. What was chiefly to be observed, he noted, was the "impassable gulf" lying between the white man and the red.

Very much of Parkman's experience on the Oregon Trail went into his study of the clash of Indian and white man in the middle of the eighteenth century. There is particularly in *The Conspiracy of Pontiac* a feeling for violence which is manifest in Parkman's journals of his Oregon Trail experience, but which he (or his editor, Charles Eliot Norton) strained out of the earlier book. The narrative in *The Conspiracy* carries the tone of having been felt as well as thought through; as artist-historian, Parkman can charge it with the symbolic value which he imputes to it in his prefatory note. What controls and shapes the life of the narrative is the idea of savagism.

He begins his history in the regular fashion, with an essay on the "Indian Tribes East of the Mississippi," first describing general characteristics and then dealing with particular peoples. His Indians are the hunters, wanderers, and warriors of the tradition, held together in loosely organized societies not by law but by custom, hero worship, and the simplicity of their life and spirit. Parkman reminds his readers at the outset that it is savage circumstances which have made the Indian into the savage:

> The very rudeness of his condition, and the absence of the passions which wealth, luxury, and the other incidents of civilization engender, are favorable to internal harmony; and to the same cause must likewise be ascribed too many of his virtues, which would quickly vanish, were he elevated from his savage state.

From this follow descriptions of the particulars of the savage state of the Iroquois and the Algonquin people and a final estimate of Indian character—hard, ambitious, vengeful, treacherous, wildly freedom-loving. The Indian sees and acts rather than thinks. And finally: " He will not learn the arts of civilization, and he and his forest must perish together." [61]

What Parkman says here and in a later chapter on the western Indians comes not so much from him as from his society. What comes from him is the narrative and the men, savage and civilized, who live through it. Chief of these is Pontiac, that Indian in whom all savage aspiration failed.

He is to be comprehended as the perfected savage. Faced with Pontiac's bravery and nobility and with his treachery and meanness, Parkman must see him whole. The problem demands repeated comment. Parkman writes of Pontiac's character in general:

> He possessed a commanding energy and force of mind, and in subtlety and craft could match the best of his wily race. But, though capable of acts of magnanimity, he was a thorough savage, with a wider range of intellect than those around him, but sharing all their passions and prejudices, their fierceness and treachery. His faults were the faults of his race; and they cannot eclipse his nobler qualities.

He explains Pontiac's strange desire to have his people live only as savages:

> There is nothing progressive in the rigid, inflexible nature of an Indian. He will not open his mind to the idea of improvement; and

[61] *Ibid.*, X, 6; X, 48.

nearly every change that has been forced upon him has been a change for the worse.

He comments upon Pontiac's attempt treacherously to take Fort Detroit:

Here, and elsewhere, the conduct of Pontiac is marked with the blackest treachery; and one cannot but lament that a commanding and magnanimous nature should be stained with the odious vice of cowards and traitors. He could govern, with almost despotic sway, a race unruly as the winds. In generous thought and deed, he rivalled the heroes of ancient story; and craft and cunning might well seem alien to a mind like his. Yet Pontiac was a thorough savage, and in him stand forth, in strongest light and shadow, the native faults and virtues of the Indian race. All children, says Sir Walter Scott, are naturally liars; and truth and honor are developments of later education. Barbarism is to civilization what childhood is to maturity; and all savages, whatever may be their country, their color, or their lineage, are prone to treachery and deceit. The barbarous ancestors of our own frank and manly race are no less obnoxious to the charge than those of the cat-like Bengalee; for in this childhood of society brave men and cowards are treacherous alike.

All this, in the end, makes Pontiac's failure intelligible and justifies it. After his defeat Parkman shows him on Lake Erie, on the way to visit his conqueror:

We may well imagine with what bitterness of mood the defeated war-chief urged his canoe along the margin of Lake Erie, and gazed upon the horizon-bounded waters, and the lofty shores, green with primeval verdure. Little could he have dreamed, and little could the wisest of that day have imagined, that, within the space of a single human life, that lonely lake would be studded with the sails of commerce; that cities and villages would rise upon the ruins of the forest; and that the poor mementoes of his lost race—the wampum beads, the rusty tomahawk, and the arrowhead of stone, turned up by the ploughshare—would become the wonder of schoolboys, and the prized relics of the antiquary's cabinet. Yet it needed no prophetic eye to foresee that, sooner or later, the doom must come. . . .

When the visit is over, and he has been kindly treated by the English ruler, he is made to realize

For [his people] the prospects of the future were as clear as they were calamitous. Destruction or civilization—between these lay their choice; and few who knew them could doubt which alternative they would embrace.

And, after the account of his murder by a drunken, vengeful Kaskaskia, the last sentences in the history are:

Neither mound nor tablet marked the burial-place of Pontiac. For a mausoleum, a city has risen above the forest hero; and the race whom he hated with such burning rancor trample with unceasing footsteps over his forgotten grave.[62]

In Pontiac's career and in the Rebellion which he led, Parkman found a subject which would take him to the vital center of American history. He could know enough about that subject—his generation knew enough about that subject—to work from within it. He could make his readers die with Pontiac, so long as they lived with America. His Pontiac is concretely and particularly and immediately the savage, conceived in a period when the actuality of the Indian was everywhere known to symbolize and to image the idea of savagism. Knowing what Pontiac meant, Parkman could show what he was. For knowing what history meant, Parkman could show what it was. His account of Pontiac, charged as it is with the most deeply felt facts of nineteenth-century American life, celebrates in an heroic vision the triumph of civilization over savagism.

When in 1867 in his *Jesuits in North America,* he published a fuller and richer account of eastern Indians, Hurons and Iroquois particularly, Parkman could still not see beyond the impassable gulf. Knowing the *Jesuit Relations* thoroughly, admiring Morgan, using Schoolcraft's data while scoffing at his interpretations, still he was bound to say, in this instance of the Iroquois, the most "advanced" of American savages:

Would the Iroquois, left undisturbed to work out their own destiny, ever have emerged from the savage state? Advanced as they were

[62] *Ibid.,* X, 191; X, 216; X, 237-38; XI, 317; XI, 323-24; XI, 331.

beyond most other American tribes, there is no indication whatever of a tendency to overpass the confines of a wild hunter and warrior life. They were inveterably attached to it, impracticable conservatists of barbarism, and in ferocity and cruelty they matched the worst of their race.[63]

The good society could sustain and prove itself only by destroying the remnant of the savage past.

[63] *Ibid.*, II, 59.

VI

The Virtues of Nature: *The Image in Drama and Poetry*

THE INDIAN over whom Americans finally triumphed was he whom they put in their plays, poems, and stories. New-rich in their discovery of the possibility of a national culture, they were certain that they could find the Indian's place in the literature into which that culture was to flower.[1] He was part of their past, they knew; and in his nature and his fate lay a clue to the meaning of their future. Yet if they would treat him imaginatively, they faced a problem for the solution of which their national experience and understanding could not wholly prepare them.

For in the overpowering English literary tradition to which, even in their sanguinary cultural nationalism, they made obeisance, the Indian had been generally conceived as a noble savage, above and beyond the vices of civilized men, doomed to die in a kind of absolute, untouchable goodness; and American experience and understanding had been directed towards destroying just such a conception and replacing it with the conception of a savage in whom nobility was one with ignobility. Certainly, as doomed noble savage the Indian could be pitied; and American literary

[1] The significance of Indian materials for a national literature is discussed in William Ellery Sedgwick, "The Materials for an American Literature: A Critical Problem of the Early Nineteenth Century," *Harvard Studies and Notes in Philology and Literature*, XVII (1935), 141-62; John C. McCloskey, "The Campaign of Periodicals after the War of 1812 for a National American Literature," *PMLA*, L (1935), 262-73; and William Charvat, *The Origins of American Critical Thought, 1810-1835* (Philadelphia, 1936), pp. 143-44.

men, sensitive to the feeling of their readers, cultivated such pity. But he also had to be properly censured, and his nobility to be denied or so qualified as to be shown not really to be nobility; and American literary men, insofar as they were to be American, could not avoid such censure, denial, and qualification.

The specifically literary idea of the pitifully noble savage had to be accommodated to that larger idea of savagism which made possible not only pity but censure. In a country searching for culture, the literary idea was strong and long-lived, and Americans respected it. In a country feeling its independent destiny, the need for accommodation was equally strong, and Americans bent to it. The literary history of the Indian in America is one in which the idea of savagism first compromised the idea of the noble savage and then absorbed and reconstituted it. What came into being in this reconstitution was the savage whom Americans had been seeking from the first, and he served them as they willed.

1

In 1766, in London, Robert Rogers, English soldier and frontier scout, published his *Ponteach; or the Savages of America.* This was an Indian tragedy which he could not get acted in spite of the success of the authoritative discourse on the Indian which he had published the year before in his *Concise Account of America.* In the *Account* there is one of those *omnium gatherum* disquisitions which, as we have seen, were published as an aftermath of the French and Indian War and the frontier disturbances which immediately followed it. It is like them, emphasizing what its author has personally seen, shaping the details into a picture, at once excited and nostalgic, of a simple, heroic, dangerous, Spartan kind of people who are being destroyed by white civilization. There is, in short, that sense of the facts of savage life which was more and more informing colonial thinking about the Indian. In the tragedy, however, literary convention completely dominates the sense of fact. Rogers intends to emphasize, as he had in the *Concise Account*, the nefariousness and evildoing of English traders and to show how the English themselves have brought on

Pontiac's Conspiracy. But he can do so only in terms of whites crudely ignobled and Indians as crudely ennobled. To make his plot work out, to show the Indians as simple savages victimized by superior and scheming whites, Rogers would have had to psychologize along the lines of his *Concise Account*. Yet his literary commitment would let him psychologize only along the lines of an *Indian Queen*.

The intended high seriousness of the play depends in great measure on its subplot, the tragic love story involving Chekitan and Philip, Pontiac's sons. Chekitan is in love with another chief's daughter, Monelia. Encouraged by his brother Philip, he determines to win glory in battle so that he will be worthy of her. But Philip, so he informs the audience, loves her too, and swears to kill her so that Chekitan cannot have her, and to blame her killing on the English. His plans go badly, of course. He kills Monelia and her brother Torax, so he thinks, and tells his father and brother that the English have killed them. But Torax lives, informs Chekitan, and Chekitan kills Philip and then himself. What all this has to do with the Conspiracy of Pontiac we never know. Meantime, the Conspiracy has failed—only, however, after Rogers has exhibited the Indians at a ceremony at which the chiefs sing a war song "To the tune of Over the Hills and far away."

Rogers' play is perhaps properly considered as an English and not an American mistake. Yet in its melodramatic ennobling of savages, in its surrendering fact (eighteenth- and nineteenth-century fact, we must remember) to convention, and in its vitiating confusions, it early indicates the direction in which the Indian play would move. Combining the worst extravagances of seventeenth-century heroic tragedy with those of domestic tragedy; veering away in its literary conventionality from even the actuality pictured in the *Concise Account*, yet ostensibly affirming a thesis of the *Concise Account*—it exhibits the predicament of the writer of Indian drama, who, although he found that pity was much easier and more pleasurable than censure, still knew that one was as real and necessary as the other.

One way out of the predicament was wholly to forget fact and actuality, accept the convention of the noble savage, and have a good time. This is the way of the first genuinely American Indian play, Ann Julia Kemble Hatton's *Tammany, a Serious Opera* (1794). *Tammany* exists today only in a few of its separately published songs. Yet the confusedly ennobled savages are clearly there. In one of the songs, for instance, Tammany's light-of-love sings of him:

At eve to lure the finny prey
As thro' their coral groves they stray,
Or, in their ousy bends supine,
They in the radiant sunbeams shine;
Beneath the morn's pale light to rove,
The aloed wood or palmy grove,
These, these are sweet; but not to me
So sweet as is my Tammany.

And he of her:

Fury swells my aching soul,
Boils and maddens in my veins;
Fierce contending passions roll
Where Manana's image reigns.[2]

At the end of the play, we know, Tammany and Manana die together like proper noble savages. We have their death song.

There is evidence of an awareness of savage inferiority in Joseph Croswell's *A New World Planted* (1802), yet no means to express it directly. Here Indians figure nobly as friends of struggling Pilgrims. One of the Pilgrims, Hampden, falls in love with an Indian princess, Pocahanta. Troubled by the problem of a mixed marriage, he decides that he can go ahead with it because she is of royal blood, beautiful, and witty. But still, being a noble savage is not quite enough; so he says,

I know she's browner than European dames,
But whiter far, than other natives are.

---

[2] *The Songs of Tammany, or the Indian Chief, a Serious Opera* [1794], *Magazine of History,* Extra No. 170 (1931), pp. 8, 12.

Pocahanta has to be ennobled, virtually civilized, into something which approximates a Caucasian. If literary convention makes her good enough for Hampden as she is, American feeling about the savage makes her need to be more than she is.

It was on the theme of noble love that much of the Indian drama was to center; and Pocahontas, transported to Virginia where she belonged, was to be a main subject of that drama. In 1808 there was performed the first of the Pocahontas plays, James Nelson Barker's *The Indian Princess; or, La Belle Sauvage.* The play recounts the classic Rolfe-Pocahontas story, but loosely and adorned with confused subplots. In the confusion it is impossible to distinguish a noble savage from a noble white man. Yet Barker apparently intends that the distinction be made. He makes Pocahontas say to Rolfe:

> O! 'tis from thee that I have drawn my being:
> Thou'st ta'en me from the path of savage error,
> Blood-stain'd and rude, where rove my countrymen,
> And taught me heavenly truths, and fill'd my heart
> With sentiments sublime, and sweet, and social.

And he has Smith say at the end:

> Methinks
> Wild Nature smooths apace her savage frown,
> Moulding her features to a social smile.
> Now flies my hope-wing'd fancy o'er the gulf
> That lies between us and the aftertime,
> When this fine portion of the globe shall teem
> With civiliz'd society; when arts,
> And industry, and elegance shall reign,
> As the shrill war-cry of the savage man
> Yields to the jocund shepherd's roundelay.
> Oh, enviable country . . .[3]

In spite of such insistence, however, there is very little of the blood-stain'd and rude in Barker's savages, for there was very

[3] James Nelson Barker, *The Indian Princess* (Philadelphia, 1808), pp. 52, 73.

little in the savages belonging to the extravagantly primitivistic tradition in which he was committed to write.

If we think back over the history of the idea of savagism, we can see that the situation which was developing was this: the Indian had to be described somehow as blood-stain'd and rude; yet the dramatic terms in which, by convention and the exigencies of melodramatic staging, he had to be conceived did not allow for blood-stains or rudeness. The difference between him and white men, a difference which supposedly made for his death, could only be imputed to him. In George Washington Custis' version of the Pocahontas story, *Pocahontas; or, The Settlers of Virginia* (first performed in 1827), the heroic English barely win out over the heroic Indians—and then only when Pocahontas aids them. She, it is pointed out, is different; above all, she is Christianized. The leader of the Indian opposition, Matacoran, talks and acts on principles identical with those of Smith, Rolfe, *et al.*; he fights the English because of his innately noble love of freedom and because he sees that he will lose his beloved Pocahontas to an Englishman if his people are defeated. With their defeat, he is offered pardon by Captain Smith; but he defies Smith and says that he will go west to die:

There [he declaims], on the utmost verge of the land which the Manitou gave to his fathers, when grown old by time, and his strength decay'd, Matacoran will erect his tumulus, crawl into it and die. But when in a long distant day, posterity shall ask where rests that brave, who distaining alliance with the usurpers of his country, nobly dar'd to be wild and free, the finger of renown will point to the grave of Matacoran.

As he rushes out, Smith comments, " Brave, wild, and unconquerable spirit, go whither thou wilt, the esteem of the English goes with thee." [4] Presumably such esteem carries with it pity and censure for savagism; for we are to take heart and to envisage the " long vista of American futurity," as Powhatan puts it in the play's final speech. And it is this way too in a later Pocahontas

[4] George Washington Custis, *Pocahontas,* in A. H. Quinn, ed., *Representative American Plays* (New York, 1930), p. 192.

play, Charlotte Barnes' *Forest Princess* (first performed 1848), in which, after a career of noble gentility and daring, Pocahontas dies in England. As she dies, she has a savage vision of her Virginia home and its future—with Washington, the Genius of Columbia, Time, Peace, and the Lion and the Eagle all taking part in the final tableau which is that vision. Even the Forest Princess in the Indian melodrama is made to envision the progress of a civilization which her very existence, her savage perfection, makes virtually meaningless.

Thus savage inferiority is repeatedly, almost unconsciously, imputed to Indians and then sentimentally or melodramatically ennobled out of existence. In Nathaniel Deering's *Carabasset* (first performed 1831), the titular hero, the last of his tribe to survive the coming of the whites, is an exceptionally noble savage; for he is said never to have slain except in the heat of battle and even to have returned "The trembling, helpless captive . . . / Back to its mother's arms." [5] Then a villainous white goads him into terrible bloodshed, and at the end, after he has achieved his vengeance, into heroic suicide. In Richard Emmons' *Tecumseh* (first performed 1834), the titular hero is above joining in savage butchery, yet at the end he must be killed by an American in heroic single combat. Of this Tecumseh it is said, that he was ". . . rude, yet great; most towering Chief that ever hatchet raised against white man"; [6] still, there is no evidence of his rudeness, except that his English is occasionally broken. In Alexander Macomb's *Pontiac* (first performed 1838), the titular hero goes down before the westward course of the empire which is beyond his ken. He is at once a hero of romance and a desperate primitive. This is part of his War Song:

On that day, when our heroes lay low, lay low,
  On that day when our heroes lay low,
I fought by their side, and thought ere I died

---

[5] Leola B. Chaplin, *The Life and Works of Nathaniel Deering (1791-1881)* (Orono, Maine, 1934), Appendix B, p. 178.

[6] Richard Emmons, *Tecumseh; or, The Battle of the Thames* (Philadelphia, 1836), p. 35.

Just vengeance to take on the foe, the foe,
Just vengeance to take on the foe.

And this is his speech after his defeat by the British: "I have no father but the Sun—no mother but the Earth. She feeds me, she clothes me. I shall recline upon her bosom."[7] This last speech contains the psychological key to Pontiac and his life and death. But the play contains mainly things like his War Song, with equivalent actions and sentiments. Macomb, like Deering and Emmons, tries to create an image of savagism in terms which deny it.

The most popular of the Indian plays, John Augustus Stone's *Metamora; or, The Last of the Wampanoags* (first performed 1829) furnishes us the richest evidence of the imbalance between the convention of the noble savage and the idea of savagism. Stone wrote *Metamora* for Edwin Forrest, who specialized in noble savages of all sorts; and the title role became one of Forrest's favorites. It is probable that the popularity of the play is mainly responsible for the great number of like plays which followed it. There were some thirty-five in twenty years, mostly unpublished, mostly recorded as being well received.

The play develops with all the trappings of its melodramatic kind. There is appropriate music, much noisy business of challenges, duels, and charges; and there is a subplot which involves a disguised regicide, villainous aristocratic passion, the discovery of a long-lost son, and a happy union of unhappy lovers. In the midst of all this, Metamora (King Philip) strives hard to preserve his people, their ways, and their lands. He is depicted as an honorable friend of the white man, a protector of female virtue, and a tender husband to a sentimental wife, until he is betrayed and driven to warfare by the white man's greed. They play is advanced now by fierce alarums and excursions, now by set pieces for Metamora; there is only the dimmest attempt to make him speak like the Indian of the savage oratorical tradition. Obviously he is Forrest. At the end, seeing his people wiped out and his son killed, having

[7] Alexander Macomb, *Pontiac; or, The Siege of Detroit* (Boston, 1835), pp. 31, 54.

killed his wife to prevent her being enslaved by the whites, he delivers himself thus:

My curses on you, white men! May the Great Spirit curse you when he speaks in his war voice from the clouds! Murderers! The last of the Wampanoags' curse be on you! May your graves and the graves of your children be in the path the red man shall trace! And may the wolf and panther howl o'er your fleshless bones, fit banquet for the destroyers! Spirits of the grave, I come! But the curse of Metamora stays with the white man! I die! My wife! My queen! My Nahmeokee!

Then he "falls and dies; a tableau is formed. Drums and trumpet sound a retreat till curtain. Slow curtain." [8]

As Stone gives Metamora to his audience, he is not the Metamora of the tradition of savagism. His psychology is not simple, his passions not limited, his life not centered on action rather than on thought, his morality on the whole not inferior to civilized morality. He is specifically of that primitivistic literary tradition which the idea of savagism was intended to refute. Yet there is in Stone's conception of him some feeling of this latter antiprimitivistic idea, so that we can see just how Stone was caught between two traditions, between two images, and how he was obliged, however unconsciously, to compromise. After Metamora's first noble appearance, the young white heroine of the subplot says to her beloved; "Teach him, Walter; make him like to us." Walter replies:

'Twould cost him half his native virtues. Is justice goodly? Metamora's just. Is bravery virtue? Metamora's brave. If love of country, child and wife and home, be to deserve them all—he merits them.

She says: "Yet he is a heathen." And Walter leaves unresolved the whole issue. He answers in his simple manly rhetoric: "True, . . . but his worship though untaught and rude flows from his heart, and Heaven alone must judge of it." [9] What we observe is

[8] *Metamora and Other Plays, ed. Eugene R. Page* (Princeton, 1941), p. 40.

[9] *Ibid.*, p. 12.

that the difference between Metamora and the Walters in the play simply is not defined; it is only imputed, nominal. One can only suggest that the form of the play, and Stone's natural talent and enthusiasm for the form, won't allow for such a definition. Like all the rest who wrote Indian plays, Stone was enthusiastically unaware of this imbalance in his work. So were his pleased audiences. In their mutual unawareness they imaged noble savages who were being destroyed because they were not noble savages.

2

The predicament of the poet who would write of the Indian was more sharply defined than that of the dramatist. Bound to write either of the noble or ignoble savage, he could produce only varying combinations of the sentimental and the melodramatic. The confused images generated in his poems eventually flowed into the image of Hiawatha, in whom melodrama and sentiment were brought into satisfying combination by the genteel folklorist, in whom a grateful reading public could find the savage and the primitive softened into the quaintly and anciently heroic. By then it was 1855, and the savage had been a long time dead. In any case, American poets could never come but weakly to grips with the problem of savagism.

Towards the end of the eighteenth century, budding American poets lined up, in a not very orderly fashion, either on the primitivistic or antiprimitivistic side. They pictured Indians as distinguished upstanding warriors, now dead,[10] as hot-hearted lovers,[11] and as strong souls exhibiting their strength in defiant death-songs.[12] Or they pictured them in their sadistic mercilessness

[10] See the anonymous "Description of a Mohawk Chief," *Massachusetts Magazine*, IV (1792), 329; William Prichard, "Character of St. Tammany," *American Museum*, IV (1789), 104; Josias Lyndon Arnold, "Fragment of an Indian Sonnet," *Poems* (Providence, 1797), pp. 53-54.

[11] See Joseph Smith, "Indian Eclogue," *Universal Asylum and Columbian Magazine*, I (1787), 146-47.

[12] See Josias Lyndon Arnold, "Warrior's Death Song," *Poems*, pp. 50-52; and the death-songs in Mrs. Sarah Wentworth Morton's *Ouâbi* (Boston, 1790) and in William Dunlap's *Cololoo* (New York, 1793?).

to captives and in their bloody glory in victory over Americans sent to punish them,[13] and in their animal-like refusal to be civilized.[14] There are in these poems—significant to us because they are intended to be poems, not because they really are—two contradictory themes: the Indian as nature's nobleman, perhaps superior to his civilized conquerors; and the Indian as subhuman, waiting fiercely to be wiped out.

The poet could with great and unconscious ease, develop the two themes side by side. This is the achievement of Francis Hopkinson in his "The Treaty," a poem written, as he said, from actual observation of a meeting "upon the banks of the river Lehigh, in the year 1761, when the author served as secretary in a solemn conference held between the government of Pennsylvania and the chiefs of several Indian nations."[15] The poem begins with a description of the beauties of the Lehigh Valley, praise of Pennsylvania's governor, and a lament for the blood which has been "Shed by barbarians' unrelenting hand." Once all was peaceful; but Indian wars brought death and destruction. This last is illustrated in the pastoral tale of Rosetta and Doris: Ro-

---

On the convention of the death-song see Frank Edgar Farley, "The Dying Indian," *Kittredge Anniversary Papers* (Cambridge, 1913), pp. 250-60; and Henry Broadus Jones, *The Death Song of the "Noble Savage,"* (University of Chicago dissertation, 1924).

[13] See the anonymous "Defeat of Stuart's Indians in the South," *Massachusetts Magazine,* IV (1792), 51-52; "Lavinia," "Indian Victory: A Fragment," *ibid.,* III (1791), 763-64; the broadside *The Columbian Tragedy* (Boston, 1791); Eli Lewis, *St. Clair's Defeat* (Harrisburg, Pennsylvania, 1792); three "Elegies" by James Lewis, *Poetical and Miscellaneous Works* (Greenfield, Mass., 1798), pp. 63-67, 69-73, 74-77.

[14] See the anonymous "On the Emigration to America, and Peopling the Western Country," *American Museum,* I (1787), 185-86; Timothy Dwight, "The Destruction of the Pequods," Part IV, *Greenfield Hill* (New York, 1794); David Humphreys, "Poem on the Industry of the United States of America" [1794], *Miscellaneous Works* (New York, 1804), pp. 89-114; Joel Barlow, *The Columbiad* (Washington, 1825), Books II and V.

[15] *The Miscellaneous Essays and Occasional Writings of Francis Hopkinson, Esq.* (Philadelphia, 1792), III, 120. The poem was first published in 1772.

setta, the shepherdess, beloved of Doris, is taken captive by a savage troop; Doris, trying to rescue her, is captured too; carried to an Indian village, he is mercilessly and gruesomely tortured to death, and Rosetta dies, brokenhearted, at his feet. It is such tragic tales as this to which the treaty will put an end, Hopkinson goes on to say; and he describes the treaty itself, participated in by Indians of a somewhat different sort from those in the tale of Rosetta and Doris:

> Solemn and grand without the help of art;
> Of justice, commerce, peace, and love, they treat,
> Whilst eloquence unlabour'd speaks the heart.
> See from the throng a painted warrior rise,
> A savage Cicero, erect he stands,
> Awful, he throws around his piercing eyes,
> Whilst native dignity respect commands.
> High o'er his brow wantons a plumed crest,
> The deep vermilion on his visage glows,
> A silver moon beams placid round his breast,
> And a loose garment from his shoulders flows.
> One nervous arm he holds to naked view,
> The chequer'd wampum glitt'ring in his hand;
> His speech doth all the attic fire renew,
> And nature dictates the sublime and grand.
> Untouch'd by art, e'en in the savage breast,
> With native lustre, how doth reason shine!
> Science ne'er taught him how to argue best,
> The schools ne'er strove his language to refine.
> What noble thoughts, what noble actions rise
> From in-born genius, unrestrain'd and free!

In this vein Hopkinson carries his poem to the finish with a complete picture of the treaty, games, feast, and war-dance,

> Till wasted nature can no more sustain,
> And down in sleep their wearied bodies fall.

As the poem demands it, Hopkinson's Indians are now subhuman killers, now nature's noblemen.

Philip Freneau began with such an ambiguous view too, and

tried to primitivize his way out of it. He came to resolve his predicament only with a primitivistic fantasy analogous to that in his social criticism. In "The American Village" (1772)[16] he describes Indians of the past, unspoiled by and superior to civilized white men:

> Nor think this mighty land of old contain'd
> The plund'ring wretch, or man of bloody mind:
> Renowned SACHEMS once their empire rais'd
> On wholesome laws; and sacrifices blaz'd.
> The gen'rous soul inspir'd the honest breast,
> And to be free, was doubly to be blest.[17]

Yet in "The Rising Glory of America," a poem written in the same year as "The American Village," he and his collaborator, Hugh Henry Brackenridge, make one of the speakers in the dialogue say of American Indians and their past:

> How much obscur'd is human nature here!
> Shut from the light of science and of truth
> They wander'd blindfold down the steep of time;
> Dim superstition with her ghastly train
> Of daemons, spectres and foreboding signs
> Still urging them to horrid rites and forms
> Of human sacrifice, to sooth the pow'rs
> Malignant, and the dark infernal king.[18]

But this passage was cut out of the poem in editions after 1786, and Freneau came, for the most part, to image Indians as a dying race, needful of recovering their original noble primitivity. (Brackenridge, we should recall, took this passage to heart and went on to become a celebrated Indian Hater.) Thus "The Prophecy of King Tammany" (1782), "The Dying Indian, Tomo-Chequi" (1784), "The Indian Burying Ground" (1787),

[16] I follow, unless otherwise indicated, the text of F. L. Pattee: *The Poems of Philip Freneau*, 3 vols. (Princeton, 1902); and the dating of Lewis Leary: *That Rascal Freneau* (New Brunswick, N. J., 1941), pp. 418-80.

[17] *Poems*, III, 387-92.

[18] *Ibid.*, I, 58-59.

and "On American Antiquity" (1790) are concerned with the Indian past, or with a present which is soon to be the past. What is emphasized is the "naturalness" of the Indian, even in his attitude towards death and dying. The tone is melancholy and marks a regret for a simpler life that is past and for the passing of beings whose simplicity has ennobled them to a degree envied by the busily civilized poet.

As in his social criticism, Freneau in his poetry of the Indian is forced to be somewhat uncertain about the positive values of civilization.[19] In "The Indian Student" (1787) and "The Indian Convert" (1797), he tells the stories of two boys who could not adjust to civilization; the former had to leave Harvard and return to Nature where he was happier; the latter, being disillusioned to find that heaven was like a church and not a taproom, would not

> consent to be lodged in a place
> Where there's nothing to eat and but little to steal.[20]

One of the savages escaped civilization, presumably, and one was corrupted by it. Another who escapes is Indian Sam, to whom a disillusioned Freneau turned for poetic material late in his life, in 1822. The poet goes to school to the Indian, for three days hears civilization denounced, and concludes that "honest Sam"

> . . . seem'd a warrior and a sage,
> And *there* I could have pass'd an age,
> For all was calm, serene, and free,
> The picture of simplicity.[21]

What, then, was the lesson to be learned from this image of the Indian? It was, for Freneau, a confused one, involving the "nature" of man. To the very end, he tried in vain to accommodate his faith in civilized America to his faith in the noble savage; for he could not subscribe to the antiprimitivism which usually

[19] See above pp. 143-46.

[20] *Poems*, III, 189-90.

[21] *The Last Poems of Philip Freneau*, ed. Lewis Leary (New Brunswick, N. J., 1945), p. 95.

sustained the former. He published in 1822 a longish poem in which he tried once and for all to teach civilized men the true virtues of nature. This was "On the Civilization of the Western Aboriginal Country." The poem begins with a general consideration of mutability: The old stars fade, new ones appear; Nature has two wheels constantly in motion—one creating as the other is destroying; only matter exists forever; forms change always. Then the poet proceeds to a consideration of "civilization"—i. e., civilizing—the western Indians. The point is that they too are simply another changing form of unchanging matter:

> THOU who shalt rove the trackless western waste,
> Tribes to reform, or have new *breeds* embraced,
> Be but sincere!—the native of the wild
> If wrong, is only Nature's ruder child;
> The arts you teach, perhaps not ALL amiss,
> Are arts destructive of domestic bliss,
> The *Indian World,* on Natures bounty cast,
> Heed not the future, nor regard the past.—
> They live—and at the evening hour can say,
> *We claim no more, for we have had one day.*
> The *Indian* native, taught the ploughman's art,
> Still drives his oxen, with an *Indian* heart,
> Stops when they stop, reclines upon the *beam,*
> While briny sorrows from his eye-lids stream,
> To think the ancient trees, that round him grow,
> That shaded *wigwams* centuries ago
> Must now descend, each venerated bow,
> To blaze in fields where nature reign'd till now.
>
> Of different mind, he sees not with your sight,
> Perfect, perhaps, as viewed by Nature's light:
> By Nature's dictates all his views are bent,
> No more *imperfect* than his AUTHOR meant.

For all forms of "moral virtue"—i. e., all the varying moral codes of different societies—the poet continues, tend towards one good end. Yet when civilized men try to reform the Indians, they give them only one virtue for a hundred vices. They do not realize that in every life, in every race, men must pursue the good in their own way, and that that good is everywhere the same.

Still, so the poet addressed civilized men, if you must go and Christianize, go with a good heart and a good will:

> Nor *selfish* motives on *yourselves* impose,
> Go, and convince the natives of the west
> That *christian* morals are the first and best;
> And yet *the same* that beam'd thro' every age,
> Adorn the *ancient*, or the modern page;
> That without which, no social compacts bind,
> Nor *honor* stamps her image on mankind.
> Go, teach what Reason dictates should be taught,
> And learn from *Indians* one great Truth you ought,
> That, through the world, wherever man exists,
> Involved in darkness, or obscured in mists,
> The *Negro*, scorching on *Angola's* coasts,
> Or *Tartar*, shivering in *Siberian* frosts;
> Take all, through all, through nation, tribe, or clan,
> The child of Nature is the *better* man.[22]

The image is that of the noble savage, his nobility minimized into universality, into a least common denominator of virtuous human nature. He is, if not superior to civilized men, in his own way as good as they are. Perhaps he is superior; for he lives according to universal Reason, as civilized men so often do not. Freneau's conclusions are not unconfused and unconfusing, certainly. They seem to be a plea for the respect of the human rights of the Indians. To establish those rights, Freneau must universalize them, must appeal to Nature. And he is forced, as it were, into finding more of Nature in Indians than in civilized whites. Thus the Indians are ennobled; and Freneau, for all his philosophical maneuvering, is back where he had started some fifty years before with the noble savage of "The American Village." The Indian lives as the image of the best man living the best life, perhaps doomed to death because he lives that life.

[22] *Ibid.*, pp. 69-71.

3

That image was most fully exhibited in a series of narrative poems beginning in the 1790's and continuing into the 1850's. The number of poems and their popularity, like the number and popularity of Indian plays, manifest the steady and sure fascination of the image for American writers and readers. It was, we must remember, an image clung to in the face of direct attacks on its validity, of a developing idea of savagism which would deny it, and, as we shall see, of a developing fiction of savagism which would reconstitute it. Why did the image persist? Certainly the sheer force of literary convention was involved. And more than that, there was the force of the primitivistic ideal, of the doubt which any civilized man must entertain as to the final rightness of his kind of civilization. Since neither the plays nor the poems concern themselves very much with attacking civilization directly, we can surmise that they furnished a safe outlet for such primitivistic doubts. In any case, they survived and thrived; and Americans read them and wrote them even while the noble savage was being destroyed.

The earliest of these narrative poems is Mrs. Sarah Wentworth Morton's *Ouâbi; or, The Virtues of Nature* (1790). Expanding upon a contemporary prose narrative,[23] Mrs. Morton makes the French Canadian official, St. Castins (i. e., the Baron Castine), into " Europe's fairest boast " and describes him fleeing civilization because he has found there—and this is his own enumeration—only terror, guilt, pain, revenge, malice, duplicity, slander, insolence, pride, envy, neglect, fear, jealousy, fraud, reproach, affectation, and passion. He flees to the Canadian woods and, roaming one day, encounters a Huron warrior who is attempting to kidnap the fair Illinois, Azakia. St. Castins rescues her and she takes him with her to her people and her husband, Ouâbi, one " form'd by nature's hand divine." Ouâbi in gratitude makes St. Castins a member of the tribe, gives him the Indian name of Celario, and makes him a member of his household. St. Castins

[23] " Azakia: A Canadian Story," *American Museum,* VI (1789), 193-98.

finds life with the Illinois all that he has wished for, with one important exception. He has fallen in love with Azakia, has told her of his love, has been rebuffed, and finds himself torn between love for her and devotion to her husband. Yet he still pursues her. And when she still rebuffs him, he is more and more impressed with the integrity of the savage character and with his own weakness as a civilized man.

So it goes until St. Castins feels that he must leave the Illinois to preserve their integrity and his. But Ouâbi will not let him go; for the Illinois are about to go to war with the Hurons, and Ouâbi depends upon his adopted tribesman to stay behind and protect Azakia. This St. Castins does, even though he knows that he will continue to pursue Azakia and thus betray his friend. Then when a lone survivor returns from the Huron war and tells him that all is lost and that Ouâbi has been taken prisoner, St. Castins immediately gathers together a few over- and under-aged warriors and sets out to rescue him. They find Ouâbi at the stake, singing his death song, and they manage to save him. Rescued and rescuers return homeward, rejoicing; and as they are returning, Ouâbi finally perceives that St. Castins loves Azakia. Magnanimously, he gives her to him, saying that he will take another bride for himself. Yet, at the double marriage ceremony that follows, Ouâbi's great heart breaks, and he falls dying. Breathing his last, he speaks to St. Castin, who has now proved that he can become a truly noble savage, and asks him to be chief in his place. Then Ouâbi expires. And the narrative ends with a kind of apotheosis and a celebration of the natural virtues of the noble Illinois chieftain.

Mrs. Morton maintained in an introductory note that she had taken her Indian material from learned sources and that she was facing all the facts of Indian life. She went so far as to admit in a distressed note to her readers that the Illinois were merciless and cruel in warfare, but she was nonetheless sure that in the main her savages were noble. A contemporary reviewer picked her up on this by setting her image of the noble savage against that of contemporary students of savagism. This reviewer took great pains to show Mrs. Morton just where she went wrong, just why her Indians would not square with any modern view of them:

> The manners of the original inhabitants of this continent have at different times been the theme of commendations. At first view there is something in them which powerfully excites our admiration. Undaunted courage, ardent patriotism, hospitality to strangers, gratitude to friends, respect to the heroes of their nation, and conjugal fidelity, form an exceedingly interesting picture. The absence of an host of vices resulting from society renders this still more attractive. A vivid imagination will readily add to this, until we at length conceive the poetical descriptions of the golden age to be realized. Poets and philosophers have joined in describing the excellencies of this state of society, and contrasting it with the miseries of civil government; and we regard with surprise the strange infatuation of mankind, who will not break the shackles imposed upon them by society, and fly to this happy state. But upon a nearer investigation, we are mortified to find, that the picture has enchanted us only from its distance, and from the obscure light in which we had viewed it. We then discover, that most of the good qualities which had excited our admiration, are produced from the situation in which this people is placed; and that what appeared to us virtue is often times the effect of apathy. If the vices of civilized life are absent, its virtues are equally unknown. Revenge, cruelty, treachery, indolence, drunkenness, and a long catalogue of black vices, convince us that the perfection of this state existed only in our imagination; and that a civil government, with all its ills and inconvenience, is still infinitely preferable to the savage state.[24]

The reviewer might well have been following Jedediah Morse's *Encyclopaedia* article, with its emphasis on character and circumstance and on the necessity of seeing the whole of Indian life, for good and for bad, and of demonstrating the integral relationship of Indian virtues to Indian vices. In any case, he was setting what was already an intellectual commonplace against what had long been a literary commonplace. The latter could survive, as it did, only by accommodating itself to the former. The history of

[24] *Universal Asylum and Columbian Magazine*, VI (1791), 105-106.

that survival in the poetry of the Indian is one of such accommodations of image to idea.

In a few instances the idea virtually destroyed the image. These instances are of poems about frontier warfare, more violent in their antiprimitivism than even the idea of savagism demanded. Joseph McCoy's *Frontier Maid* (1819) centers on the attack by British-maddened Indians on idyllic frontier farmers. In an appended note, McCoy admits that he has overdrawn both his Indians and his frontier farmers—this for contrast. The point is that the design of his poem, which is the design of frontier life, demands that he attack violently the image of the noble savage. The anonymous *Ensenore* (1840) exhibits its titular hero rescuing his beloved from the fate worse than death which is captivity, and manifests in its Indians only animals deserving civilized destruction. Andrew Coffinberry's *Forest Rangers* (1842) is a long " Poetic Tale of the Western Wilderness in 1794." In the midst of a narrative of frontier war and frontier love, Coffinberry has two soldiers of Wayne's army debate the nature of their foe. The upshot is that they find the Indians to be so beastly in warfare and in their rejection of civilized ways that they must be not of the race of men.

But these poems, which really only continue the tradition of the sensationalistic captivity narrative, represent distinctly minority views. The noble savage could not be thus summarily got rid of. A more significant strategy for dismissing him—because it was a strategy that allowed the poet also to hold on to him—was to show that it was his very savage nobility which had brought him to his death. This was a strategy which, even if it did not completely accommodate the noble savage to the idea of savagism, at least made his destruction intelligible in relation to the progress of American civilization.

There is thus a whole series of miscellaneous narrative and descriptive poems, ranging from the crude to the innocuously competent, which celebrate the death of the noble savage and the coming of civilization. The pattern of these poems is uniform enough itself to constitute a received way of imaging American relations with the Indians. The Indian is described for what he is, a noble savage. The coming of the white man is described for what it is, the introduction of agrarian civilization. And the Indian is shown dying or moving west, often with a vision of the great civilized life which is to come after him, occasionally with the hope that he himself can become civilized. The tone is now bitter, now melancholy. The end is said to be good.

Taken most generally, this is the form of the Indian passages in Charles Mead's *Mississippian Scenery* (1819), of James Eastburn and Robert Sand's *Yamoyden* (1820), of the anonymous *Land of Powhatan* (1821), of Lydia Sigourney's *Traits of the Aborigines of America* (1822), of the Indian passages in Bryant's "The Prairies" (1832), of Job Durfee's *What Cheer; or, Roger Williams in Banishment* (1832), of Mrs. M. M. Webster's *Pocahontas* (1840), of Seba Smith's *Powhatan* (1841), of George H. Colton's *Tecumseh* (1842), and of Elbert Smith's *Ma-Ka-Tai-Me-She-Kia-Kiak*; or *Black Hawk and Scenes in the West* (1848). Even Henry Rowe Schoolcraft was obliged, when he put Indians into poetry, to conceive of them as doomed noble savages; his *Alhalla* (1843), a romance of the Creek War, and his descriptive *Rise of the West* (1841) are cast in terms identical with those employed by Mead, Bryant, and the rest. The image of the noble savage was to be sustained at all costs.

In these pieces, the inevitable destruction of the noble savage is not explained; it is merely accepted. The fact of destruction serves only further to ennoble the savage. Thus in Eastburn and Sand's *Yamoyden*, it is said of the dead King Philip:

> . . . and if indeed,
> The jewelled diadem thy front had prest,
> It had become thee better, than the breed
> Of palaces . . .[25]

Moreover, noble perfection, once destroyed, can well suggest imperfection. Thus in her *Traits of the Aborigines* (a poem sup-

[25] James Eastburn and Robert Sands, *Yamoyden* (New York, 1820), p. 254.

ported by 102 pages of learned notes), Mrs. Sigourney first contrasts civilized whites unfavorably with noble savages and then, recalling frontier warfare and the butchery on both sides, pleads for the Christianization of the noble savages. She addressed her countrymen:

> Oh! make these foes
> Your friends, your brethren, give them the mild arts
> Social and civiliz'd, send them that Book
> Which teaches to forgive, implant the faith
> That turns the raging vulture to the dove,
> And with these deathless bonds secure the peace
> And welfare of your babes.[26]

Like the Indian of the heroic drama, Mrs. Sigourney's noble savages, and those of many of her contemporaries, are being destroyed because they are not noble savages.

Another strategy for sustaining the image of the noble savage was to deal with him as he was when he was yet out of contact with a white civilization, to put him safely in the past and to see him as the embodiment of a heroic American antiquity. This would be to give still another literary image of civilized progress; but the Indian would be so indirectly involved in that progress that the poet would not need to concern himself with the real complexity of the savage's fatefully inferior relationship to civilized man.

This strategy is worked out in a group of poems which culminates in *Hiawatha* (1855). William Hayne Simmons' *Alasco*, for example, begun as *Onea* in 1820 and picked up again and continued under its second title in 1857 in order to capitalize on the popularity of *Hiawatha*, is a fragment dealing with long-dead Indians as " venatic " Spartans. Among them, Simmons writes:

> Wealth pamper'd not the few, nor poverty
> The many crush'd; but in community
> Born Nature's gifts they generously shared.

---

[26] Lydia Sigourney, *Traits of the Aborigines of America* (Cambridge, 1822), pp. 177-78.

Bred up in Spartan discipline, they knew
No riches, or none prized. Desert in arms,
Wisdom and eloquence in council,—these
Alone conferr'd pre-eminence and place.
Equality's just rights enjoy'd by all,
On Nature's plan, by reason's dictates plain,
Guided, in social harmony they lived.[27]

In the fragment—two cantos—the plot hardly gets moving; but we are told that there was intended a great tale of love, warfare, defeat; for the Yamasees by the Creeks, and an account of the Yamasees' retreat to a distant place where they would establish a lonely paradise. Samuel Beach puts his *Escalala* (1824) even farther back in history, to the time of the moundbuilders in their fight to sustain their noble primitivity against the incursions of Norwegian invaders; Indians who have lived the life of lotos-eaters are forced to become Spartans; they are as good at one as the other. Isaac McClellan in his "Fall of the Indian" (1830) sets out systematically to recapture an even more pristine savage past when the Indian

. . . sharpened . . . his arrow but to slay
The animal that howled around his hut,
Or drive back to the desert some wild Tribe
Of hostile savages . . .

Yet he admits in his prefatory note that such absolute heroicism is a little "at variance with [the Indians'] real character." [28] And Henry Whiting, in his *Sannillac* (1831) celebrates a savage way to love and honor which, as he concludes explicitly in a series of commentary stanzas, although it has gone forever, nonetheless makes the past glorious.

But it was Longfellow who fully realized for mid-nineteenth-century Americans the possibilities of this image of the noble savage. He had available to him not only the examples of such American poems on the Indian as I have instanced above, but also

[27] William Hayne Simmons, *Alasco* (Philadelphia, 1857), p. 15.

[28] Isaac McClellan, *The Fall of the Indian, with Other Poems* (Boston, 1830), p. 6.

the general feeling that the Indian belonged nowhere in American life but in dim prehistory. He saw how the mass of Indian legends which Schoolcraft was collecting depicted noble savages out of time, and offered, if treated right, a kind of primitive example of that very progress which had done them in. Thus in *Hiawatha* (1855) he was able, by matching legend with a sentimental view of a past far enough away in time to be safe and near enough in space to be appealing, fully to image the Indian as noble savage. For by the time Longfellow wrote *Hiawatha*, the Indian as direct opponent of civilization was dead, yet was still heavy on American consciences. He might well be conjured up in a comforting vision of American antiquity, so that everything would be shown to have gone as planned. The noble savage, that is, would be shown to have had his part in the plan; he could be loved and Americans could feel tender toward his manliness, because he was part of the plan. That manliness, in turn, could only be of the sort toward which Americans could feel tender. The tone of legend and ballad (this follows from Longfellow's opening statement of the qualities of the poem) would color the noble savage so as to make him blend in with a dim and satisfying past about which readers could have dim and satisfying feelings. In *Hiawatha* the image of the noble savage was sustained as such, yet was finally accommodated to the idea of savagism.

From the beginning of the poem to its end, the hero is carefully kept apart from the life of civilization. These are "voices from afar off" which

> Call to us to pause and listen,
> Speak in tones so plain and childlike . . .

This is a poem of savages in whose bosoms

> There are longings, yearnings, strivings
> For the good they comprehend not . . .

Kept apart from that good, these people may well be noble savages; yet their nobility will take on a kind of expression which will make it virtually irrelevant to civilized life. The history of Hiawatha follows naturally. He, as every schoolboy was to come to know, is in all things an aboriginal Prometheus who leads his people into an age of idyllic peace, an age of true primitivity. Yet time passes, the white man comes, and at the end Hiawatha must report his vision:

> I beheld the westward marches
> Of the unknown, crowded nations.
> All the land was full of people,
> Restless, struggling, toiling, striving,
> Speaking many tongues, yet feeling
> But one heart-beat in their bosoms.

He has seen, too,

> . . . the remnants of our people
> Sweeping westward, wild and woful . . .

One day the missionaries come and Hiawatha, according to Longfellow's understanding of the fate of the American noble savage, must welcome them. As they sleep that night, he slips quietly out and goes westward alone. Thus dies still another noble savage.

In the main, as we know,[29] Longfellow followed Schoolcraft's version of a cycle of Chippewa legends, assuming, even as Schoolcraft had assumed, that the Chippewa demigod Manibozho was identical with the Iroquois statesman Hiawatha. Schoolcraft had felt a strong antipathy to the trickster element in the Manibozho legends and had done as much pruning of the sexual and obscene as he could. Longfellow pruned even more and virtually omitted this part of the legends. Above all, he humanized Manibozho-Hiawatha according to the ideals and beliefs of healthily civilized Americans of the nineteenth century. He created a conventionally romantic love story for Hiawatha and so brought him down to the American earth. Yet he preserved him as superman by making him part of the earliest history, even prehistory, of that earth. The point is that his qualities as superman are colored by the quality of legends selected and trimmed so as to make him in no way gross, cruel, and conniving, in no way a savage. Legendary deeds are somehow not savage deeds. The mood of Hiawatha is the mood

[29] See Stith Thompson, "The Indian Legend of Hiawatha," *PMLA*, XXXVIII (1922), 128-43.

of *Idylls of the King*. And it is Longfellow's use of legendary materials, as opposed to his predecessors' use of historical and quasi-historical materials, which lets him fully exploit this mood. Casting his poem is a folk-meter (we would say pseudo-folk-meter, but we must view this as Longfellow did), giving it a quality of childlike charm, he was further able to characterize his Indians as living in America's dim and distant childhood. He was able to create a noble savage who accommodated his readers', his culture's, and his own needs. Thirty-eight thousand copies of the poem were sold during the first year of publication. And the noble savage lived on in spirit precisely because he no longer lived on in the flesh. Longfellow preserved the noble savage by making him an ancient culture hero after the common reader's heart's desire.

4

Even as all these plays and poems were being written and were achieving their popularity, the Indian was being studied and his nature comprehended by that idea of savagism which directly related him to civilized men and their nature. Yet in these plays and poems the idea of savagism exists only by imputation and accommodation. The convention of the noble savage, which it was to destroy, is in them at once affirmed and compromised. It is the fact of compromise which lets us mark the presence of the idea of savagism—a dim, almost negative presence, exhibited only in the strategies which playwrights and poets use to avoid it. The strategy which is common to almost all of these writers is that of killing off the noble savage (a matter forced on them by historical fact) and of giving him a vision of the higher and better life which was to come (a matter forced on them by their sense of civilized mission). The problem was to avoid the confusion of making superior savages envy inferior civilized men, yet to show the righteness of the victory of civilization over savagism. The characteristic solution of the problem was to separate the savage from the civilized by such a great span of time or distance as to make immediate comparisons and judgments irrelevant and unnecessary. Here was Longfellow's ingeniousness: to discover the possibility of the noble savage as prehistorical culture hero, thus to save history, or at least modern history, for his own civilization.

Yet American experience of the savage had been immediate and hard and bitter. The Indian was a perversely contemporary actuality. A man like Henry Schoolcraft, who could go against all his researches in drawing the noble savages of his *Alhalla*, still had to stop short and write of civilizing the Iroquois, in a volume filled for the most part with sentimental pieces on the Indian:

> This is the law of progress—kindlier arts
> Have shaped his native energies of mind,
> And back he comes—from wandering, woods and darts
> Back to mankind.[30]

The Indian's nobility was something which existed not for white men to aspire to, but rather something for white men to outgrow. Thinking about it, one was thinking about his childhood; and one could afford to sentimentalize, even to celebrate, childhood—as with Longfellow. One would be returned to the reality of adulthood, of growth, of progress—to the actuality of the westward course of civilization.

The task forced upon playwrights and poets by the convention of the noble savage was to consider the Indian as part of American prehistory. The task forced upon writers of fiction by the idea of savagism was to consider the Indian as part of American history. The two tasks were not antipathetic if they were considered in their proper relationship. The idea of savagism had destroyed the convention of the noble savage by subsuming it, by showing that savage nobility was part of man's earliest nature and that it was integral with the savage ignobility of that nature. If playwrights and poets chose to celebrate that nobility, they were perforce confined to the childhood of man in America. Writers of fiction would treat of the relation between childhood and adulthood, the relation of the savage to the civilized, of red man to white. Noble savages would be viewed not in terms of what was lost when they died, but what was gained. Savagism would be comprehended, as in the end it had to be, in its relation to civilization.

[30] Henry Rowe Schoolcraft, "On the State of the Iroquois," *The Myth of Hiawatha, and Other Oral Legends* (Philadelphia, 1856), pp. 322-23.

VII

Red Gifts and White: *The Image in Fiction*

WE cannot say why the storyteller's image of the Indian did not take shape and meaning as did the dramatist's and the poet's, why novelists and writers of tales did not generally adopt themes and strategies involving the noble savage of drama and poetry. Nor can we say why they did not adopt from the captivity narrative the convention of the bloodily ignoble savage. Perhaps the nineteenth-century storyteller's professional involvement in problems of society, as opposed to the dramatist's and poet's in problems of sensibility and the captivity narrator's in those of propaganda, gave him a means of avoiding the extremes represented by both the noble and the ignoble savage. Perhaps fiction was loosely enough conceived of as an imaginative form not to demand strict observation of literary or propagandistic convention. Perhaps the sheer dimensions of a novel or tale forced the author to go beyond immediate convention. Perhaps the fact of a Cooper's writing as he did itself established a new convention. In any case, we can see how the either-or convention of the noble and the ignoble savage dominated the slender amount of fiction of the Indian until Cooper's time and how after him it was subsumed by a larger, more inclusive convention, that comprehended by the idea of savagism.

To be sure, writers of fiction after Cooper sometimes expressed American guilt feelings by celebrating the noble savage. Sometimes—not very often however—they expressed American hatred by reviling the ignoble savage. Sometimes they did both at once.

But always they tried to argue feelings of guilt and hatred, of pity and censure, out of existence by showing how Indian nobility was one with Indian ignobility. We can observe how Cooper set the pattern for writers who would treat of the Indian, and how after him imaginative realization of the idea of savagism became a prime means to the understanding of American progress in its glories, tragedies, and risks.

1

Before Cooper, at the beginnings of American fiction, we can see a scattering of savages, noble and ignoble. Of noble savages, there are first the magazine Indians—those, for example, in "Azakia: A Canadian Story" (1789),[1] which furnished Mrs. Morton with the outline of *Ouâbi*, and those in "Yonora: An American Indian Tale" (1797),[2] in which a whole tribe saves its honor from white civilization by stoically accepting execution or committing suicide. And there are, somewhat later, noble redskins even more fully portrayed in such blood-and-thunder historical fiction as that of John Neal and James Kirke Paulding. In Neal's *Logan* (1822), the chief is one of the tribe of Aurung-Zebe who, apparently dying, commands his long-lost son:

> Be thou the Indian leader . . . Unite them; head them; perfect their confederacy. Drive the whites back to the banditti of Europe—back to—(his voice faltered) to—back to England! (His articulation was convulsive and passionate.) Rescue thy inheritance; avenge thy mother—Oh, God! Oh, God! where art thou, dearest! Lo, I am coming! I am coming—*Yo me muero.*[3]

The son is named Harold, and is doomed to die as a Byronic hero should. He denies his Indian blood, becomes a leader of the whites, and at the end is killed by his father, who has kept himself alive just to wreak his vengeance on his cowardly offspring. In Paulding's confusedly expansive *Konigsmarke* (1823), noble

[1] *American Museum,* VI (1789), 193-98.

[2] *South-Carolina Weekly Museum,* I (1797), 107-11.

[3] John Neal, *Logan, A Family History* (Philadelphia, 1822), I, 110.

savages are half-satirically introduced as critics of white civilization. The hero and his people are taken captive by Indians who torture them all, kill some, adopt the hero and his lady, and only then show them the noble virtues of savage life. The hero debates religion with an Indian philosopher, Ollentangi; what the Indian learns of civilized religion so upsets him that he determines to send missionaries from his people to the whites. The criticism implied is hardly serious; still, the situation hardly makes for a good joke. The image of savage nobility is accepted by Paulding and the others and used for what it seems to be worth at the time—as a stimulator of female pathos, of Byronic excitement, or of supposedly playful satire.

The image of savage ignobility, taken over bodily from the captivity narrative, is in our earliest fiction a means to literary terror. Ann Eliza Bleecker's *History of Maria Kittle* (1793) is simply a captivity narrative turned novel of sensibility; that it is based on a type of true frontier experience only makes the story more appealing to the sensibilities. Horror is piled on horror. Indian raiders come, shoot Maria's brother-in-law (her husband is away), tomahawk the brother-in-law's pregnant wife, and tear Maria's infant son from her arms and "dash his little forehead against the stones." Her daughter hides herself in a closet and is burned alive when the Indians set fire to the house. Maria and another brother-in-law are taken prisoner; and the march begins. On all this she soliloquizes:

> O barbarians . . . surpassing devils in wickedness! so may a tenfold night of misery enwrap your black souls as you have deprived the babe of my bosom, the comfort of my cares, my blessed cherub, of light and life. . . .[4]

Pitched thus, the *History* goes on through suffering, struggling, and bloodshed to eventual rescue, ransom, and reunion. Mrs. Bleecker works hard, as she says, to open the sluice gates of her readers' eyes and to achieve the luxury of sorrow.

Charles Brockden Brown is interested in the luxury of horror.

[4] Ann Eliza Bleecker, *The History of Maria Kittle* [1793] (Hartford, 1797), p. 22.

Striving for a specifically American Gothicism, he achieves it by centering his *Edgar Huntly* (1799) on the image of the ignoble savage. He involves his hero in a series of frightening adventures with savages, carefully builds up the horrific, and makes him try to analyse the overpowering fear which results. The explanation goes back to the fact that his parents had been murdered by Indians. This psychology of trauma is simple:

> Most men are haunted by some species of terror or antipathy, which they are, for the most part, able to trace to some incident which befell them in their early years. You will not be surprised that the fate of my parents, and the sight of the body of one of this savage band, who, in the pursuit that was made after them, was overtaken and killed, should produce lasting and terrific images in my fancy. I never looked upon or called up the image of a savage without shuddering.[5]

The lasting image is that of the ignoble savage of the captivity narrative. Its function is to arouse Gothic terror in the soul of the American searching for the dark meaning of his past. As in Mrs. Bleecker's little horror, it has become a native means to a conventional and stylish kind of literary experience. The point is that in our earliest fiction the image of the ignoble savage, like that of the noble, has no meaning intrinsic to itself.

2

The double image of the Indian, noble and ignoble, had by the end of the first quarter of the century, we must recall, been firmly resolved into one image, that of the savage whose life was to be comprehended by the idea of savagism. Placed in the context of the whole life of American society, his life could not be said to be one totally superior or totally inferior to that of a civilized man. It did not make sense to view his state as one either to be aspired to or to be dismissed with unfeeling contempt; rather it was to be seen as the state of one almost entirely out of contact, for good and for bad, with the life of civilized men. Indian nobility and

[5] Charles Brockden Brown, *Edgar Huntly* [1799], ed. D. L. Clark (New York, 1928), pp. 181-82.

ignobility, Indian virtues and vices, had to be at once admitted and praised and dispraised for what they were, qualities tied together and delimited by the special nature of Indian society. That society was found as a whole to be morally inferior to civilized society; and its moral inferiority was found to be a product of its historical anteriority. The American Indian had long been out of contact with the main stream of civilized life, so long that he could never participate in that life unless by some miracle he should stop being an Indian. Meantime he lived as an example of the savage life out of which civilized Americans had long grown. He was, in fact, a means to measuring that growth. It was this Indian who gave writers of fiction a way imaginatively to understand American progress, which was American progress westward. It was this Indian whom James Fenimore Cooper, concerned from the first with the nature and fate of American civilization, cast into the major image of savagism.

Cooper was interested in the Indian not for his own sake but for the sake of his relationship to the civilized men who were destroying him. So far as we can tell, Cooper had little personal contact with Indians. Rather, he read widely in the best authorities on individual tribes; in particular, we know that he read of the Delawares in Heckewelder and of the Plains Indians in Biddle's account of the expedition of Lewis and Clark and in James' of the expedition of Major Long.[6] There was thus an essential " author-

[6] The matter of particular sources is still a vexed one which it does not seem profitable to more than glance at here. Cooper told Sir Charles Augustus Murray, " I never was among the Indians. All that I know of them is from reading, and from hearing my father speak of them." (James Grant Wilson, *Bryant and His Friends* [New York, 1886], p. 237.) His daughter Susan Fenimore Cooper insisted that he had seen treaty-deputations of Indians in Washington, Albany, and New York and that he read in the best authorities (" Introductions " to *The Last of the Mohicans* and to *The Prairie* in the Globe edition of Cooper's novels; *Pages and Pictures from the Writings of James Fenimore Cooper* [New York, 1861], pp. 129-30, 142-44; James Fenimore Cooper, *The Legends and Traditions of a Northern County* [New York, 1921], pp. 216-17). And recent scholars have managed to work back from novels to probable major sources in Heckewelder, Biddle's *Lewis and Clark*, and James' *Long*. (See

ity " in the Indian materials out of which he constructed his series of stories on the nature of American progress westward. That even before him those materials had been so conceived of as to comprehend and to justify that progress could only make his theme the more easily realizable. Perhaps it made his theme possible. When in *Notions of the Americans* (1828), a treatise on American society, he studied the Indian's fate, he could say what was regularly and obviously being said: " As a rule, the red man disappears before the superior moral and physical influence of the white . . . ." [7] In the *Notions* he might hope for gradual civilization of the Indians, but he was forced to admit that savage heroism, as he called it, was doomed, even in the west, to go down before civilized heroism. The Indian and his fate were intelligible only in their relationship to the white man and his future, as savagism was intelligible only its relationship to civilization.

It is in terms of this relationship that we must read the Leatherstocking Tales, because it is precisely this relationship which Cooper images in the Tales. The Tales are Leatherstocking's; and the Indians serve only to define him and his nature and his end. Yet Cooper, we must remind ourselves at this point, was not forcing his Indians into such a use. He was taking them as his culture gave them to him. And he was to give them back to his culture imaged so powerfully that they could never be rejected, yet imaged so powerfully that no one could doubt that they had to be destroyed.

The Leatherstocking Tales constitute an examination of the heroic, adventurous progress of American civilization westward and of the very process of civilizing the savage frontier. At the center of the Tales is neither a savage nor a civilized man but rather Natty Bumppo, Leatherstocking, somewhere between savagism and civilization, the *beau ideal* of the frontiersman, with all

Gregory L. Paine, " The Indians of the Leatherstocking Tales," *Studies in Philology,* XXIII (1926), 16-39; E. Soteris Muszynska-Wallace, " The Sources of *The Prairie,*" *American Literature,* XXI (1949), 191-200.)

[7] *Notions of the Americans: Picked Up by a Travelling Bachelor* (London, 1828), II, 368. The entire account of the Indians (pp. 367-83) is of a piece with most travellers' accounts in the 20's and 30's.

the goodness and greatness that the pioneer could have in the circumstances of pioneering. Yet even he, no Indian, is steadily pushed westward until he dies on the prairies; and the progress which makes for his death is known ultimately to be good. To look at the story of the Tales objectively, according to Leatherstocking's chronology: In *The Deerslayer* (1841) he is young, at times unsure, not having yet proved himself; offered the love of a woman of the civilized world, he will have none of it, for his loyalties are to Chingachgook and the Indians with whom he has matured. In *The Last of the Mohicans* (1826) and in *The Pathfinder* (1840) he is Leatherstocking *triumphans*, fighting Indian-style to make the world safe for civilization and for the romantic love of men and women more civilized than he. In *The Pioneers* (1823) he is old, driven westward with his now debauched friend Chingachgook, albeit by a kindly, understanding civilizer. And in *The Prairie* (1827) he is alone in the west, and he dies at peace with his simple world, aware that in the richer, complex life which is coming to the west he can have no part. Leatherstocking's Tale, in all its abundant adventurousness, is thus to be taken to be a kind of tragedy; the progress of civilization is to have the tragic meaning which is part of any growth to maturity. Cooper's task was to trace that growth as it was to be seen in American movement westward and as it was to be remarked in the difference between conditions of the civilized and the savage in America. We may observe in Cooper's Indians and the part they play in the Leatherstocking Tales exactly what we have observed in the evolution of the idea of the savage upon which the Tales depend. The interest is not in the Indian as Indian, but in the Indian as a vehicle for understanding the white man, in the savage defined in terms of the ideas and needs of civilized life.

The Indians are most often ennobled, but not in the fashion of the proper primitivist. Chingachgook and his son Uncas are classically the last of their kind, Mohicans joined with the Delawares in befriending the white man. Marked by all the qualities of savage nobility, bravery, cunning, courage, artfulness, they yet are limited by their life of hunting and warfare. Since Cooper closely follows his source, Heckewelder, they are set against the villainous Mingoes (i. e., Iroquois); yet even the Mingoes can be noble in their villainy. The Indians, that is to say, are of a piece in their savagism. If the Huron Magua (in *The Last of the Mohicans*) is made the consummate villain by his passion for liquor, so is Chingachgook (in *The Pioneers*) shown in the end to be debauched and corrupted by liquor, civilization, and their discontents. And only when Cooper takes Leatherstocking west can he find among the Sioux and the Pawnees Indians who will at once exhibit the complex of good and bad which makes for savage life. He sums up his total view of the Indian in the Introduction to the revised edition (1850) of *The Last of the Mohicans*:

> Few men exhibit greater diversity, or, if we may so express it, greater antithesis of character, than the native warrior of North America. In war, he is daring, boastful, cunning, ruthless, self-denying, and self-devoted; in peace, just, generous, hospitable, revengeful, superstitious, modest, and commonly chaste. These are qualities, it is true, which do not distinguish all alike; but they are so far the predominating traits of these remarkable people as to be characteristic.[8]

Constantly he must keep this diversity, this antithesis, in view; for it is his means to comprehending Leatherstocking.

Leatherstocking, as the *beau ideal* of the frontiersman, mediates between the civilized and the savage. He is a type which is created as an intermediate result of the civilizing process. To the east there is an ordered complex way of life; to the west there is unordered simple nature. To the east there are civilized Americans; to the west there are savage Indians. The Leatherstocking Tales focus on the area between east and west, between the civilized and the savage. In the Tales the mediating frontier type is understood essentially as a savage variant of the civilized; our recognition that Leatherstocking's disappearance is necessary, albeit tragically necessary, must be a product of such an understanding. We are, then, to understand that the frontiersman is inadequate for the kind of life for which he clears the way simply

[8] *The Last of the Mohicans,* Globe edition, p. v.

because he is, to a significant degree, a savage—even though he may be so noble a savage as Leatherstocking.

Leatherstocking is made to recognize this inadequacy in himself and his type again and again. Such recognition forces him ever westward, however much he knows that those who are coming after him are living a better kind of life than his; for being as he is, he cannot participate in that life. And Cooper makes those who do come after Leatherstocking know just this, however tritely and awkwardly. Thus in *The Prairie*, what is virtually Leatherstocking's epitaph is spoken, significantly, by the grandson of that Duncan Heyward (of *The Last of the Mohicans*) whom he had helped long ago in the east: "In short, he was a noble shoot from the stock of human nature, which never could attain its proper elevation and importance, for no other reason, than because it grew in the forest." [9] Having grown in the forest, having participated in a savage way of life, Leatherstocking is not good enough for the very society for which he has cleared the way. Americans had thus been able to account for the cultural and moral lag among Indians. Cooper is thus able further to account for the death of the frontiersman. And for him there is triumph in that death, because it occurs as civil society is moving westward. He observes toward the beginning of *The Prairie*:

> The gradations of society, from that state which is called refined to that which approaches as near barbarity as connection with an intelligent people will readily allow, are to be traced from the bosom of the States where wealth, luxury and the arts are beginning to seat themselves, to those distant and ever-receding borders which mark the skirts and announce the approach of the nation, as moving mists precede the signs of day.[10]

Progressing thus towards high civilization, American society sweeps over Leatherstocking, the man of the forest mythically perfected. For even such perfection as his must disappear, since it is in the end not civilized perfection.

Cooper defines Leatherstocking's character as he is a man of the forest, as one who shares savage ways but is not a savage.

[9] *The Prairie, ibid.*, p. 129.

[10] *The Prairie, ibid.*, p. 70.

Leatherstocking's radical inadequacy for civilized life derives from the portion of savagism he shares. Hence the Indian as savage furnishes a primary dimension of meaning in the Tales exactly as he images at once what Leatherstocking is and is not. Cooper is here explicit. Leatherstocking is forever finding it necessary to explain the savage man to the civilized and the civilized man to the savage. What we must remark is that Leatherstocking's explanations are always set in terms of the idea of savagism.

In the Tales the explanations most often come as part of a discussion of Indian and white "gifts." In *The Deerslayer*, Leatherstocking is the philosopher of nature discussing savage religion:

"I am too christianized to expect anything so fanciful as hunting and fishing after death; nor do I believe there is one Manitou for the red-skin, and another for a pale-face. You find different colors on 'arth, as any one may see, but you don't find different natur's. Different gifts, but only one natur'."

"In what is a gift different from nature? Is not nature itself a gift from God?" [he is asked.]

"Sartain; that's quick-thoughted and creditable, . . . though the main idee is wrong. A natur' is the creatur' itself; its wishes, wants, idees, and feelin's, as all are born in him. This natur' never can be changed in the main, though it may undergo some increase or lessening. Now, gifts come of sarcumstances. Thus, if you put a man in a town, he gets town gifts; in a settlement, settlement gifts; in a forest, gifts of the woods. A soldier has soldierly gifts, and a missionary preaching gifts. All these increase and strengthen until they get to fortify natur' as it might be, and excuse a thousand acts and idees. Still the creatur' is the same at the bottom; just as a man who is clad in regimentals is the same as the man that is clad in skins. The garments make a change to the eye, and some change in the conduct perhaps; but none in the man. Herein lies the apology for gifts; seein' that you expect different conduct from one in silks and satins from one in homespun; though the Lord, who didn't make the dresses, but made the creatur's themselves, looks only at his own work. This isn't ra'al missionary doctrine, but it's as near it as a man of white color need be . . . ."[11]

[11] *The Deerslayer, ibid.*, p. 458.

This is practically an outline of the theoretical basis for the idea of savagism. Elsewhere in *The Deerslayer*, Leatherstocking is made to apply the theory of gifts more particularly, so to arrive at the idea of savagism itself:

" God made us all, white, black, and red; and, no doubt, had his wise intentions in coloring us differently. Still, he made us, in the main, much the same in feelin's; though I'll not deny that he gave each race its gifts. A white man's gifts are christianized, while a redskin's are more for the wilderness. Thus, it would be a great offense for a white man to scalp the dead; whereas it's a signal vartue for an Indian. Then ag'in, a white man cannot amboosh women and children in war, while a red-skin may. 'Tis *cruel* work, I'll allow; but for them it's lawful work; while for *us*, it would be grievous work." [12]

This, with its cultural relativism and its moral absolutism, is a kind of analysis which is made abundantly explicit throughout the Tales. Materialistic religion, scalping, torture, horse-stealing on the plains—virtually all savage traits are accounted for and explained and rationalized in their place. Leatherstocking's regular gambit for such explanations is talk about red gifts and white. The heroic Indian and the villainous—each is to be accepted in the context of his kind of life. For good and for bad, that kind of life is inferior to civilized life; taken all in all, white gifts are superior to red. And always the man of the frontier is found to be caught between surrendering to such Indian gifts as his frontier situation would develop in him and preserving the culture which he has brought from the east. What fascinates Cooper, and was to fascinate his contemporaries and successors, was the problem of the kind of semicivilized character which would, as a result of inevitable progress westward, develop on the Indian frontier. Cooper's analysis and evaluation of that character are almost exclusively in terms of the savage side of the frontiersman's nature and its inadequacies. There are in the Tales frontiersmen, bloodthirsty, cruel, uncontrolled, who have developed only the bad side of the Indian character; and there is Leatherstocking who has developed only the good side. Good or bad, it does not matter in

[12] *The Deerslayer, ibid.*, p. 36.

the end; for good or bad, Indian gifts are not white gifts, the frontier is not the ordered east, and the savage is not the civilized. So Leatherstocking and his kind, frontiersman and Indians, must pass. Their passing and its significance is defined in the end by what are known to be the inadequacies of savage life, taken in its relationship to civilized life. In the figure of Leatherstocking, facing his fate squarely, intuitively aware of its grand meaning, at times even a Christ-figure offering himself for sacrifice, Cooper justifies the ways of civilization and progress to man. As the Indian could not have any real part in civilization, so Leatherstocking could not.

Thus, for all the aboriginal blood and thunder of the Tales, the savage Indians are not at the center of the narrative and its meaning; rather they are at one side, with the civilized Americans at the other. Focus is on the middle world of the frontier. Cooper can assume that his civilization automatically argues its own virtues; so he lets it be symbolized almost entirely by a group of static, typed dignitaries whose function is to stand ready to replace the frontiersmen who go before them and die just for the replacing. This failure fully to explore the civilized may disappoint us artistically; annoyed by the woodenness of the Heywards, Middletons, Temples, and their kind we may find our attention caught only by the richly textured life of Leatherstocking, Chingachgook, and their kind; so we may not wholly sense the tension Cooper would reproduce for us. We are asking, as we have a right to, that Cooper be a major artist. He is not; rather, he is satisfied to take his materials as they come and, affirming the meaning inherent in them, to tell as best he can the simple, exciting story which derives from that meaning; western alarums and excursions are enough, for they are what Americans had to discover and to know.[13] Concerned with justifying the desperate need for American civilization westward, Cooper needs to define his frontiersmen only as they absorb or resist savage life, not as they make a civilization; the civilization is already made and must be super-

13 I have discussed this problem in "The Leatherstocking Tales Re-Examined," *South Atlantic Quarterly*, XLVI (1947), 524-36.

imposed on savagism, so as to dissolve it. Thus a cruel frontiersman like Hurry Harry in *The Deerslayer* is made out to be much worse than even a villainous savage because he has no right to the cruel gifts of savagism. Thus Ishmael Bush in *The Prairie* is made out to be a dishonest squatter about to go native and to be even worse than savage. Even Leatherstocking himself must find that his chief gifts are those of the Indians, gifts of acting, not thinking; and so he must go west, and so he must die. The life of these men is a new, often dangerous, always inadequate, kind of life and must be explored as such; the life of civilization is old, self-contained, above all adequate, and can be counted on to take over when the time comes. Ultimately what interests Cooper, as a civilized man, is what these frontiersmen are not—what they are not measured positively in terms of the savages which, for good and for bad, they have become. It is the negative of civilization which Americans must discover and understand.

In 1852, reviewing the revised edition of Cooper's novels, a man as historically minded as Francis Parkman saw just this.[14] He objected to Cooper's Indians as being softened out of reality; they were, he concluded, "for the most part either superficially or falsely drawn." Yet he had nothing but praise for Cooper's conception of Leatherstocking:

> There is something admirably felicitous in the conception of this hybrid offspring of civilization and barbarism, in whom uprightness, kindliness, innate philosophy, and the truest moral perceptions are joined with the wandering instincts and hatred of restraint which stamp the Indian or the Bedouin.

And he set forth Leatherstocking's meaning:

> Civilization has a destroying as well as a creating power. It is exterminating the buffalo and the Indian, over whose fate too many lamentations, real or affected, have been sounded for us to renew them here. It must . . . eventually sweep from before it a class of men, its own precursors and pioneers, so remarkable both in their virtues and their faults, that few will see their extinction without

[14] *North American Review,* LXXIV (1852), 147-61.

regret. Of these men Leatherstocking is the representative; and though in him the traits of the individual are quite as prominent as those of the class, yet his character is not on this account less interesting, or less worthy of permanent remembrance. His life conveys in some sort an epitome of American history, during one of its most busy and decisive periods.

Now, we may find Cooper's Leatherstocking as contrived as his Indians, and we can show how the contrivance of one is the contrivance of the other. But as late as 1852, Leatherstocking and his fate seemed not at all contrived, even if his Indians did. Parkman could not know, as we do, that Leatherstocking's life is defined in terms of that of the very Indians in whom he cannot believe, that the lives of both are equally the product of a civilized imagination making a civilized fiction.

Indeed, all Cooper's Indian stories are civilized fictions in which the Indian is imaged as a measure of the noncivilized and is made to die as both Chingachgook and Leatherstocking have died. *The Wept of Wish-ton-Wish* (1829) is in the main set at the time of King Philip's War; the Indians are dying heroes; the white who dies with them is not a Leatherstocking but a captive married to a chief and completely Indianized. *Wyandotté* (1843) is a study, as Cooper says in his preface, of Indian morality; the morality is that of the outcast, debauched Tuscarora, Saucy Nick-Wyandotté, who recovers his savage manhood by killing his white master, then fulfills that manhood by returning freely to serve his master's family; he has, it is said, " lived according to his habits and intelligence. . . ."[15] The novels which make up the Littlepage series successively contrast the savage with the civilized as a means of pointing up the necessity of private property. In *Satanstoe* (1845) the faithful Onondaga Susquesus helps the first Littlepage and his friends preserve themselves on the frontier; in *The Chainbearer* (1845) another Littlepage, engaged in keeping squatters off his lands, lectures Susquesus on the great civilized gift, that of the sense of private property; and in *The Redskins* (1846) a group of western Indians come to visit Susquesus and furnish a welcome

[15] *Wyandotté*, Globe edition, p. 464.

contrast to antirenters who, disguised as Injins, still try to squat on property now descended to a third Littlepage. And *The Oak Openings* (1848) exhibits Indians as the victims of Americans and Englishmen in the War of 1812. The strongest Indian motif in the novel is that of the missionary risking his life to save the unsavable.

In none of these novels is savagism imaged so richly as in the Leatherstocking Tales; for in none of these is there a Leatherstocking for whom such imaging has to exist. It is the Leatherstocking Tales to which we must in the end return for Cooper's fullest and most explicit understanding of the Indian whom his culture gave to him. This is most fully the Indian informed by the idea of savagism. In the Leatherstocking Tales the nineteenth-century idea of the savage has been sufficiently absorbed to furnish a symbol by means of which American destiny, civilized destiny, could be located immediately, made fictive, recounted in detail, and so comprehended imaginatively. Cooper could most fully image the Indian of savagism because he could relate that Indian to the Leatherstocking of the frontier, and through Leatherstocking to men of civilization. In the Leatherstocking Tales, the idea of savagism is realized in the image of an Indian in his gifts at once noble and ignoble, an Indian whose fate it was to be a means of understanding a civilization in which he, by civilized definition, could not participate.

Cooper, then, did not create the savage of nineteenth-century American fiction, but he brought him forth. However much writers after him were constrained to show that his Indians were not sufficiently true to reality, they never forgot that in the long run their own Indians had to be exactly what his were, images of creatures who symbolized savagism. If the details of savage life had to be further explored, its general form was known once and for all. Such knowledge made that exploration possible.

Cooper was attacked for ennobling his Indians so much after the manner of Heckewelder as to make them unreal—for example in 1826 and 1828 by Lewis Cass, who had had official relations with Indians in Michigan and who said he knew whereof he spoke.[16] Cooper's defense, in the revised edition of *The Deerslayer* (1850) was that Cass himself had not known Indians at their best and, more important, that he was writing the sort of romance in which effects had to be heightened and colored to register as poetically true. (Margaret Fuller, concerned with savage harmony and wholeness, put it thus: " [Cooper's] is a white man's view of a savage hero, who would be far finer in his natural proportions; still, through a masquerade figure, it implies the truth.")[17] Denying that he was a Chateaubriand dreaming of noble savages, he had written earlier of *The Prairie* to his French publisher, " . . . of course my description is a little poetic, as it should be, but in the main it is correct enough."[18]

The problem was to get at poetic truth and yet to be correct enough, to get at truth yet not to violate fact. The truth was that the Indian as savage defined precisely what the civilized man was not. The facts were the abundant and rich details of American progress westward and the Indian's decline and fall in the face of that progress. Writers after Cooper were often to agree with Cass; yet they were by the same token always to follow Cooper's lead. They were to deal in harder, less agreeable, more " realistic " facts about the nature of Indian life; yet they were to make those facts argue the idea of savagism. Whether or not this is owing to Cooper's direct influence is no great matter here. We can say, if we wish, that the idea of savagism and the image of the Indian which it supported were articles of belief which had to be subscribed to by Americans who wanted to put their progress into fiction. And we can say, if we wish, that Cooper was the first to

[16] Cass's statements appeared in review-articles of books dealing with the Indian in the *North American Review,* XXII (1826), 53-119 and XXIV (1828), 357-403. The controversy is discussed in Marcel Clavel, *Fenimore Cooper, sa Vie et son Oeuvre: La Jeunesse* (*1789-1826*) (Aix-en-Provence, 1938), pp. 567-87.

[17] Margaret Fuller, *Writings,* ed. Mason Wade (New York, 1941), p. 25. The statement occurs in the posthumously published *At Home and Abroad* (1856).

[18] The letter appears in the American Autograph Shop *Catalogue* (April 1937), item 42, pp. 695-96. I am very grateful to Mr. James Beard, who pointed it out to me.

fall under this necessity, and thus first to fill out imaginatively the symbol of the Indian as savage.

3

The truth for writers of fiction, as for other Americans who thought seriously about the matter, was that the Indian might well have been a noble savage but that his nobility, inferior to civilized nobility, could not survive the pressures of civilization. Their task came to be to put this truth down imaginatively, at once publicly to admit that the Indian had been cruelly destroyed and to satisfy themselves and their readers that that destruction was part of a universal moral progress which it was the special destiny of America to manifest. The myriad Indian fictions after 1823 are so many attempts to expiate the sin rising from the cruelty which was a necessary quality of American progress westward. In the fictions of the Indian, American pity and censure came to find their fullest and most public expression. Beginning with Cooper and issuing in the 1850's into the dime novel, moving irregularly from the heroic to the sentimental to the noisomely bloodcurdling, appealing to readers at any and all levels, deriving now from careful historical study, now from hackworked inventiveness, that image of the Indian which was maintained by the idea of savagism was a means of making men know the triumph, the pain, and the final glory in being a civilized American.

A story of an Indian, then, as in Cooper, would be meaningful primarily as a story of the tension between savagism and civilization. Tension implies a simultaneity of existence and means that one factor must be treated in relation to its opposite. So fictions of the Indian fall, for our analysis here, into two groups, the nature of each depending upon its narrative focus. There are, first, stories of the effect of civilized on savage life (the image in Cooper is that of Chingachgook and his kind); and second, stories of the effect of savage on civilized life (the image in Cooper is that of Leatherstocking and his kind). The groups, as we shall see, do not and cannot exist independent of one another. But they can and must be so separated if we are to look at the welter of

Indian fictions as a whole, clearly to see their primary images, and firmly to fix their largest meanings.

How might the Indian be depicted as a truly noble savage? Only as he aspired to the higher nobility of civilized life. This is the way of four novels I have seen. In Gardiner Calkins' *Fort Braddock Letters* (1824), the Indian Weshop proves himself good, in spite of civilized opinion to the contrary, by befriending and rescuing a white man; only at this point can he be differentiated from his tribesmen. In Mrs. Eliza Cushing's *Saratoga* (1824), a Christianized Mohawk is ennobled by his devotion to the Americans in their Revolution; his British-loving tribesmen, ignobled by *their* love, hate him for this. In J. L. E. W. Shecut's *Ish-Noo-Ju-Lut-Sche; or, The Eagle of the Mohawks* (1841) and in its continuation *The Scout* (1844), a Mohawk sachem, Christianized and reared in civilization, strives to make his people become like himself; these last are fictionalized tracts on civilizing the Indians, the point of which is that their true nobility lies outside their savage ways.

But these four are minority reports on the problem, reflecting a continuing but steadily fading hope of saving the Indian for civilization. The real fact seemed to be that Indian nobility was something that could not survive the inroads of civilization. In her *Hobomok* (1824), Lydia Maria Child is at pains to demonstrate this fact and the Indian's noble recognition of it. *Hobomok*, as she says in her preface, is her version of *The Pioneers*—that is, of the destruction of heroic savage life. She measures that destruction in terms of its work upon a group of civilized sensibilities. The novel is a kind of portrait of a Puritan town in the first decade of its history. At the center of the portrait is the figure of Mary Conant who, lonely, oppressed by the rigor and discipline of Puritan society, having, so she thinks, lost her Anglican beloved, gives herself in marriage to Hobomok, an Indian who worships her. Hobomok has all the spiritual attributes, if not the manners and language, of a noble savage; Mary has the sensibilities of a proper heroine. She feels, so she says, " lost and degraded," even though she knows that Hobomok truly loves her.

And she is saved only when her white beloved returns from the dead and noble Hobomok divorces her and disappears forever, doomed to celebrate his nobility in savage loneliness. It was only apart from civilization that that nobility could survive. So Miss Child wrote in a sketch published in 1832 of a " Lone Indian," a Mohawk chief whose child had died of a fever caught from the English, whose wife had died of a broken heart, who himself could now only wander in the west and appear, nobly lamenting, at their graves once a year.[19]

This was the most abundantly developed motif, how civilization, for all its greatness and goodness, inevitably destroyed the fabric of savage nobility. The burden of the anonymous *The Christian Indian; or, Times of the First Settlers* (1825) is that even the savage further ennobled by Christianity is destroyed by civilization. In Catherine Maria Sedgwick's *Hope Leslie; or, Early Times in Massachusetts* (1827), the heroine suffers in her recognition that the Indians are noble children of darkness who should be enlightened, not destroyed, by the Puritans. Her means to this recognition is the fine sensibility she finds in the female Indian Magawisca, who herself is torn between her loyalty to her people and to the noble English. Hope Leslie's sister, taken captive and reared as an Indian, directly discovers the existence of this noble sensibility and insists on being an Indian herself; but Magawisca, we are constantly reminded, is one of the last of the Pequots, and the Indians are said generally to be doomed. In Karl Postl's *Tokeah; or, The White Rose* (1829) there is another white girl reared by Indians, only she always instinctively holds herself aloof, even from the Creeks who befriend her; we are to approve and admire the Creeks' fierce opposition to Removal, but we are to accept them as doomed and to be relieved when in the end The White Rose is restored to civilization and the white man she loves. Timothy Flint's *The Shoshonee Valley* (1830) is a narrative, at once moral and prurient, of the destruction of the Shoshones and their peaceful valley by evil whites; even those good

[19] Lydia Maria Child, " The Lone Warrior," *The Coronal* (Boston, 1832), pp. 3-19.

whites who live in peace and love with the Indians are caught in this destruction. James Birckett Ransom's *Osceola; or, Fact and Fiction* (1838) is concerned with accounting for Osceola's present status as a noble savage by inventing a meaningful past for him. Ransom, conceiving of the Seminole leader as born of a white father and a Creek mother, has the father give his son to the Indians to rear, since he realizes that the boy, being even part savage, will be destroyed by civilization. Robert Strange's *Eoneguski; or, the Cherokee Chief* (1839) is devoted to chronicling the heroics of its title character; although these heroics include fighting with the Americans against the British in the War of 1812, at the end Eoneguski and his people are caught by Removal and driven to the Far West. M. C. Hodge's *The Mestico; or, The War-Path and Its Incidents* (1850) is a novelized defense of such Removal; yet Hodges accepts the fact of the nobility of savage life. His immediate attitude is far removed from that of a Child or a Sedgwick, but he puts down explicitly the sense of accomplished fact which ultimately informs their attitude as well as his:

> [The Indians] were doubtless in their pristine state more entitled to the noble epithets which poesy has liberally bestowed, but in the contact with the whites, the savage unfortunately evinced an aptitude for the vicious teachings of the race of strangers, and under it the native bad propensities struggled into preponderance and swelled into a fearful controlling influence over his character and habits. Whatever was noble in the native character was unfortunately impaired and rendered wholly inoperative by the process of grafting into the parent stem, artificial desires, strong, unhealthy, and wicked.[20]

All this, of course, is merely to note the iteration and reiteration of this motif, and only to glance at its different developments, its shifting tone, and its varying contexts. What we should remark, I think, is that the motif is obsessive; that such popular writers as these took it up because they knew their readers wanted them to; that therefore the iteration and the obsession mark a deep need in

[20] M. C. Hodges, *The Mestico; or, The War-Path and Its Incidents* (New York, 1850), pp. 55-56.

the collective American imagination of the second quarter of the century.

Searching out more of development, tone, and context, we can study the motif as it is developed by the writer who, after Cooper, was most celebrated for his Indian fictions. This is, of course, William Gilmore Simms. One of the ways in which Simms comprehended the savage was to put him in a legendary past, much as Longfellow did. So in short stories he retold southeastern Indian legends, humorous and romantic; for example, that of a man who finally got rid of his shrewish wife by wishing her the prisoner of a magical tree in which he had been caught and from which he could escape only by wishing someone else in.[21] The tone is that of quaint and safe and sane folklore. Simm's view of the Indian, set apart from his legends, was the opposite of quaint and safe and sane.

In the short story, "Oakatibbe; or, The Choctaw Sampson," Simms concerns himself with the fatal inability of the Indian to accept the ways of civilization. This is a distinctly southern development of the motif; for the story is set in the context of a racial theory worked out by the narrator and his companion at the beginning. It is simply this: that Indians had best be treated like Negroes, as members of a conquered, enslaved race, and kept together and gradually brought to civilization, if that is possible, through forced education into the ways of agrarian living. The story of Oakatibbe shows how few are the chances of this scheme working out. Oakatibbe, who has heretofore been a "superior" Indian, quarrels with a drunken tribesman, later himself gets unaccountably drunk, and then kills the man with whom he has quarreled. He freely confesses and stoically awaits the eye-for-an-eye death which his tribesmen owe him. Then white friends urge him to run away, and he does; for he decides that he wants to live for the whites and not for the Indians. Still he is enough like his savage kind to have to return for his punishment:

[21] "The Arm-Chair of Tustenuggee," *The Wigwam and the Cabin* [1845], new and revised edition (Chicago, n. d.), pp. 121-48. Cf. "Jocassée," *ibid.*, pp. 209-33.

. . . he had taken one large step in resistance to the tyrannous usages of custom, in order to introduce the elements of civilization among his people. But he could not withstand the reproaches of a conscience formed upon principles which his own genius was not equal to overthrow.[22]

If the principle of Indian genius could not accept civilization, still that principle could not sustain itself in the face of civilization. This is the meaning of Simm's account, in *The Yemassee* (1835), of the young Indian whose savage nature is corrupted by his contact with civilization. Occonestoga is the son of the great and incorruptible Yamasee chieftain, Sanutee. Sanutee will lead his people to fight the white man to the finish; for he sees how civilization degrades them and disintegrates their way of life. He sees, in fact, that his son Occonestoga, who has shown promise of greatness, has himself been disintegrated by the white man's liquor. Occonestoga, who can now do nothing but serve the white man, has become a slave and so has destroyed his nature as a savage, as a free hunter and warrior. Sanutee disowns his son and likewise leads his people in disowning all those chieftains who would make peace with the English. When Occonestoga would return to his people, his father demands that the disowning be formalized; the totem which the son bears on his skin must be cut out to show that he has no tribal identity, that he is in no way a man. Occonestoga is saved only by death, this at the hand of his mother who would help him preserve his savage self. Likewise, when his father dies, killed in the war against the English, we recognize that, in his own way, he has saved his self.

For Simms, Sanutee's heroicism is a principle of Indian genius. He admires Sanutee and his kind and makes him die like a noble savage; and he pities Occonestoga in his loss of identity and self and makes him die miserably, losing his nobility. Yet he recognizes the brutality of their lives, and he exploits it as fully as he can. The account of Occonestoga's trial and his murder and the accounts of Indian warfare are detailed in the great, gory patches of rhetoric in which Simms moves most easily. But we must

22 "Oakatibbe; or The Choctaw Sampson," *ibid.*, pp. 204-205.

remember that the story of Sanutee, Occonestoga, and the Yamasee War is nominally only the subplot of the novel. The main plot deals with those who will certainly defeat the Yamasees—with the English civilizers, their lives, struggles, and loves. As Simms thinks of his Indians as being portrayed realistically for their times,[23] so he sees Sanutee as aware of their inevitable doom:

He well knew that the superior must necessarily be the ruin of the race which is inferior—that the one must either sink its existence in with that of the other, or it must perish.

On this Simms comments in his own person:

An abstract standard of justice, independent of appetite or circumstance, has not often marked the progress of Christian (so called) civilization, in its proffer of its great good to the naked savage.[24]

Appetite and circumstances form, for Simms, means to the great rationale of the progress of the white man over the Indian. For Indians, appetite and circumstance are marked, as Simms makes his white hero summarize explicitly, by a life of hunting and wandering—and the personal and social qualities which rise from that life.[25] In the context of civilization and progress, such appetite and circumstance are marked also by death. Sanutee's death is tragic, because he finds meaning in his life as bounded by its mutually dependent appetites and circumstances. Occonestoga's death is pathetic, because at the end his life is meaningless.

The problem disturbed Simms, and he returned to it in 1859 (six years after the second edition of *The Yemasseé* had appeared) in a novel of less vigor and more direct, motive-hunting rationalization, *The Cassique of Kiawah.* At the outset of *The Cassique,* Simms describes the Indian as a creature set apart from civilized men, " savage rather in his simplicity than in his corruptions." [26] The Cassique (i. e., proprietor) of the little colony in seventeenth-

[23] *The Yemassee* [1835], ed. from ed. 1853 by A. Cowie (New York, 1937), p. 4.

[24] *Ibid.*, p. 22.

[25] *Ibid.*, p. 137.

[26] *The Cassique of Kiawah* (New York, 1859), p. 15.

century South Carolina, unlike other Englishmen of his time, proceeds on such an assumption. He gets as hunter the son of a powerful chieftain; his hope is to free the boy from his savage ways. (Here Simms takes the opportunity to interpose in his own person a long discussion of the special nature of the savage; it is cast in the regular language of such discussions and is focussed primarily on the education of the Indian boy to hunting and warfare.) [27] The boy Iwatee is caught between his savage past and his civilized present. His father has allowed him to go to the whites only so that he may help in a surprise attack on them. Yet Iwatee has come to know the daughter of the white proprietor and to love her for her tender, civilized ways. Simms makes him struggle within himself.

He has the proprietor think of the boy as one who will link his people to civilization but who will never achieve it for himself. He says of Iwatee, whom he sees domesticating a fawn for his daughter,

> "The wild for the wild; else would it never be made tame! But when, in the great forests, the wild beasts shall all be subdued or slaughtered, will the wild man rise to higher uses? Hath his humanity a free susceptibility for enlargement and other provinces? Shall he feel the growth, in his breast and brain, of higher purposes? Will his thought grow, and provide for newer wants of his soul? If it may not be thus, then must he perish, even as the forests perish; he will not survive the one use for which all his instincts and passions seem to be made! It is, perhaps, his destiny! He hath a pioneer mission, to prepare the wild for the superior race; and, this duty done, he departs: and, even as one growth of the forest, when hewn down, makes way for quite another growth of trees, so will he give place to another people. Verily, the mysteries of Providence are passing wonderful!" [28]

The mysteries of Providence in the end destroy Iwatee. For he dies, insane with grief and anger, when his father's attack fails, his father is killed, and he discovers that he can have neither the love of his people nor of the proprietor's daughter.

[27] *Ibid.*, pp. 250-54.

[28] *Ibid.*, pp. 513-14.

At the conclusion, the proprietor of Kiawah is told by one who is more practically minded than he:

" Make [Kiawah] a world to itself, and *your* world. You can transplant civilization to the wilderness, and so train it as that refinement and art shall be triumphant without excess or sensualism. That is the nice point for the study of the philosopher—how to secure the blessings of the higher moral of society, involving the full development of the best human powers, without endangering or degrading the essential manhood of the race. But you must abandon all your wild notions of philanthropy. You will never reform or refine the savage. You must subdue him." [29]

If the drive is towards a purer world, it is one purified also of savagism. The simplicity of the savage, however much Simms has been concerned to make his readers see it in *The Cassique* and in *The Yemassee*, is not available to them as civilized men. What kind of simplicity, what kind of refinement and art without excess or sensualism, Simms does not say. Likely it is that of the agrarian idealism associated with Jefferson, an idealism whose actuality persisted stubbornly in Simms' own region and in Simms' own time. What is important from our perspective is that it is the simplicity, refinement, and art of that civilization in which the savage cannot participate.

Narrative of the effect of civilized on savage life, then, only argued the idea of savagism and filled it out into a palpable image. Even a direct and " realistic " treatment of the Indian from first-hand observation argued this idea and filled out this image. Thus William Joseph Snelling's *Tales of the Northwest* (1830) represents a firm effort to write of the " real " Indian, in this case of Sioux, Sauks, Foxes, and Iowas, from fresh, direct observation. Snelling is sure that only those who, like him, have lived with the Indians can write of them. When he says that he wants a balanced view of savages as being " neither more nor less than barbarous, ignorant men," [30] he talks like many of his contemporaries. His

[29] *Ibid.*, pp. 597-98.

[30] William Joseph Snelling, *Tales of the Northwest* [1830], ed. J. T. Flanagan (Minneapolis, 1936), p. 4.

view is one which, as we have seen, derives from defining the savage almost exclusively in terms of the theoretically noncivilized. Yet Snelling insists that he is describing the genuinely savage, apart from any theory. Some of his tales do deal exclusively with Indians, apart from contacts with whites. Still, for all their richness and literalness of detail, they stand as wholes and make integrated sense only when read as accounts of noncivilization. They are completed, as it were, by tales of civilized men who act like savages and who must be understood in terms of the civilization they have lost.

The Indian tales are straightforward enough. " The Captive " is the story of a young Iowa who must betray his white friends and must bravely and stoically accept death as his due. " The Hokays " describes an Indian blood-feud involving a stolen wife and a series of murders. " Weenokhenchah Wandeetekah " centers on a Sioux squaw's love for her husband—a love so very deep that when in order to raise his status he takes another wife, she commits suicide. These tales are cast in simple, direct, baldly descriptive language; the plots function to demonstrate, as Snelling writes in his preface, that the Indian is in all things " the child of nature, and her caprice will dictate his course " and that " inconsistency " is at the heart of savage character.[31] What we come to observe is that Snelling gives meaning to his directly observed details by categorizing them, in all their freshness, according to the idea of savagism. He is talking about red gifts, talking more directly than most of his contemporaries certainly, but nonetheless talking as they had talked. Such talk assumes white gifts.

Properly enough, Snelling studies white gifts in a series of counterpart stories which focus on the " rude adventurers " who settled among the Indians on the northwestern frontier. Of such men he writes generally:

A very short residence among the aborigines learns them to despise the refinement and artificial wants of civilized society, and spurn the restraints legally and conventionally established to bind men to each

[31] *Ibid.*, p. 4.

other. The wild, independent habits of the wilderness are at first pleasing from novelty, and soon become riveted by custom. . . .[32]

This note prefaces a sketch of the exciting life of the trader Charles Hess. " Pinchon " is the story of the heroic " enormities " of a Frenchman gone native; Snelling regrets, but can only record, the " misapplication of his great natural gifts." [33] And the long story called " The Bois Brule " contains as background material a whole gallery of sketches of life on the frontier. Snelling's frontiersmen make most sense as their frontier situation makes them lose their civilization and as they take on savage gifts to which they have no right. For them too, savage gifts are gifts of loss.

Much of Snelling's effort is to achieve a direct description of Indian life; item for item, detail for detail, his descriptions are of Indians and the gifts peculiar to them. But the details come to be true in the ensemble only as they explain how Indians differ from white men—what civilized men are not, not what savages are. The literature of the Indian, even for a Snelling, is essentially a literature of the white man, particularly a literature of the white man who might lose part of his civilization and become a savage.

We are moved, then, to the second large group of Indian fictions, those dealing with the effect of savage on civilized life, those in which the loss of civilization is the subject, those rising in the image of Cooper's Leatherstocking.

4

That men who were the instruments for bringing civilization to the frontier ran the danger of becoming savages and semisavages was not a discovery of writers of fiction, but had long been known as a fact of American life and been so commented upon. Conventionally it was said, as by the essayist Albert Pike in 1836, that although the frontier meant freedom from the business of the civilized world and a chance for the sublime loneliness and the Indian-like life of the hunter, Americans would have to remember that such a life could not long endure, that the higher life called for

[32] *Ibid.*, p. 62. [33] *Ibid.*, p. 221.

the fireside, society, a sense of social obligation.[34] Frontiersmen were said, as by Judge James Hall (he of McKenney and Hall's *History*), only to be clearing the way for another kind of pioneer, who would settle down, farm the land properly, and make the beginnings of American civilization in the west.[35] It was observed that, by virtue of his achievements on the frontier, the frontiersman might destroy his chance of the civilized happiness which those very achievements made possible. This was a prime mystery of the law of progress. Storytellers strove to get at its heart.

Their means was the creation of characters who, like Leatherstocking, mediated between savagism and civilization, yet who, unlike Leatherstocking, were not ennobled into martyrdom. We have seen that Leatherstocking was said to have taken on no evil red gifts, yet had become enough of a savage to have to die. For Americans after Cooper, he was too much the *beau ideal*, and it was as hard to find or to invent others like him as it was to sustain his creator's over-poetic image of savagism. (I know of only one clear imitation of the heroic Leatherstocking; this is Adherbal in John Treat Irving's *Hawk Chief* [1837].) The " real " frontiersman was as hard and as cruel as the " real " Indian. Yet however much one envied or was grateful to him, one would have to admit that he could never have what that Indian had—the nobility of savagism. He could have only the ignobility of savagism; this was the price he would have to pay for surrendering part or all of his civilized self.

After Cooper, the figure of Leatherstocking as frontiersman was

[34] Albert Pike, " The Philosophy of Deer Hunting," *American Monthly Magazine*, VII (1836), 154-59. Cf., for example, Timothy Flint, " Editor's Preface," *The Personal Narrative of James O. Pattie* [1833], in R. G. Thwaites, ed., *Early Western Travels*, XVIII (Cleveland, 1905), 25-28, and Flint's *The First White Man of the West; or, The Life and Exploits of Col. Dan'l Boone* [1833] (Cincinnati, 1850), pp. 170-71, 249; Rufus Sage, *Western Scenes and Adventures* [1846], 3d ed. (Philadelphia, 1855), pp. 17-18; T. B. Thorpe, *The Hive of " The Bee Hunter "* (New York, 1854), pp. 135-44. And recall Parkman on Cooper's frontiersmen, discussed above, pp. 208-209.

[35] James Hall, *Sketches of History, Life, and Manners in the West* (Philadelphia, 1835), I, 22-23, 241, II, 54.

either heroicized into a son of civilization temporarily on the frontier or was naturalized into a permanent victim of the frontier. The hero, the man who, detached from the problem of savagism and civilization, issued into the dime novel Kit Carsons, Deadwood Dicks, Buffalo Bills, and their fry, is not our concern here.[36] Our concern is with the victim, the man who had taken on so many red gifts that he hated them, even had come sometimes to hate himself.

In Indian fictions after Cooper, the image of Leatherstocking as victim issued into that of the Renegade and the Indian Hater. The innocent, martyred *beau ideal* was no longer there to trouble the conscience of those who had destroyed him, even as he had cleared the way for them. His place was taken by the civilized man who had become the moral victim of savagism and who, as a consequence, was destroying himself.

In our Indian fiction, the Renegade is simply defined. He is a man who has wilfully given himself over to savagism and deliberately turned against civilization. Timothy Flint describes the type towards the beginning of his *Shoshonee Valley* (1830). On men of this sort, it should be remembered, he blames that inevitable corruption of savage life which was his main theme; yet he makes them fight decent civilization too. These are Mountain Men, fur-trappers, who have become "more adroit, and more capable of endurance, than [the Indians] themselves." They are consciously expert in their kind of studied savagism, and with liquor and vice they corrupt the Indians to whom they have gone to school. Why have they come to live and love this hard, primitive life? Because they were all "imbued with an instinctive fondness for the reckless savage life, alternately indolent and laborious, full and fasting, occupied in hunting, fighting, feasting, intriguing, and amours, interdicted by no laws, or difficult morals, or any restraints, but the invisible ones of Indian habit and opinion."

[36] I refer here, and am much indebted to, the definitive analysis of the Leatherstocking figure as it survived into the 1860's and beyond in Henry Nash Smith's *Virgin Land, The American West as Symbol and Myth* (Cambridge, 1950), pp. 51-120.

And the moral for civilized men follows: " None know, until they have experimented, for how many people, who would be least suspected to be endowed with such inclinations, this life has its own irresistable charms." [37]

What makes the Renegade significant is what he has given up, how far behind he has left civilization for savagism. Thus in his *The Renegade* (1848) Emerson Bennett sets Simon Girty, wholly a savage, against a heroic Boone; Girty is made out to be the consummate villain, worse than a savage, for he is nothing but a destroyer of the civilization which Boone is made to represent. But perhaps the extreme of such Renegades, because his savagery is infused wtih a highly civilized intelligence, is the villain of Charles Webber's *Old Hicks the Guide* (1848). By the time the dénouement comes around, he turns out to be a decadent French aristocrat who has come to Texas, corrupted properly savage Comanches to his own evil purposes, and contaminated even bountiful western nature with his vile presence.

> In him [Webber writes], it seemed as if the social bravo had grown tired of sneaking murder with the polished tongue thrust amid courts, and had sought the avowed license of savage life to slake a rampant thirst for blood, bringing along with him the keen intellect and consummate tastes of a nobler development to aid an imperious will in wielding these simpler elements of mischief.[38]

This is to blame the temptation to savagism on over-civilization, so to speak. Webber's villain has in common with Flint's trappers and Bennett's Girty only the savagism which comes to be a means to the perpetration of villainy.

The Indian Hater is at once more complex of analysis and, as fictive image, more readily accessible than is the Renegade, since he is a man paradoxically kept by his hatred from falling entirely into the very state which defines it. Moreover, he fights on the side of civilization, not against it. In his life, good is accomplished through evil; for only by living as a savage is he able to destroy

[37] Timothy Flint, *The Shoshonee Valley* (Cincinnati, 1830), I, 20-22.
[38] Charles Webber, *Old Hicks the Guide* (New York, 1848), p. 205.

savages and thus, consciously or not, to contribute to the advancement of civilization. In his evil life as a savage, he must be destroyed; but since he accomplishes good, his fate and its meaning must be comprehended and celebrated as one of the tragic or pathetic works of progress.

The fullest imaging of the Indian Hater and the charms and risks of Indian hating is that in the stories and sketches of the ubiquitous James Hall. The very Indians who stalk through Hall's western writings give him a means of defining the character of those civilized men who go west and are obliged to wipe them out. His general subject, held in common with most writers of Indian fiction, was, as he put it in 1835, the " mutual antipathy " of red men and white.[39] One aspect of this subject, as we have seen, was the nature of savage life and its relation to civilized life; this Hall explored, as others had done, in sketches of Indian legends and studies of the effects of civilization on savagism.[40] But he was more interested in studying the character of those pioneers who cut themselves off from a civilization in order that they might make one. He said, looking over the stories in the second edition of his *Legends of the West* (1854, first published in 1832), that he was trying to describe a frontier growing into civilization—in this case that Ohio frontier which he had known as a pioneering young lawyer. This, he knew, had been the time of the " dawn of civilization," whose makers were properly " all farmers," but " rather pastoral than agricultural . . . ." [41] His task was to deal not only with these pioneers, but with the men who pioneered for them, with men whose state was pre-pastoral. These latter were the Indian Haters and their kind. With them,

[39] James Hall, *Tales of the Border* (Philadelphia, 1835), p. 11.

[40] See for example, " The Black Steed of the Prairie " and " The Red Sky of the Morning," collected in *Wilderness and the War Path* (New York, 1849), pp. 1-31, 83-111; " The New Moon," collected in *Tales of the Border* (Philadelphia, 1835), pp. 213-76; and the Indian materials in *The Harpe's Head* (Philadelphia, 1833).

[41] James Hall, *Legends of the West*, 2d ed. (New York, 1854), pp. vii-xiv.

as Hall's stories abundantly show, civilization on the frontier became possible.

In "The Backwoodsman" (collected in *Legends of the West* [1833]), the hero's function is to help out in the rescue of a fair maid taken captive and to make articulate the opinions of a first-class Indian Hater. Towards the beginning he soliloquizes:

"They [the Indians] have no more bowels of compassion than a wolf. But after all, the Indians have some good qualities. They are prime hunters, I will say that for them, and they are true to one another. I don't blame them a grain for their hatred to the Long Knives. That game is fair, for two can play at it. But their thirst for human blood, and their cruelty to women and children is ridiculous."

This Backwoodsman is an Indian Hater out of duty. And he finds later that he hates civilization as much as he does savagism:

"Nature [he says] did not make these clear waters and beautiful woods merely for the use of treacherous Indians,—no, nor for land speculators and pedlars. Here is quiet and repose, such as they know nothing of who toil in their harvest fields or bustle about in crowded cities . . . ."[42]

So his frontier idealism, a frontier primitivism, cuts him off, as it does Leatherstocking, from both kinds of society available to him, the higher and the lower. But at least, like Leatherstocking, he finds a kind of peace not accessible to less philosophically inclined, more "realistically" conceived backwoodsmen. These others, a more dangerous and more pitiful sort, are Indian Haters out of obsession.

Among them is Samuel Monson, whom Hall describes in a tale collected in *The Wilderness and the War Path* (1846) and Colonel John Moredock, described in a tale collected in *Sketches of History, Life, and Manners in the West* (1835). However, Hall's fullest account of the obsessed Indian Hater, one in which he does his best to study the psychology of obsession, is in the tale called "The Pioneer," collected in *Tales of the Border* (1835).[43] "The

[42] *Ibid.*, pp. 255, 257.

[43] Hall, *Tales of the Border* (Philadelphia, 1835), pp. 13-101.

Pioneer" is introduced by a description of frontier society in its rude warmth, in its struggle to be of the natural frontier and yet not be enveloped by it. The tale proper which follows is an *apologia pro vita sua* of a frontier circuit rider. As a child he had known a father killed, a sister stolen, and a mother kidnapped by Indians; the experience had colored his life and moulded his faculties, had made him crueller than even his fellows on the frontier; his whole life, as he describes, analyses, and accounts for it, was one of fear and hatred of the savage.

He had become the classical Indian Hater, had trained himself to out-savage the savage, knowing that one day he would get his vengeance:

> I learned especially that patience, that forbearance, that entire mastery over my appetites, fears, and passions, which enables the Indian to submit to any privation, and to delay the impending blow until all his plans are ripe, however alluring may be the temptation for premature action.

In context, this is irony; for, as he discovered, in gaining savagism he was losing civilization. If this was "unnatural," he declares, it was a product of having "been raised upon the frontier." So he continued in his frontier-natural fashion, organizing a band of avengers as skillful as he, killing all Indians he could find, making himself into a scourge of savagism.

The life claimed its due. Although he had soon become exhausted and retired from a career of active Indian-hating, he could not forget his hatred. It had, as he says:

> rendered me moody and unsocial. It kept me estranged from society, encouraged a habit of self-torture, and perpetuated a chain of indignant and sorrowful reflections.

He was obliged to kill occasionally, just to feed his obsession.

He was saved, however, by a wonderful, miraculous coincidence. One day he happened upon an Indian warrior, his squaw, and their child, and, unseen, stole upon them, intending his usual vengeance. A certain uneasiness, a burdensome conscience, and the weight of his guilt-feeling (as we should say) made him hesitate. But he would go on. About to shoot, he noticed that the squaw looked like his mother, and it occurred to him that she might be his long-lost sister. So he went to the Indians as a friend and learned what he had to learn—that she was his sister. He learned, moreover, that she was happy and that she scorned to return to civilization. What he had to face was this:

> Between my sister and myself there were no points of sympathy, no common attachments, nothing to bind us by a tie of affection or esteem . . .

Moreover his sister was "contented, perhaps *happy,* in the embraces of a savage, at the very time when I was lying in ambush by the war-path." The moral was pressed on him. He had almost lost his sense of civilization and its responsibilities; as an avenger he had been a savage. Only as a savage had he the right to such vengeance; for only as savages did the Indians have a right thus to protect themselves from the white men and their ways. It is, once more, the doctrine of red gifts and white. In this crisis, the Indian Hater recovered his true civilized self and, in public expiation, became a circuit-riding preacher.

Hall's Pioneer saves himself in a way that most Indian Haters cannot. Their creators regularly give them the Pioneer's biography or one analogous to it, portray them as men somehow cut away from civilization and made incapable of returning to it, and leave them there, neither civilized nor savage; regularly they define their Haters in terms of the savages whom they hate. In James McHenry's *Spectre of the Forest* (1823), the earliest Indian Hater of our fiction, Hugh Bradley, is said to be justified, but is nonetheless shown going mad and so dissociated from civilized life. In N. W. Hentz's *Tadeuskund* (1825), the Hater becomes so vicious that civilized men drive him from them. In James Kirke Paulding's *Dutchman's Fireside* (1831), the historical frontiersman, Lewis Wetzel, is translated into one who lives up to his name, Timothy Weasel. In Robert Montgomery Bird's *Nick of the Woods* (1837), the Hater is a Quaker, Nathan Slaughter, so deeply obsessed by his hatred that he disguises himself as a monstrous savage and seeks at once to terrify and to kill. Bird's means of demonstrating Nathan's obsession is first to brutalize his Indians (he feared that Cooper had too much ennobled his) and then to brutalize Nathan beyond them, to un-Quaker the Quaker and make him mad. In Mrs. Anna L. Snelling's *Kaboasa; or, The Warriors of the West* (1842), the Indian Hater refuses to join an expedition against Tecumseh solely, as he makes it clear, because he is bound by the origin and nature of his hatred to achieve a lonely, savage vengeance. In Samuel Young's *Tom Hanson, the Avenger* (1847), Hanson the Indian Hater is set against Pesquet the White Hater; they hate for identical reasons, their families having been destroyed by each other's people. When Hanson finally triumphs over him, a dying Pesquet explicitly recognizes that this is savage justice. (Hanson is one of the very few Haters who, like Hall's Pioneer, is allowed fully to return to civilization, apparently purged of his hatred.) In James W. Dallam's *The Deaf Spy* (1848), the Texas hero Deaf Smith is celebrated as the lone frontiersman (made more lonely by his deafness) who hates for the usual reasons, even as he can see the justice of Indian attempts to wipe out whites; his special hatred is reserved for the renegade Cordova who leads the Indians in their raids and who thus for Smith is the lower-than-savage Renegade. In the stories of Emerson Bennett the Hater is also set against the Renegade and the Indians to whom the Renegade has sold his civilized soul. In *The Renegade* (1848), it is an Indian-hating, but at the same time potentially civilized, Boone, of course, who pursues Simon Girty; and in *Kate Clarendon* (1848), the heroine is protected from renegade aristocrats by a run-of-the-mill Indian Hater. Bennett conventionally images the type when in his *Prairie Flower* (1840), he writes of some Rocky Mountain fur-trappers who, as he describes them, have to hate to survive:

> . . . as the trapper or hunter is but little removed from [the Indian] by civilization, and not a whit by knowledge gained from letters, it is hardly reasonable to suppose that he would [not] imbibe ideas at war with those among whom the most of his eventful life is spent. In his earliest venture, he learns and adopts the habits of his enemy, and in some cases it would seem his very nature also; and the result

is, that he becomes at last neither more nor less than what I may venture to term a civilized savage.[44]

By Bennett's time the moral significance of Indian-hating has virtually been lost sight of in the welter of blood-and-thunder good times into which the popular novelist must plunge his characters. Indeed, such a hyper-conventionalized story as James Quinlan's *Tom Quick, the Indian Slayer* (1851) is said to be composed of half-truth, half-fiction; and Quinlan feels bound to try to separate one from the other, thus to cleanse of fable what is significant in Quick's life. At the end there is even a chapter of apocrypha. On Quick's career—one whose particulars is according to the regular pattern as I have outlined it—Quinlan comments:

> . . . the writer cannot attempt to palliate and excuse Quick's conduct, nor can he account for the admiration which his doings excited among the hardy pioneers, in any other way than by supposing that in the struggle for mastery between the aborigines and those who supplanted them, the refined and humane sentiments which are promoted by civilization and Christianity, were obliterated by the dark and unfeeling dogmas which obtain a lodgment in the human mind during perilous and bloody times.[45]

Nor, according to the tale, had Quick's society palliated and excused his conduct. He had died a lonely old man, "outlawed" by a government whose existence he had helped make possible.

Here, as in Bennett's work, the image of the Indian Hater and all that it conveys is made to persist, even in its fading; and we can see it on its way to becoming the image of the Indian fighter of the dime novel, in whom aggressiveness and success are all, in whom there is no memory of civilization and its responsibilities, hence no feeling for savagism and its irresponsibilities. But that is a later and different story, one which develops when the Indian and his way of life no longer can furnish imaginative writers, big

[44] Emerson Bennett, *The Prairie Flower; or, Adventures in the Far West* [1849] (Cincinnati, 1850), p. 58.

[45] James Eldridge Quinlan. *The Original Life and Adventures of Tom Quick, the Indian Slayer* [1851, as *Tom Quick, the Indian Slayer*] (Deposit, N. Y., 1894), p. 101.

and little, with the means of defining Indian-hating as one of the hazards of bringing civilization to the west. So long as the idea of savagism seemed meaningful, we can observe, it furnished such a means. The image of the Indian Hater, like the image of the Renegade, is evidence of that means.

5

Late in the eighteenth century, Americans had set out to comprehend the Indian in such a way as to establish a meaningful relationship between his savagism and their civilization. They were to define savagism in terms of civilization, or noncivilization, so as to mark with it all that civilized men could not be, if they wished to save their civilized souls alive. By the second quarter of the nineteenth century, the definition had been made so many times and with so much self-assurance that it could body forth an image of the savage powerful and substantial enough to fill out a literature of progress. At the last, however, Americans ended where they had begun, with their civilized selves and the dangers in store for those selves should they venture west toward noncivilization. What they had gained was deep affirmation of the role of civilization in America. It turned out, as it had to, that what Indians signified was not what they were, but what Americans should not be. Americans were only talking to themselves about themselves. But they had succeeded in convincing themselves that they were right, divinely right. Only with such conviction—cruel, illogical, and self-indulgent as it was—could they move on.

It is this image of the savage which will in the end not let us separate frontiersmen from Indians, men who became (or almost became) savages from men who were savages. We saw how closely they were bound one with another in The Leatherstocking Tales. To see them in their full development we had to analyse them out of their contexts and to separate them. We can at this point join them once more by seeing how they function together at their melodramatically most popular—this in James Strange French's *Elkswatawa; or, The Prophet of the West* (1836). French, like the great majority of his fellows, does not set out to write about savagism and civilization; he is, in his own way, just a storyteller. Yet granting the subject of his story, he cannot help but write about savagism and civilization. That is to say, in selecting his subject, he also takes from his culture the mode of analysis which had shaped it. If his primary concern is with his story, still we can see in it the problem of savagism and civilization which makes its telling possible, which informs its subject matter so completely as, for its author, not to have a separate existence.

French early announces that *Elkswatawa* is a novel of the destruction of Indian life in America; its terms, he indicates, are to be not crudely realistic but poetic. As Cooper had been, he is concerned with essential truth, but he will not rudely violate literal truth. The place is the Ohio country; the time is early in the nineteenth century; and the background is Wayne's victory of 1794 and its aftermath of mistreatment of Indians, broken treaties, and a continual civilized push westward. The narrative commences in 1809 and centers on the struggles against civilization of Tecumseh and his brother, Elkswatawa, the Prophet. The subject is, simply enough, the last stand of the Indian in the Ohio country. Yet it is whites, the victors not the victims, who dominate the action.

At the beginning there is an account of an Indian attack on an American family going down the Ohio. All are killed, except a daughter who is taken captive and carried off to adorn some Indian household. Immediately we are moved to two travellers who overhear the commotion, realize what is happening, and set out to pursue the Indians and to rescue the fair captive. The two men are an easterner (i. e., a non-westerner) temporarily turned frontiersman and a veteran indigenous to the frontier. Rolfe, the easterner, is a "high-toned chivalrous Virginian," a poor young lawyer, unlucky in love, who has come west to share in "the high, yet pleasing excitement produced by being alone in the wild woods, where danger is known to be abroad." The veteran is one named Earthquake, Earth for short, one whose name contains his proper self; he is the Leatherstocking figure, bereft of some of Leatherstocking's more philosophical qualities, speaking always in a low style, yet gentle in his earthly roughness. When the two travellers come upon the slaughtered family, Earth lets flow tears of sensibility and says that he also has lost " a father, and a mother, and a sis." Thus he exhibits his right to be at once an Indian Hater and a frontier man of feeling. From the very beginning, his potential share of savagism is softened—softened, one supposes, to ease French's and his readers' tender feelings; for savagism is not an easy thing to face. Earth's and Rolfe's attempts to rescue the captive maiden (who later turns out to be Rolfe's Virginia beloved) furnish the structure and substance of the novel. Its grand morality, however, derives from the meaning for American civilization of the Indian war into which they walk in their pursuit.

French wishes us clearly to understand Tecumseh, the Prophet, and the origin and nature of their fear and hatred of whites. So he portrays heroic savages, banded together through the trickery and idealism of the Prophet, sworn literally to purify themselves and their lands of white civilization. Half the novel is filled with details of Indian ways and Indian warfare, which, taken together, constitute a conventional treatise on savagism. If French is sympathetic toward the Indians, yet he must insist that their very way of life, the very principles which ennoble them, doom them forever. For him the incompatability of red gifts and white is absolute. He wants his readers to understand the savage and, understanding, to accept the sad necessity of the victory of the white man over the red.

The implications of such acceptance center around the true frontiersman, the Indian Hater, Earth, and his attitude toward the savages. In this, Earth at once shocks and tutors Rolfe. Once he cares for a wounded Indian boy so, as he says, that he may have a full-grown warrior to kill later. Once he and Rolfe debate the question of Indian resistance and depredation:

" How beautiful are these plains," said Rolfe, " Earth, do you blame the Indians for not surrendering them? "

" No, I cannot say that I do: nor do I blame the whites for endeavouring to take them away."

" Why? are not the Indians the rightful owners, and have not their fathers owned them time out of mind? "

"Rolfe, it will not do to argue this matter: we have treated the Ingens so badly, that we cannot now live in peace, but are obliged to add insult to injury. You know I've a great many grudges agin 'em, and use them up on all occasions, for I well know they would have killed me long before this, if they had had a good chance."

"And because you have treated them badly, you think you ought to kill them? Is that your argument?"

"No, I never argue about it; if one comes near me, and he gives me a cause, I'm very apt to kill him. Somehow or other it is bred in me, and I hate them; for you see they are always straggling along the frontiers, and committing murders."

"Yes, and you see our frontiers are always extending, so that the Indians are compelled either to move or else to be continually at war."

"The fact is," said Earth, "I believe I think as most of the whites do, and that is, that these lands are too good for them; they should be cultivated instead of lying waste for them to prowl over." [46]

If a Rolfe can think in terms of eternal right and wrong, an Earth cannot. His "somehow or other" is that of an Indian Hater and of a semisavage harbinger of American progress. He prowls over the lands to kill those who should not prowl over them. He might well be the doomed Indian Hater, cut off from Rolfe and his kind forever.

But French, searching for the completely happy ending, will not let him be. He makes the victory of civilization over savagism all the greater by letting Earth have his full share of it. So Earth loses even his Indian-hating identity in the conventionally melodramatic confusions of the later parts of the novel and is saved for civilization. The contrivance is purely mechanical and adventitious, aimed at a tying-up (or a cutting-off) of loose ends. Earth and Rolfe for a time give up their search, go to Kentucky and settle down, Rolfe as a lawyer and Earth as a sheriff. When they finally learn that the fair captive is Rolfe's Virginia sweetheart and that she is alive, they return to the pursuit. Meantime the Indians have gathered for warfare and, urged on by the Prophet, move toward Tippecanoe. So do Rolfe and Earth. For the In-

[46] James Strange French, *Elkswatawa* (New York, 1836), I, 93.

dians it is defeat and death; for Rolfe and Earth, rescue, return to civilization, and happiness ever after. If all this serves no other purpose, it does save Earth from his Indian-hating self. For once the Indians are disposed of, the Indian Hater has no function. Earth, in fact, is saved from his own savagism by helping to destroy it in others. Early in the story, his life and his character manifest the incompatability of red gifts and white, and he surrenders to those red gifts which will make him a proper frontiersman. Yet French will not be the complete realist and let Earth be fully the white man who is lowered by red gifts into tragedy, or pathos, or degradation. Saving Earth, he avoids the implications of the terms in which he must conceive of him; saving Earth, he sacrifices only the Indians. The nineteenth-century Common Reader must have been pleased. For in Earth, it is shown how the American could become a savage in order to do his duty and crush savagism, and then could recover his civilized self. The victory of civilization over savagism could be complete. The victory was complete.

PART 3

Afterthoughts: 1851–

" Queequeg no care what god made him shark . . .
wedder Fejee god or Natucket god, but de god
wat made shark must be one dam Injin."

Herman Melville, *Moby-Dick,* 1851

" And Indian-hating still exists; and, no doubt, will
continue to exist, so long as Indians do."

Herman Melville, *The Confidence-Man,* 1857

" . . . the scholastic philosophy of the wilderness
to combat which one must stand outside and laugh
since to go in is to be lost."

Marianne Moore, " New York," 1924

" For I was born in the shadow of the great forest. . . ."

Thomas Jefferson, speaking in
Robert Penn Warren's *Brother to
Dragons,* 1953

VIII

After a Century of Dishonor:

The Idea of Civilization

IN the 1840's, Americans discovered that the West, to which they had consigned the Indian, itself needed the creative hand of civilization. The notion of Removal, of pushing the Indian to the Great Plains, somewhere west of the Mississippi, no longer seemed practicable; for then he would stand between Americans and Santa Fé, Oregon, and California. He had to be dealt with; his newly acquired lands had to be taken over; and still he had to be brought to civilization, or die. What eventually resulted was the Reservation system, whereby Indians were segregated and gathered together on specific pieces of land assigned to specific tribes. These were to be savage islands in the midst of civilized seas. The good hope was that once they were on their islands, Indians would be at long last liable to proper civilizing.

But this hope failed too, as it had always failed. Such a failure could seem nothing less than a divine success to a booming westerner like Senator Thomas Hart Benton, whose eye was always on the bigger and better and richer life that was to rise when the West was civilized. In 1846, speaking to his colleagues on the Oregon question, he judged that Indians (red men) were inferior to Orientals (yellow men), and proclaimed that the red had been destroyed so that Americans (white men) could get to the yellow—once great, now "torpid and stationary"—by commerce, conquest, and intermarriage, and so bring them to full life and high civilization. "It would seem," he said, "that the white race alone received the divine command, to subdue and replenish the earth!" And then:

For my part, I cannot murmur at what seems to be the effect of divine law. I cannot repine that this Capitol has replaced the wigwam—this Christian people, replaced the savages—white matrons, the red squaws—that that such men as Washington, Franklin and Jefferson, have taken the place of Powhattan, Opechonecanough, and other red men, howsoever respectable they may have been as savages. Civilization, or extinction, has been the fate of all people who have found themselves in the track of the advancing Whites, and civilization, always the preference of the Whites, has been pressed as an object, while extinction has followed as a consequence of resistance. The Black and the Red Races have often felt their ameliorating influence.[1]

Benton's expansionist " civilization or extinction " echoes Sullivan's officers' revolutionary " Civilization or death." The speech must have sounded even nobler than the toast; for it put the burden of destruction on a civilized God, not on civilized men.

1

The history of the Indian problem in the 1850's and after is not our concern here, except as it was the result of the victory of civilization over savagism. We must note, then, that beginning in 1851, the American government began once more to acquire western Indian lands. The aim was to protect travellers west, to assure safe settlement of needed lands, and to clear the way for roads and railroads and the civilization which they would bring. There was no longer a question of a permanent Indian danger to civilization; there was only a question of managing to civilize as peacefully as possible. On the side of the civilizers there was little but dishonor; on the side of those to be civilized there was little but desperation; on both sides there was little but violence. The

[1] I quote from the text of the speech as given in William M. Meigs, *The Life of Thomas Hart Benton* (Philadelphia, 1904), pp. 309-10. The entire speech appears in *Congressional Documents*, 29th Cong., 1st Sess., pp. 851-919.

Department of the Interior sent out its agents to care for the Indians; as often as not they cared only for themselves. The War Department sent out soldiers to keep Indians pinned down to lands newly assigned to them and to protect Americans in the West; Indians would not be pinned down, attacked Americans encroaching on what they took to be their lands, and were punished for violating sacred agreements. In the 1860's, the 1870's, and the 1890's, the Sioux tried violently to assert their independence; in the 1860's the Cheyennes and the Arapahoes tried to assert theirs; in the 1870's the Modocs tried to assert theirs and the Nez Percés theirs. These were the most celebrated campaigns, but there were others like them. Civilized Americans still cried out in pity and censure. The end was always the same: defeat and death or confinement.

The American conscience which was hurt by these events could only be a philanthropic, humanitarian conscience; for American censure in the past century had reduced the Indian to a state so pitiful as to be comprehended only by philanthrophy and humanitarianism. Henry Schoolcraft was one among many to set the theme early in the 1850's:

> Whatever defects may, in the eyes of the most ardent philanthropist, have at any time marked our system of Indian policy, nothing should, for a moment, divert the government or people, in their appropriate spheres, from offering to these wandering and benighted branches of the human race, however often rejected by them, the gifts of education, agriculture, and the gospel. There is one boon, beside which their ignorance and instability, and want of business and legal foresight, requires, in their present and future state—it is protection.[2]

After the Civil War, in the midst of troubles with the Plains Indians, protection was loudly called for, particularly by Helen Hunt Jackson, who in 1881 traced the history of American treatment of the Indians and denounced it in a name that stuck—A

[2] Henry Rowe Schoolcraft, *Historical and Statistical Information*, III, viii. Cf. Emerson Davis, *The Half-Century* (Boston, 1851), pp. 31-40; and Robert Baird, *The Christian Retrospect and Register* (New York, 1851), pp. 27-28.

Century of Dishonor. Protection gradually was being given. In 1871 the government had ended the practice of making treaties with Indians and had stopped pretending they were anything but wards of their betters. The Indian Service was cleansed and overhauled, especially under the administration of Secretary of the Interior Carl Schurz. Attempts to educate and to civilize were stepped up. In 1887, with the Dawes Act, tribal lands were distributed among individual Indians, according to civilized notions of land tenure. Finally, in 1924, Indians were made American citizens. They had at last paid enough for protection and had fully earned philanthropy and humanitarianism.

Yet even philanthropy and humanitarianism would not work. He on whom it was to work was in fact no Indian but an image which the civilized conscience had created just for the protecting, which the civilized intellect and the civilized imagination had earlier created just for the destroying. Civilization had created a savage, so to kill him. Idea had begotten image, so to kill it. The need was to go beyond image and idea to the man.

Recent attempts of our government have been to go that far—as it were, to begin over again: to grant the Indian what remains of his cultural heritage as an Indian and to encourage him to hold on to it and still to become integrated in the American civilization which has been brought to him and which can yet raise him. Our enlightened aim now is, in the words of one who has recently been concerned with the Indian's welfare, to let him learn all the devices the white man has and still be an Indian.[3]

2

Thus far our civilization has come, and we can say that it is more civilized than it was. Yet the idea of savagism has a monument which it will pay us to examine closely, since it stands where we all must see it. This is the Rescue Group, by Horatio Gree-

[3] Oliver La Farge, *As Long as the Grass Shall Grow* (New York, 1940), pp. 134-40. A detailed account of recent Indian policy is in A. Grenfell Price, *White Settlers and Native Peoples* (Melbourne, 1950), pp. 41-58.

nough, which stands at the East Portico of our Capitol and at the beginning of this book. Commissioned in the late 1840's, executed while the sculptor was in Italy trying to bring forth a major American art, erected in 1853 a year after his death, it raises the meaning of its subject to generalization and permanence. The conception is grandiosely heroic, not tied down to the particular facts of frontier life. The frontiersman and the Indian are in their ways classicized, simplified, abstracted from their "real" images and made to bear out as simply and as clearly as possible the largest significance of their struggle. The Indian's look is one of fierce resignation to his fate; the frontiersman's, of a defender's stern and sad necessity at being the administrator of such a doom; the wife's, of gentle, civilized terror in the presence of the savage. The frontiersman, we see, has no choice. As he looms over his enemy, he bears that burden of victorious pity and censure which suffused the American understanding of the Indian and his inevitable destiny.

The statue was explicitly intended to epitomize the meaning of our progress westward. It illustrated, in the words of the cataloguer of Greenough's works in 1853, "a phasis in the progress of American civilization, viz., the unavoidable conflict between the Anglo-Saxon and the aboriginal savage races." Greenough himself is said by a friend to have declared that he wished to depict "the peril of the American wilderness, the ferocity of our Indians, the superiority of the white-man, and why and how civilization crowded the Indian from his soil . . ."[4] I suggest that looked at through the eyes of our age, the Rescue Group epitomizes the perils not only of the American wilderness, but of American civilization.

The suggestion of course comes easily, because it comes so long after the fact. And it is moreover now an obvious one,

[4] The catalogue description is from Henry Tuckerman, *A Memorial of Horatio Greenough* (New York, 1853), p. 56. Greenough's "story" of the Group is recounted in a letter from E. G. Loring, a friend of his family, to Senator James Pearce, July (?), 1858, in the files of the Architect of the Capitol.

widely made, and with the appropriate sentiments. We would do well, then, to meditate hard upon it, so as fully to understand it—not only to know what we feel, but to feel what we know. One way into such a meditation is to read those sections of Melville's *Confidence-Man* (1857) which center on a chapter called " The Metaphysics of Indian-Hating." Herein Melville, in one of the great creative outbursts in his fading career, proceeds by parody and satire to indict the idea of savagism for what it precisely was: hatred justified by piety, piety rationalized by hatred, civilization cultivating and then feeding upon its discontents. Melville assumes that his contemporary readers will be ready for his story. He assumes that they will know as much as, or more than, we now know, thanks to our historical researches, about savagism and civilization. He thus is addressing readers as immediately involved as he in living with a culture's commitment to move west, no matter what the cost, and with the violent ambiguities in all attempts to justify and rationalize that movement. The art of *The Confidence-Man* is powerful enough virtually to make us Melville's contemporaries, and so to bring this study to its proper conclusion. But then, he is ever our contemporary.

The Confidence-Man as a whole is the fantastic story of a nineteenth-century shape-shifter, who, on a voyage on a riverboat, ironically called the *Fidèle*, in various guises plays on the naïve, optimistic trust of a body of representative Americans. The working motto of the novel is in fact " No Trust " and its end is to project a vision of ante-bellum American culture lost in its own crazy pursuit of quick and easy ways to spiritual and material wealth. One way of those ways is that of " Metaphysics of Indian-Hating "; and it is detailed to us as it centers on the career of Colonel John Moredock, in a version Melville not only derives from, but explicitly credits to, James Hall, in his *Sketches of History, Life, and Manners in the West* (1834-35). Hall, it will be recalled, was in fact one of the age's prime authorities on the west and its indigenous inhabitants. And Melville constructs his version of Hall's account of Moredock in such a way as to transform Hall into an appallingly blind apostle of progress. We may well take Melville's Hall as an ideal type, a possible author of all the writings which have been examined in this study; and we may likewise take Melville's version of Hall's account of Moredock as a composite, perfected version of those writings. The effect of the composition and the perfection is to plunge us directly into the life of Hall's culture and to make us know, only barely mediated, the component of death—in the idea of savagism—with which, all unknowing, it sustained itself.

In Chapter XXV of *The Confidence-Man*, Melville introduces a stranger "with the bluff *abord* of the West." Having overheard the affair of the ursine Missourian who has almost successfully resisted the confidence-man in one of his guises but who has fallen victim to him in another, the stranger is reminded of Judge James Hall on Moredock the Indian-hater; and he tells the story to the cosmopolitan. The Indian-hater, thus, figures as the Missourian carried to a logical extreme; and in him resistance to the confidence-man is carried to its logical—and, I think, horrible—extreme.

At the outset, the cosmopolitan is shocked, says that he admires Indians, and goes into a paean to celebrated heroic chiefs—this, too, part of a tradition of writing on the Indian in Melville's time. As one would expect him to, the cosmopolitan as confidence-man, endowing even the natural man with his kind of (false) confidence, can see nothing but noble savages. But in spite of this pious interruption, the stranger will go on with his story. In Chapters XXVI and XXVII, he discusses first the "Metaphysics of Indian-Hating" and then the life and work of that prime Indian-hater, Colonel Moredock. Both the story and the Metaphysics are said to be quoted verbatim from Hall. And both fall into the traditional pattern as it has been outlined above, but with critical variations.

For Hall's brief, traditionally cautious and progressivist apologia for Indian-hating, Melville substitutes (crediting it to Hall) one which is long, detailed, frank; one in which progress figures not at all: an analysis of the compulsively lonely, thoughtful, violent, self-willed, self-reliant, ungodly pathfinder who, even though he is a "provider of security to those who come after him, for himself asks nothing but hardship." In the *Sketches* Hall concludes simply: "It is not from a desire of conquest, or thirst of blood, or with any premeditated hostility against the savage, that the pioneer continues to follow him from forest to forest, ever disputing with him the right to the soil, and the privilege of hunting game." In *The Confidence-Man* Melville, speaking through the western stranger, makes Hall conclude: "Thus, though he keep moving on through life, he maintains with respect to nature much the same unaltered relation through-out; with her creatures, too, including panthers and Indians." The relation is one of single-minded hatred; the Indian-hater is a man who will have no contact with other men, who is compelled in his self-willed loneliness to face down nature and fight her to the death. So Melville's narrator (still nominally quoting Hall) fills out the rest of his introductory metaphysics with accounts of frontier hardships and savage villainy—all told from the point of view of the Indian-hater, hence all serving to justify that point of view and to furnish it a metaphysics. What results is a definition of the "Indian-hater *par excellence*"—the Indian-hater of the tradition, with the regular biography, but now interpreted entirely in terms of the hatred and loneliness he embraces as positive goods: "Ever on the noiseless trail; cool, collected, patient; less seen than felt; sniffing, smelling—a Leather-stocking Nemesis." This is virtually (if, on the part of Melville's Hall, unconsciously) to make him into an animal, so that the conclusion comes naturally enough: "'Terror' is his epitaph." The admiration of this Hall (and presumably of the western stranger who quotes him) for the Indian-hater is so extravagant as to force us to reject it. The irony is almost too heavy.

Whereas the actual Hall and the rest who wrote in the tradition had tried to rationalize the terror and loneliness of Indian-hating into part of some larger, glorious, progressivist scheme of things, Melville makes his Hall dwell only on terror and loneliness. This Hall is made to be caught up in the violence of the men whom he is describing; such violence clearly comes to be an end in itself. We are moved from the commonplace, quietly ordered, straightforward narrative of the Hall of the *Sketches* to the flamboyantly eruptive rhetoric of the pseudo-Hall of *The Confidence-Man.* The attempt is, I think, to make us know the terrors of hatred as directly and as fully as we have known and shall know those of false love and confidence.

Then, in Chapter XXVII the stranger, still largely quoting Melville's Hall, comes to the story of Moredock himself, and our knowledge of hatred is realized not as metaphysics but as action. And, as always, action is not quite so logically complete or extreme as metaphysics. For Moredock is not an Indian-hater par excellence; no man could be, as no man could be a real Leatherstocking out of Cooper—both being examples of the *beau idéal* of their types. But Moredock will do. At this point Melville makes his Hall follow most closely the Hall of the *Sketches.* Changes that are made from the original account are such that will make Moredock's action so palpable that the metaphysics which informs them cannot be denied. Moredock's mother in the *Sketches* has been married and widowed by the tomahawk "several times"; in *The Confidence-Man* it is "thrice." Her "large family" becomes a family of "nine children." The massacre of the family, John excepted, is told in more gruesomely concrete detail in *The Confidence-Man* than it is in the *Sketches.* In general, what Melville does to Hall's account can best be illustrated by comparing a paragraph from the *Sketches* with its rendering in *The Confidence-Man:*

Hall

John Moredock was just entering upon the years of manhood, when he was thus left in a strange land, the sole survivor of his race. He resolved upon executing vengeance, and immediately took measures to discover the actual perpetrators of the massacre. It was ascertained that the outrage was committed by a party of twenty or thirty Indians, belonging to different tribes, who had formed themselves into a lawless, predatory band. Moredock watched the motions of this band for more than a year, before an opportunity suitable for his purpose occurred. At length he learned that they were hunting on the Missouri side of the river, nearly opposite to the recent settlements of the Americans. He raised a party of young men and pursued them; but that time they escaped. Shortly after, he sought them at the head of another party, and had the good fortune to discover them one evening, on an island, whither they had retired to encamp the more securely for the night. Moredock and his friends, about equal in numbers to the Indians, waited until the dead of night, and then landed upon the island, turning adrift their own canoes and those of the enemy, and determined to sacrifice their own lives, or to exterminate the savage band. They were completely successful. Three only of the Indians escaped, by throwing themselves into the river; the rest were slain, while the whites lost not a man.

Melville

He was just entering upon manhood, when thus left in nature sole survivor of his race. Other youngsters might have turned mourners; he turned avenger. His nerves were electric wires—sensitive, but steel. He was one who, from self-possession, could be made neither to flush nor pale. It is said that when the tidings were brought him, he was ashore sitting beneath a hemlock eating his dinner of venison—and as the tidings were told him, after the first start he kept on eating, but slowly and deliberately, chewing the wild news with the wild meat, as if both together, turned to chyle, together would sinew him to his intent. From that meal he rose an Indian-hater. He rose; got his arms, prevailed upon some comrades to join him, and without delay started to discover who were the actual transgressors. They proved to belong to a band of twenty renegades from various tribes, outlaws even among Indians, and who had formed themselves into a marauding crew. No opportunity for action being at the time presented, he dismissed his friends; told them to go on, thanking them, and saying he would ask their aid at some future day. For upwards of a year, alone in the wilds, he watched the crew. Once, what he thought a favourable chance having occurred—it being midwinter, and the savages encamped, apparently to remain so—he anew mustered his friends, and marched against them; but getting wind of his coming, the enemy fled, and in such panic that everything was left behind but their weapons. During the winter, much the same thing happened upon two subsequent occasions. The next year he sought them at the head of a party pledged to serve him for forty days. At last the hour came. It was on the shore of the Mississippi. From their covert, Moredock and his men dimly descried the gang of Cains in the red dusk of evening, paddling over to a jungled island in midstream, there the more securely to lodge; for Moredock's retributive spirit in the wilderness spoke ever to their trepidations now, like the voice calling through the garden. Waiting until the dead of night, the whites swam the river, towing after them a raft laden with their arms. On landing, Moredock cut the fastenings of the enemy's canoes, and turned them, with his own raft, adrift; resolved that there should be neither escape for the Indians, nor safety, except in victory, for the whites. Victorious the whites were; but three of the Indians saved themselves by taking to the stream. Moredock's band lost not a man.

Thus, following the Hall of the *Sketches*, Melville's Hall traces Moredock's career—emphasizing that Indian-hating did not completely destroy his civilized character, that he was, in spite of everything, a good family-man, a good storyteller, a good singer of songs. Yet he was also a good enough Indian-hater to make one think of the ideal, the hater par excellence. The Hall of the *Sketches* concludes with the simple statement that Moredock late in life once refused to be a candidate for the governorship of Illinois. Melville's Hall explains that Moredock refused because he realized that it would be improper for a governor, Indian-hater or not, to steal out now and then "for a few days' shooting at human beings. . . ." Further: "In short, he was not unaware that to be a consistent Indian-hater involves the renunciation of ambition, with its objects—the pomps and glories of the world; and since religion, pronouncing such things vanities, accounts it a merit to renounce them, therefore, so far as this goes, Indian-hating, whatever may be thought of it in other respects, may be regarded as not wholly without the efficacy of a devout sentiment."

The cosmopolitan is at this point most deeply disturbed by the narrative; for this is the antithesis of his kind of love and confidence. And we are to be disturbed too—but not into siding with Moredock or, beyond him, with an Indian-hater par excellence. Hatred is hatred; and Melville will not let us see it as anything but hatred. To remake the traditional Indian-hating story in general and Hall's version of it in particular into something that will justify calling hatred "a devout sentiment"; to let us see Hall, as it were, forcing himself into celebrating loneliness, isolation, godlessness, and terror—that is, one of Melville's critics says, to give "a strong purge" [5] for the disease spread by the confidence-man; but not on that account the right purge. Its artistic function is to be too violent a purge, a terrible irony. If one takes to the story, as Melville must have assumed his readers would, a minimal awareness of the tradition, one can see that Melville has no more praise for Indian-hating than he does for confidence. Both are false, blind, unreasoning. The frightening thing—in the total context of *The Confidence-Man*—is that he who escapes one seems, by virtue of his very escape, to be driven to the other.

4

Whatever the final truth of the propositions Melville discovers and elucidates in *The Confidence-Man*, the facts of the case are there, and, in the power and passion of their presentation, may confirm our sense of them as they have been developed in this study. For the historical fact surely is that our civilization, in subduing the Indian, killed its own creature, the savage. The living fact is that it has not yet been able entirely to kill the Indian, but having subdued him, no longer needs or cares to. Still, it might be that there will always be somebody who needs to be subdued—men to play the part of Indians and so become savages standing in the way of civilization. (We can see this happening in Benton's speech on the Oregon question, from which I quoted toward the beginning of these Afterthoughts.) Civilized men continue to forget—and to explain that the difficulties of the situation force them to forget—that there is a difference between raising men and exploiting them and that civilization should

[5] John W. Shroeder, "Sources and Symbols for Melville's *Confidence-Man*," *PMLA*, LXVI (1951), 379.

always mean life, not death. It is very easy to come to a hard conclusion like that of the bluff westerner whom Melville makes retell Hall's tale of Moredock: "And Indian-hating still exists; and, no doubt, will continue to exist, so long as Indians do."

Yet, meditating the nineteenth-century victory of our civilization over savagism, profiting from both victory and meditation, bearing the burden of the facts, we may hope not and work with the hope. We may say with the Melville who in 1849 had objected to what he termed Parkman's "almost natural" but "wholly indefensible" disdain for the Indian: "We are all of us—Anglo-Saxon, Dyaks, and Indians—sprung from one head, and made in one image. And if we regret this brotherhood now, we shall be forced to join hands hereafter. A misfortune is not a fault; and good luck is not meritorious. The savage is born a savage; and the civilized being but inherits his civilization, nothing more." And we may even try to remember, out of *Moby-Dick* and 1851, Queequeg and what is said to be his savage idea of civilization: "It's a mutual, joint-stock world, in all meridians. We cannibals must help these Christians." [6]

[6] Herman Melville, *The Confidence-Man* [1857] (London, 1923), p. 191; review of Francis Parkman's *The California and Oregon Trail*, in *The Literary World*, IV (1849), 291; *Moby-Dick* [1851], ed. Willard Thorp (New York, 1947), p. 59.

INDEX

"Reasonings from a State of Nature are fallacious, because hypothetical. We have not the facts. Experiments are wanting. Reasonings from Savage Life do not much better. Every writer affirms what he pleases. We have not the facts to be depended on."

— John Adams, *c.* 1790